*Through creative storytelling and practic[...]
Hanah Polotsky and Lisa Williams did a s[...] ....g physicians in
translating clinical skills into healthcare leadership mastery.*

Scott Smith, MD, SVP & Medical Director Value Based Care,
Millennium Physician Group

Physician Leader *is a must read for any physician jumping into the
turbulent waters of healthcare leadership.*

Bruce Schroffel, MS, MPH, President and CEO,
University of Colorado Hospitals (Retired)

*Why wouldn't physicians translate their exam room skills to lead successfully
as physician leaders? Hanah and Lisa demonstrate how to apply scientific
thinking and problem-solving to self-development as a physician leader. They
skillfully use coaching and story-telling to illustrate how to capitalize on
exam room skills to lead daily improvement.*

John E. Billi, MD, Professor Emeritus of Internal Medicine and Former
Chief Engineer, Michigan Quality System, University of Michigan

*The GUIDES Framework for self-development is a brilliant and indispensable
tool for sharpening your leadership skills. Whatever stage your transition
from physician to physician leader is in – from just starting your first
leadership role to many years as an established physician leader – this book's
straightforward and concise advice will resonate and educate. I only wish it
had been available during my own career transitional years.*

Harley A. Rotbart, MD, Professor and Vice Chair Emeritus,
Department of Pediatrics, University of Colorado School of Medicine

*Primarily written for physicians tasked to step into new administrative
roles, Hanah and Lisa thoughtfully and eloquently coach them in how to
apply familiar exam room problem-solving to leadership and management.
Real world experiences, along with sample case studies, infuse new
perspectives into previously mundane leadership lessons, combining to create
thoughtful – and practical – information for both new and experienced
physician leaders.*

Justin Chang, MD, President, CirrusMD Provider Network

Physician Leader

Physicians are often asked to lead healthcare teams, departments, divisions, practices, and hospitals. Though many of them are experts in their fields, they are rarely prepared or educated in business management and leadership. Based on the authors' interviews with many physician and non-physician executives and leaders, medical training contributes little to leadership skills. Many physicians leave medical training with a command-and-control leadership style that later has to be unlearned to succeed in a team-based healthcare environment.

This book will help physician leaders to shed derailers and authoritarian leadership tendencies picked up in years of medical training. It is intended for (1) physicians who are transitioning to healthcare leadership roles, (2) senior-level physician and non-physician leaders as a coaching model to develop their physician leader direct reports, and (3) administrative leaders who are partnering with physician leaders.

Both authors progressed from mid-level leadership roles to the C-suite, one as a physician leader and one as an administrative leader. As such, they have leveraged their operational excellence expertise to design the Iterative Leadership Model that includes the leader's mindset, Leadership Strategies, and a coaching framework: GUIDES (Gather, Understand, Identify, Design, Execute, and Self-Reflect) that is based on the scientific method, PDSA (Plan, Do, Study, Act), A3 thinking, and the SOAP (Subjective, Objective, Assessment, and Plan) note format.

The authors masterfully integrate personal reflections, coaching examples, illustrative fictional vignettes, and GUIDES exercises to support leaders in the self-development and self-improvement of seven critical Leadership Attributes: strategic thinking, effective communication, coaching, team building, change management, continuous learning, and problem-solving.

Physician Leader
How Exam Room Experience Drives Leadership Excellence

Hanah Polotsky, MD, MBOE
and Lisa Williams, MPPA
with Cheryl Kirk

Routledge
Taylor & Francis Group

A PRODUCTIVITY PRESS BOOK

First published 2024
by Routledge
605 Third Avenue, New York, NY 10158

and by Routledge
4 Park Square, Milton Park, Abingdon, Oxon, OX14 4RN

Routledge is an imprint of the Taylor & Francis Group, an informa business

ISBN: 9780367370190 (hbk)
ISBN: 9781032690322 (pbk)
ISBN: 9780429352355 (ebk)

DOI: 10.4324/9780429352355

Typeset in Garamond
by Newgen Publishing UK

To my father, Lev Nadelson. You were my role model, a source of endless inspiration, and a beacon of light in the darkness of the Soviet Union.

Hanah Polotsky

I dedicate this book to my dear husband, Mark. Without you, I would not be here. Though you are no longer with me on earth, you are forever in my heart, my thoughts, my memories. Thank you for believing in me and continuing to be by my side. I love you.

Lisa Williams

Contents

Foreword

To become a surgeon, I went through four rigorous years of medical school, six intense years of residency training, and a thorough certification process to prove my readiness to practice. My transition into organizational leadership was not anticipated nor planned and it meant a lot of "on the job" training, often "just in time." This accelerated learning in times of change meant a lot of trials and tribulations to succeed.

Though artificial intelligence is creeping its way into clinical medicine, physicians, in a perpetual state of burnout with many hurdles between them and their patients, are reluctant to embrace even old technologies, often struggling through the electronic medical record. We need innovative and forward-thinking physician leaders who can remove barriers to effective clinical practice and inspire clinicians to embrace waves of unprecedented healthcare change. An intentional and thorough approach to leadership education is critical to achieving that.

To bridge the gap between physician clinical and leadership development, the authors undertook a monumental and timely task to design and teach a leadership self-development model using the GUIDES Framework (Gather, Understand, Identify, Design, Execute, and Self-Reflect) that is steeped in the scientific method, operational excellence, and continuous improvement.

Though this engaging book is intended for physicians early in their leadership careers, it is equally applicable to clinical and administrative leaders at various levels of the leadership ladder.

Through colorful stories and examples, the book GUIDES leaders on the self-improvement journey in strategy, communication, coaching, team building, change management, learning, and problem-solving. These excellent knowledge and skills will increase competence and confidence to lead.

Physicians intentionally or unintentionally have a disproportionate influence on healthcare. They can passively watch change passing them by or design the healthcare of today and the future.

Jack Cochran, MD
Served as Executive Director (CEO) of the Permanente Federation at Kaiser Permanente from 2007 until 2015. Author of *Healer, Leader, Partner: Optimizing Physician Leadership to Transform Healthcare*, and co-author, with Charles Kenney, of *The Doctor Crisis: How Physicians Can, and Must, Lead the Way to Better Health Care.*

Foreword

When physician leaders are asked why they accepted a leadership role in medicine, many jokingly reply that they were "the last to step back." While a sense of duty to patients, colleagues, and teams often draws reluctant physicians to lead, they often feel they haven't developed the skills and competencies to facilitate improvement on behalf of their people and patients.

Medical training frequently prepares lonely heroes whose command-and-control style disempowers those they serve. Unlearning authoritarian tendencies requires a systematic approach to developing habits and behaviors that unleash the creativity and ingenuity of both individuals and teams.

In *Physician Leader: How Exam Room Experience Drives Leadership Excellence*, Hanah Polotsky and Lisa Williams introduce an Iterative Leadership Model that facilitates an important shift in leadership mindset. Combining this mindset shift with the practical Leadership Strategies outlined by the authors is vital to elevating the physician from clinician to successful leader, whether they hold a formal administrative leadership role or informally lead their clinical team in improving patient-care every day.

The authors are steeped in the proven tenets of operational excellence. Throughout the book, they masterfully infuse the concepts of respect for people, continuous improvement, leaders as teachers and coaches, and team problem-solving capabilities.

Hanah and Lisa vividly portray their own leadership journeys as well as lessons learned from others. Their honest and humble depiction of their coach–coachee interactions during Hanah's Master of Business Operational Excellence studies at The Ohio State University is refreshing and inspiring.

The ability to lead effectively is not an innate skill. It requires learning productive behaviors and habits while unlearning unproductive ones. It necessitates focused attention on continuous self-development, not dissimilar from the lifelong journey physicians carefully attend to in order to continuously improve their clinical expertise and skills. This book is a long-awaited self-improvement guide for physician leaders and the administrative leaders they partner with to improve the lives of the patients and colleagues they serve.

Jeff Krawcek, MD, MBOE
President and Executive Medical Director
Colorado Permanente Medical Group

Preface: The Case for Physician Leadership

Everyday leadership: manage yourself, develop great leaders and teams, learn relentlessly.

Jack Cochran, MD

Before you are a leader, success is all about growing yourself. When you become a leader, success is all about growing others.

Jack Welch

The US healthcare system is broken. With ever-changing reimbursement models, healthcare remains a schizophrenic mix of fee-for-service (FFS) payment structures, Accountable Care Organizations (ACO), and Patient-Centered Medical Home (PCMH) models. Patients, payers, policymakers, and physicians are frustrated and disillusioned with the rate of healthcare spending, quality outcomes, and the perceived value of the care delivered. Some of the statistics are alarming. Healthcare spending continues to rise with no relief in sight. The Centers for Medicare and Medicaid Services (CMS) reported the National Health Expenditure grew 2.7% to $4.3 trillion in 2021 and accounted for 18.3% of the Gross Domestic Product. The cost of healthcare is expected to continue to increase by more than 5% each year between 2021 and 2023 (2023). Further, in a 2013 *Harvard Business Review* article by Robert Kocher, in the last few decades, the healthcare workforce exploded by 75%, but most of the growth was in administrators, not physicians (2013).

With the ranks of administrators swelling, physicians are losing the autonomy to run their practices. Sadly, many physicians are in desperate need of care themselves. Sensational news stories about physician burnout are regularly in the headlines. Mayo Clinic's recent study of physician burnout reported that almost 63% of physicians exhibit at least one symptom of burnout (exhaustion, inefficiency, and cynicism) compared to 43% five years ago (Shanafelt et al., 2015).

The financial cost of physician burnout is high. In 2019, Han et al. noted in the *Annals of Internal Medicine* that between $2.8 and $9.6 billion annually is attributed to turnover and decreased productivity costs and is a conservative estimation of the direct costs of burnout. Indirect costs due to decreased patient satisfaction, increased errors, and malpractice lawsuits are much higher.

Many organizations are asking physicians to move into leadership positions to have a bigger voice in helping develop approaches to decreasing burnout, improving care, and meeting financial demands.

In recent years, researchers and thought leaders argued that well-trained physician leaders are indeed the answer to solving our country's healthcare challenges, and the research may bear this out. Amanda Goodall showed in her often-cited 2011 study published in *Social Science and Medicine* that hospitals led by physician executives ranked higher in quality and represented disproportionately higher ranked hospitals (2011). In her 2016 *Harvard Business Review* article, Goodall and her co-authors argued, based on studies from Brazil, Canada, France, Germany, India, Italy, Sweden, the UK, and the US, that clinically trained leaders had higher performance scores:

> *Physician leaders who have greater credibility may act as role models for medical staff and their presence may help hospitals to attract talented medical personnel. Physician leaders share the same values as other medically trained staff, and therefore may create better working conditions for doctors, surgeons and nurses.*

(2016)

Physician leaders are uniquely qualified to create the perfect patient experience, curb medical costs, and decrease physician burnout, and they can and should play an outsized role in creating exceptional, safe, and high-quality patient care. Goodall posits that "Doctors want to be led by other doctors," and they are trusted to redesign healthcare delivery, "balancing quality and cost."

Regrettably, physicians are not taught to be leaders. In a 2018 *Harvard Business Review* article by Rotenstein, Sadun, and Jena, the authors lament the lack of physician leadership training: "Nearly all physicians take on significant leadership responsibilities over the course of their career … [yet] physicians are neither taught how to lead nor are they typically rewarded for good leadership" (2018). Dike Drummond, author of the blog, *happymd*, writes that most physician leaders automatically adopt a dysfunctional physician leadership style based on "giving orders" (2019). Authors Cochran and Kaplan explained in their 2014 article: "Historically, physicians have been trained to work and make decisions autonomously and have been rewarded for individual achievement" (2014). In a frustrating paradox, physicians are not formally trained to be leaders, and the transition from physician-to-physician leader can be disorienting and unsettling.

COACH'S CORNER: RETHINKING LEADERSHIP

My husband and I met in medical school, and while our medical school education was superb in clinical care, akin to many other medical school programs, leadership training was not included. One day my husband came home absolutely shaken after a residency shift in obstetrics and gynecology. One of his patients, who happened to be exactly his age, went into cardiac arrest after delivery. The supervising physician stalled in shock. My husband jumped in, redirected the team, and performed an emergency hysterectomy to save the mother's life.

My husband's experience is emblematic of the leadership style that most physicians learn, where life-or-death decisions are made fast, and authority is not delegated. In training, especially surgical, one is working non-stop under conditions of extreme stress, with very little time left for reflection or processing emotions. It is a chaotic work environment where verbal orders are flying, and the "why" behind them is rarely explained. It is not surprising, then, that physicians, including myself, must confront and question our own authoritarian tendencies years later as we lead multi-disciplinary teams in hospitals and clinics. Our residency and fellowship training simply did not contribute to our development as physician leaders.

Yet physicians do have many of the skills needed to be effective leaders. Physicians may not realize that they learned management and problem-solving skills in medical school. Each and every one of them is trained in the scientific method. They have been practicing it for five, ten, 20, or more years. When a patient comes to see a clinician, they do not just give them a treatment. First, they learn about the patient's background and understand the problem by taking a detailed history and performing a physical exam. They come up with a hypothesis (diagnosis) and then prescribe a treatment. And if it does not work, they readjust the thinking and try something else.

Why can't physicians manage their teams and healthcare organizations just like they manage patients in exam rooms or on hospital floors?

Many physicians and physician leaders demonstrated during the Covid-19 global pandemic that they can indeed. In fact, the pandemic has highlighted the versatility of physician leaders to lead care redesign with flexibility, agility, and unprecedented speed. The response to the pandemic quickly demonstrated the value of physicians' clinical training in scientific thinking and problem-solving, preparing them better than anyone to iterate quickly under conditions of extreme uncertainty.

Our patients – including our own family, friends, and community members – deserve a healthcare system that ensures excellent care, better outcomes, and exceptional value. We must leverage the momentum that our response to Covid-19 has created and engage physician leaders in reimagining our healthcare system. In our opinion, there has never been a better time for physicians to intervene and change the course of healthcare.

We believe that physicians with the right leadership training and skills can, should, and will transform healthcare. What makes physician leaders well-positioned to lead a healthcare organization?

- Physicians intimately understand patients' complex clinical pathways.
- Physicians "walk the walk and talk the talk" of fellow physicians.
- Physicians have an inordinate impact on reducing healthcare spending.
- Physicians can drive improvements in quality and population health.

The purpose of this book is to guide your leadership transformation by translating physician experience into the effective Leadership Attributes, skills, and behaviors critical to your success. The activities in this book will help you map a clear path for advancing your leadership skills. In Chapter 1, we introduce the Iterative Leadership Model, which demonstrates how you can apply clinical practice experience directly to leadership. We apply the GUIDES Framework (Gather, Understand, Identify,

Design, Execute, and Self-Reflect) – based on scientific thinking – to transform your leadership mindset, skills, and behaviors. In Chapter 2, we introduce seven critical Leadership Attributes: strategic thinking, effective communication, coaching, team building, change management, continuous learning, and problem-solving. Subsequent chapters dive deep into each Leadership Attribute. The intent is to enrich and broaden your leadership armamentarium, and that can only be accomplished with your commitment to invest in your own professional development.

Are you ready to immerse yourself in this new learning experience? Your leadership journey starts with you.

Bibliography

Centers for Medicare and Medicaid Services. "NHE Fact Sheet." Last modified June 14, 2023. www.cms.gov/Research-Statistics-Data-and-Systems/Statistics-Trends-and-Reports/NationalHealthExpendData/NHE-Fact-Sheet

Cochran, Jack, Gary S. Kaplan, Robert E. Nesse. "Physician Leadership in Changing Times." *Healthcare* 2, no. 1 (March 1, 2014): 19–21. https://doi.org/10.1016/j.hjdsi.2014.01.001

Drummond, Dike. "Physician Leadership – 3 Reasons Doctors Make Naturally Lousy Leaders." Accessed July 4, 2019. www.thehappymd.com/blog/bid/290715/Physician-Leadership-Skills-3-Reasons-Doctors-Make-Poor-Leaders-and-What-You-Can-Do-About-It

Goodall, Amanda. "Physician-Leaders and Hospital Performance: Is There an Association?" *Social Science & Medicine* 73, no. 4 (August 2011): 535–539. https://doi.org/10.1016/j.socscimed.2011.06.025

Han, Shasha, Tait D. Shanafelt, Christine A. Sinsky, Karim M. Awad, Liselotte N. Dyrbye, Lynne C. Fiscus, Mickey Trockel, and Joel Goh. "Estimating the Attributable Cost of Physician Burnout in the United States." *Annals of Internal Medicine* 170, no. 11 (June 4, 2019): 784. https://doi.org/10.7326/M18-1422.

Kocher, Robert. "The Downside of Health Care Job Growth." *Harvard Business Review* (September 13, 2013). https://hbr.org/2013/09/the-downside-of-health-care-job-growth

Rotenstein, Lisa S., Raffaella Sadun, and Anupam B. Jena. "Why Doctors Need Leadership Training." *Harvard Business Review* (October 17, 2018). https://hbr.org/2018/10/why-doctors-need-leadership-training

Shanafelt, Tait D., Omar Hasan, Lotte N. Dyrbye, Christine Sinsky, Daniel Satele, Jeff Sloan, and Colin P. West. "Changes in Burnout and Satisfaction with Work-Life Balance in Physicians and the General US Working Population Between 2011 and 2014." *Mayo Clinic Proceedings* 90, no. 12 (December 2015): 1600–1613. https://doi.org/10.1016/j.mayocp.2015.08.023

Stoller, James, Amanda Goodall, and Agnes Baker. "Why the Best Hospitals Are Managed by Doctors." *Harvard Business Review* (December 27, 2016). https://hbr.org/2016/12/why-the-best-hospitals-are-managed-by-doctors

Acknowledgments

Writing a first book, especially a how-to book like this one, can be intimidating. Readers assume that authors are subject matter experts on the transition from clinicians to physician leaders – or at least, highly knowledgeable. In this regard, we, as authors, are well trained, skilled, and have many years of combined immersive experience in our fields and the subject matter of this book, and yet we approached this book with enormous humility. Hubris would not be our downfall as authors. We knew that we couldn't base the book just on our own learnings and experiences. Thus, we have asked many respected healthcare leaders to share diverse viewpoints on physician leadership. They generously shared their rich perspectives and insights that we quoted throughout the book or weaved into fictional case studies and Leadership Attributes. We are forever grateful to the following individuals: Eli Y. Adashi, MD; Gina Altieri; Jenny Bajaj, MD; Janelle Banat; Myron Beard; John E. Billi, MD; Justin Chang, MD; Jack Cochran, MD; Imelda Dacones, MD; Lloyd David; Alan Decherney, MD; Dianne Dickerson; Edward Fitzgerald, MD; Larry Gray; W. Gray Houlton, MD; Pat Houlton; David Kaplan, MD; Ryan Kramer, MD; Jeff Krawcek, MD; Barbara Ladon; Bruce O'Neill, MD; Danielle Orli, MD; Christopher Pepin, MD; Craig Pepin, MD; Mitchell Peterson, MD; Umesh Prabhu, MD; Steve Quach, MD; M. Sean Rogers, MD; Harley A. Rotbart, MD; Nanette Santoro, MD; Scott Smith, MD; Andy Wiesenthal, MD; Nancy Wollen; Debbie Zuege.

Additionally, we owe a special debt to Cheryl Kirk who quickly transitioned from our manuscript assistant and project manager to a co-author.

This book would not be the same without our editor and writing coach extraordinaire, Carolyn Varvel. Though we found you just months before the manuscript submission, you jumped in enthusiastically to get us to the finish line.

Our beta readers Bridget Hurley, RPh, and Sarah Van Scoy, MD, were gracious to read the entire manuscript and point out where to clarify, omit, or expand content. We are thankful for their candid feedback.

This book would not have come to fruition without unconditional love and support from our families and friends. Hanah especially wishes to thank: Ella Shteingart – you are my best friend and not just a cousin; your editing and cheerleading were invaluable. Maya Balakirsky-Katz – you inspired me with your writing and became my informal writing coach. My brother Gene Nadelson – thank you for introducing me to the world of operational excellence and being my sounding board. My mom Galina Zakharina – you are my rock. I would never be who I am and where I am without you. My kids Esti, Avi, Yael, Eli, and Yoshi – I was so incredibly lucky that you shopped, cooked meals, and entertained each other while I was busy working and writing. Alex – I can fill pages with my gratitude for you as my life partner and a father of amazing children. You inspired me, encouraged me, challenged me, and pushed me beyond what I thought was possible in writing this book.

Lisa wishes to thank: My sisters, Lori Grimes and Belinda Arrington – you are the best sisters in the world; loving and supporting me unconditionally, through thick and thin. My amazing daughter, Haley Brock – you are my light, my sunshine. You have helped me and taught me more than I could have ever imagined. I love you, cutie. My stepsons, Brian Williams and Christopher Williams – you have always been there for me, no matter what, and I am eternally grateful. I am so thankful to have you in my life. My wonderful daughter-in-law, Rita von Lehe – I have come to rely on your warm heart and beautiful spirit. You have no idea how often I channeled you while writing this book. Lynda Herrington – my wonderful mother. I am who I am because of your love, support, role modeling, and friendship. Thank you, mom. My dad, Billy Thames – even though you're no longer here, I feel your presence and love every day. My dear husband, Mark. I know you're here in spirit to see this dream finally come true. You have always been my rock and my best friend, and I attribute my successes in life to you. You even flew to Denver with me when Hanah and I were working on this book. You helped us in so many ways, including occupying her dog, Calvin, while we worked. I miss you terribly and will always be thankful to you for giving me the best years of my life. Until we meet again, my love.

We are also indebted to Kristine Rynne Mednansky, Senior Editor at Taylor and Francis. Thank you for your guidance and patience.

And finally, we must express our gratitude to every patient, physician, and leader we have had the pleasure of serving and learning from over the years. Without each of you, our learning journeys would be incomplete. Each encounter with you helped us grow and mature as leaders and humans, and we are thankful for your generosity.

If anyone who made this book possible was accidentally omitted, we apologize sincerely.

About the Authors

Humility is the simple recognition that you don't have all the answers, and you certainly don't have a crystal ball.

Amy C. Edmondson

Hanah Polotsky, MD, MBOE

My leadership journey started at Albert Einstein College of Medicine and Montefiore Medical Center in the Bronx, where I did all my medical training. When I became an attending physician, I had an opportunity to lead resident teams as well as direct the Internal Medicine Clerkship, training future physicians. I also stepped into a leadership vacuum in my clinical practice, assigning myself an informal role as a team leader of five physicians and 20 residents. In 2010, we moved from New York to Colorado, and I joined Colorado Permanente Medical Group (CPMG). Six months later, I was promoted to chief of Internal Medicine. I was motivated to learn all I could about management and leadership in my new position. I wanted to decrease physician burnout and create an enjoyable work environment for physicians and staff while providing excellent and timely care to our patients. However, I understood that I lacked the knowledge and experience to lead and started reading leadership books and taking leadership courses. My brother, a Lean/Six Sigma master black belt working in the pharmaceutical industry, introduced me to Operational Excellence, or lean management. He sent me a copy of *The Machine That Changed the World*, by James Womack, Daniel Jones, and Daniel Roos. This book changed my world, especially my views on leadership.

As an early student of Operational Excellence, I recognized that this structured approach to leadership and management parallels a clinician's training and daily work. As a physician, I was already on a continuous learning path to improve my communication and problem-solving skills.

I knew I would have to undertake a similar journey if I aspired to grow as a leader. Soon I was promoted to lead a multispecialty clinic, in partnership with non-physician administrative leaders. With more leadership responsibility came the realization that I needed a formal business education to be more effective. So, I enrolled in the Master of Business in Operational Excellence (MBOE) program at The Ohio State University, where I met my co-author, Lisa Williams.

In the MBOE program, I saw more similarities and parallels between successful physicians and first-rate leaders. As physicians, we learned that getting data and involving patients in our clinical decisions, also known as shared decision-making, drives better outcomes. John "Jack" Billi, MD, Chief Engineer for the Michigan Quality System and an MBOE instructor at The Ohio State University, challenged us to manage our teams and healthcare organizations using the SOAP (**S**ubjective, **O**bjective, **A**ssessment, and **P**lan) framework we use daily on the hospital floors or in exam rooms. Physicians are trained in the scientific method, and many have practiced iterative problem-solving for decades.

I practiced what I learned in MBOE with my teams, first as Medical Office Chief and later as Director of Operational Excellence. A structured approach to problem-solving allowed teams to achieve results faster. Instead of me having all the answers, people closer to the work developed and tested hypotheses, determined meaningful metrics, and experimented with solutions or countermeasures. Furthermore, when I was promoted to oversee primary care, behavioral health, urgent care, and telehealth for 550,000 patients, I applied a similar leadership approach to strategy, execution, and cross-functional process redesigns.

I was fortunate to recognize early in my leadership journey that I needed to overcome my authoritarian leadership style. Learning how to listen, ask questions, and not give answers was challenging, and I continue to practice those skills to this day. Still, at times, I revert to the command-and-control approach when I am under extreme stress. When it happens, I stop in my tracks, reflect on my behavior, and apply the same Leadership Strategies we share with you in this book.

Lisa Williams, MPPA

I didn't exactly choose to pursue a career in healthcare; it's more like healthcare chose me. My early career was in behavioral health simply because that is where I could get a job as a recent college graduate. In the 30 years since that first job in healthcare, I have been privileged to have worked in many patient care settings. I managed a long-term care facility, a blessing for my family and me because I could look after my grandmother and grandfather, both residents there. From there, I became the hospital administrator for a Level One trauma center, followed by a two-hospital health system administrator role. In each of those positions, I was humbled to discover that even with a master's degree and a few years of experience, I was unprepared to partner with physicians and physician leaders. Interestingly, business schools and programs do not teach healthcare administrators how to co-lead or partner with physicians.

For this reason, my time at the Level One trauma center remains, in my mind, the most challenging time of my career. In my next hospital administrator role, I focused more on how to partner with physician leaders. Together, we navigated Joint Commission and Department of Health surveys, audits, legal inquiries, and the ongoing battle of developing budgets. We struggled to balance meeting our patients' needs within the budgetary and regulatory constraints we constantly faced. Working within financial, operational, and regulatory limitations was difficult, but our administrative and clinical leadership teams worked together to meet those challenges. Throughout the process, we frequently clashed as our management approaches seemed very different. I often wondered if administrators and physician leaders were trained differently in business management and leadership – resulting in divergent thinking about how to approach and solve business problems. Looking back, I realized that our approaches to leadership had similarities; we just didn't know how to communicate effectively to bridge that gap. As a young administrative leader, I didn't understand how to help my physician partners translate their clinical training and exam room experience into effective leadership. However, I was committed to learning. I've spent years on this journey, taking advantage of countless interactions, conversations, and experiences with clinical teams: listening, watching, and learning.

This journey took my career path to executive coaching and consulting. For the last 15+ years, I've provided various services (such as strategy development and deployment, operational improvement, and leadership development) to healthcare settings and clients across the country: clinics, hospitals, health plans, and educational institutions. In addition, I partnered with other consulting businesses. In my years of experience as a consultant and executive coach, I learned repeatedly how critical it is for administrators to partner with clinical leaders.

A few years ago, serving as an adjunct healthcare coach at The Ohio State University, I had the great fortune to coach Hanah Polotsky in her MBOE program. I promptly discovered that we enjoyed expanding our conversations into leadership situations outside her school requirements and her capstone project. She helped me understand the clinical voice and I reciprocated with the administrative voice. Even after completing her master's program, Hanah and I often talked about how great it would be to share our stories and insights to help other physicians translate their medical training and skills to the world of leadership. This book is the culmination of our many in-depth, broad-based, and always-collaborative conversations. I encourage you to approach this book with an openness to learning and development. I wish you well on your leadership journey.

Chapter 1

Introducing the Iterative Leadership Model

Every now and then a man's mind is stretched by a new idea or sensation, and never shrinks back to its former dimensions.

Oliver Wendell Holmes, Sr.

Long-term commitment to new learning and new philosophy is required of any management that seeks transformation. The timid and the fainthearted, and the people that expect quick results, are doomed to disappointment.

W. Edwards Deming

Introduction

Do you recall your early days as a new physician? Or perhaps your first days as a physician leader? Taking on a new professional role can feel like approaching an unfamiliar abyss; your stomach may lurch, and your legs may wobble as you peer down from the edge into the deep chasm. At the same time, you may also feel an exciting thrill as your gaze stretches across the chasm to a new and unknown horizon. Though it can feel unsettling to leave behind the familiar territory of yesterday, your new professional role is an exciting and enticing destination that invites adventure and discovery.

DOI: 10.4324/9780429352355-1

Transitioning from a practicing physician to a new leadership role is a significant milestone in your career. This moment marks the beginning of a journey that will take you into the world of operations, finance, strategy, market competition, regulatory requirements, compliance, health insurance plans, and people management processes. You are no longer working independently in your practice; instead, you now find yourself working with a team of administrators and operations managers focused on small and large issues like employee development, operational efficiencies, market share, and business strategy. You may even have an administrative dyad partner with whom you will co-lead or share leadership responsibilities in a department, clinic, or region.

■ Do you feel comfortable in this new environment?
■ Are you confident that your current leadership skills can help you successfully navigate your new responsibilities?
■ What leadership skills, attributes, and behaviors need sharpening?

To new leaders, I'd advise patience and curiosity. The best physician leaders I know are great listeners, build relationships, and extend their caring skills to their role as administrators.
Dianne Dickerson, *Vice President, Integrated Work*

Fortunately, as a physician, you are already an expert in many essential leadership skills that you practice daily with your patients: change management, scientific thinking, and problem-solving.

How can you leverage and mold your existing physician expertise into effective leadership? That is the purpose of this book. We are unaware of any other books that map the path from a practicing physician to that of an effective operational and administrative leader. This book is designed to guide you across the chasm and introduce you to the new landscape. You will learn to leverage your current physician skill set to become a more effective leader. As authors, our leadership journeys and combined years of coaching healthcare leaders compel us to share our knowledge, experience, and observations to benefit and accelerate your leadership growth. This book will help you to better understand yourself: how you best operate; how others see you; your personal strengths and weaknesses; and what you need to learn to be effective and influential.

The Iterative Leadership Model

The Iterative Leadership Model (ILM) is a systematic approach to leadership growth designed to engage professionals in an action-oriented and self-directed learning model that is easy to use. It helps you focus the right level of attention on the areas of your leadership to improve, in consultation with your coach, mentor, or trusted colleague.

The ILM design draws on the experiences and learnings of both authors, as well as their colleagues and other professionals. This is the model we have used in our practice of coaching others in leadership roles, and it shares commonalities with other improvement and change models you may be familiar with, such as PDSA (Plan-Do-Study-Act/Adjust) and ADKAR (Awareness, Desire, Knowledge, Ability, Reinforcement). In this book, the ILM is applied to seven Leadership Attributes critical in your maturation as a leader:

1. Strategic Thinker
2. Effective Communicator
3. Coach
4. Team Builder
5. Change Manager
6. Learner-in-Chief
7. Problem-Solver

Chapters 3 through 9 apply the ILM as the systematic approach to understanding, learning, and improving each attribute. Along the way, we share leadership best practices, personal experiences, case studies, and the expertise of other leaders. In addition, we emphasize the crossover concepts between clinical practice and business that will ease the transition from practicing physician to physician leader. Mindset shifts and practical strategies that have benefited others on their leadership journey are also suggested.

Throughout this book, the components of the ILM create a roadmap for achieving your leadership potential, leveraging what you do well, and helping you identify and continuously improve the areas where you want to become more skilled. There are three main components that form the ILM, as shown in Figure 1.1, and described next.

Figure 1.1 Components of the Iterative Leadership Model.

Leader Mindset

Effective leadership and leadership development depend heavily on your beliefs, assumptions, and notions. Throughout the book, we highlight the significance of shifting your mindset and invite you to approach mindset change with humility, openness, commitment, and curiosity.

Leadership Strategies

Essential and practical strategies are presented to sharpen your skill level with the seven Leadership Attributes. Colorful examples, stories, case studies from other leaders, and the authors' personal experiences bring these strategies to life. In addition, we demonstrate how to apply the GUIDES Framework to one Leadership Strategy in each chapter.

The GUIDES Framework

This is central to the ILM. It is a process used to map and guide leadership development. GUIDES is comprised of six elements: **G**ather, **U**nderstand, **I**dentify, **D**esign, **E**xecute, and **S**elf-Reflect. Each element of GUIDES is explained more fully in the next section. GUIDES provides structure to the ILM and produces a comprehensive leadership development portfolio as its output.

The ILM is highly versatile and can serve in multiple situations regardless of your starting point and where you are in your career. For physician leaders in a new organization or working in a new department, clinic, or medical center, this model can help you evolve your leadership skills and ensure your successful navigation and integration into the new environment. Consider engaging a coach, a mentor, or a trusted colleague as you apply the model. Your coach can also use the ILM and its corresponding processes, tools, and activities to complement their coachees' ongoing leadership development efforts. Though we are focused on the seven Leadership Attributes mentioned previously, the same iterative model for improvement can be used to sharpen technical business skills and other soft skills. As we demonstrate in Chapter 9, once you become familiar with the ILM and practice the GUIDES Framework, you can successfully use it to tackle personal, team, and company problems, big and small.

GUIDES: Gather, Understand, Identify, Design, Execute, and Self-Reflect

The GUIDES Framework is the centerpiece of the ILM. The six elements of GUIDES – Gather, Understand, Identify, Design, Execute, and Self-Reflect – are the building blocks of the model. Following these sequential steps of the GUIDES process, you will create an iterative development plan for each of the seven Leadership Attributes: Strategic Thinker, Effective Communicator, Coach, Team Builder, Change Manager, Learner-in-Chief, and Problem-Solver. This section describes each building block, how it contributes to your professional development of the Leadership Attributes, and how it connects to the next block. Each attribute chapter will have an example of a completed GUIDES development plan for one of the Leadership Strategies. The first step is Gather.

Gather

The purpose of the Gather step is to collect and record information about a specific Leadership Attribute. For example, let's assume you want to improve your ability to be an effective communicator. Begin by documenting your starting point with this Leadership Attribute. Conduct a self-assessment of how well you communicate with various constituents in diverse settings, and your level of confidence with each of the four Leadership Strategies: (1) create deliberate communication pathways,

(2) listen with respect and empathy, (3) deliver compelling messages, and (4) foster a culture of feedback.

Once you have completed the brief self-assessment, wrap up the Gather step by:

1. Checking in with your coach, mentor, or trusted colleague. Ask for their perspective on your ability to perform these skills and their suggestions for improvement with this attribute.
2. Checking in with peers, other leaders, and people you coach for their input. What do they see as your strengths and development opportunities with this attribute and the four strategies? Be open to their feedback. Constructive feedback can feel personal even if you solicited it. These moments can make you defensive and expose vulnerabilities. Carefully consider your partners in this step, as it must be a relationship of trust and goodwill.
3. Conducting research. Based on your self-assessment and input from others, what more do you think you need to learn about this attribute? Go on a research mission: read articles, attend webinars, and talk with leaders you consider excellent in this area.
4. Recording your strengths and areas of opportunities.

Figure 1.2 is an example of what the Gather step might look like for a physician leader who rates themself as "Somewhat Confident" in their ability to "Listen with respect and empathy." After checking in with a few of their peers and direct reports, the leader gathers more specific examples of how well they perform as a listener. More detailed descriptions help them better grasp the skill gap they need to close, such as:

> *When I interrupt, people may think I don't care, don't listen, and don't connect to their concerns.*
> *I dominate the conversation, leaving no space for others to share ideas.*

Additionally, after several observations of the physician leader's performance by the leadership coach, the coach mentions that empathetic listening can be improved by paraphrasing what the speaker has said and clarifying their intent. With that feedback added to the notes (as shown in Figure 1.2), the physician leader reviews the content in Chapter 4

Step 1: GATHER inputs to evaluate your skills gaps and opportunities for development.

    1. Record your own assessment of your degree of confidence in these skills.

To what extent are you confident in your ability to:	Not at all	Somewhat	Great deal
Listen with respect and empathy		x	

    2. Reflect on your answers to the questions above. Record your additional thoughts. *It's sometimes hard for me to give my undivided attention to others. I usually have a lot of ideas and solutions I want to share, plus it is not unusual for me to multitask.*

    3. Ask for feedback from others (e.g., trusted colleagues, your coach, or direct reports) on the skills, and take notes. *My coach observed that I rush with solutions and don't restate, paraphrase, or clarify what people share with me, so they don't feel heard.*

    4. What does your additional research tell you about this attribute? *It's ok to not always know the "right" thing to say in response to someone. Empathetic listening demonstrates that I'm intentional about listening and care about their feelings – I don't always have to have the solution to their problem.*

Figure 1.2   Example of the Gather step.

and conducts additional research to find techniques to enhance their listening ability. Sources such as a TEd Talk or journal article can provide improvement ideas.

With the Gather step now complete, the documented results become the input into the next step in the GUIDES process: Understand.

Understand

The purpose of the Understand step is to interpret the data you collected in the Gather step. In the Understand step, you begin to make sense of the data you've gathered. Leaders often short-change this step. It is easy to do, as some leaders often think they know the answers and understand their strengths and opportunities. As a result, they rarely take the time to study the inputs honestly and objectively.

Take time to journal or record the information gleaned from the Gather step. There is something powerful about seeing information and data on paper. It removes some of the emotion attached to the observations. Reflect on the data and ask yourself:

■ Does my self-assessment align with what others observe?
■ What ingrained habits do I have that interfere with my listening skills?
■ How did my self-assessment, feedback from others, and research help me better understand the "why" and the root causes of the counterproductive habits and behaviors I often display?

As you consider these questions, enter descriptive responses in your journal, such as:

As my mind moves very fast, I don't have much patience to listen attentively.
I can grasp the information being shared very quickly and jump into action mode.

Figure 1.3 continues developing the "Listen with respect and empathy" example by reflecting on the data gathered, then recording thoughts to the prompts in the Understand section.

With the data gathered and its interpretation underway, we can proceed to the next step in the GUIDES process: Identify.

Identify

The purpose of the Identify step is to recognize and prioritize improvement opportunities. Using the data and insights from Gather and Understand, identify specific areas you choose to focus your professional growth and development. The Identify step is multilayered, with each layer revealing

Step 2: UNDERSTAND and interpret the data you collected.

The following questions help you understand and interpret the data you collected in the GATHER step. Spend a few minutes thinking about these questions. Record your thoughts and responses.

1. **What did you learn from your self-assessment?** *I've paid attention to my behavior over the past few weeks and noticed that I often missed important points in a conversation and had to ask people to repeat what they said.*

2. **How did you interpret feedback from others (e.g., trusted colleagues, your coach, or reports)? Were you surprised? Did their feedback match your self-assessment?** *I heard from my coach and others that I focus on hearing a problem and jumping right in with my perspective, not allowing others to reflect on the next steps. It makes sense that leaders who report to me often feel I am in a rush to give my perspective, and they don't feel heard.*

3. **What were your key takeaways from the research? Were you surprised by anything you learned?** *I learned from the research that empathetic listening is not waiting to jump with your opinion but the process that allows the other person to feel heard and understood, and perhaps then coaching them to find the answers to their problem.*

Figure 1.3   Example of the Understand step.

subsequent layers: (1) list top areas of focus, (2) discuss top areas of focus with your coach, mentor, or a trusted colleague, and (3) refine areas of focus.

The first layer in the Identify step is to take a few minutes to list your top areas of focus. How many areas of focus do you want to tackle now? One? Three? Ten? More? Keep in mind that it is hard to focus on several things simultaneously. For example, if you work on empathetic listening, meeting management, and electronic communication at the same time, your new skills are unlikely to become habits. It is better to dive deeper into learning and practicing in one area than try many changes only superficially. Similarly, you are likely to give up if you focus on multiple complex measures and try to improve the skill without internalizing the basics. It is like starting a weight-lifting program. Begin with good technique and posture before adding more weights to the barbell. Increasing the difficulty level and intensity will come later with time and practice; focus first on the fundamentals.

The second layer of the Identify step is to share what you have learned so far with a coach, mentor, or trusted colleague. Does this person share your perception of the self-assessment, analysis, research findings, and what you heard from others? What would they add or change? Hopefully, the in-depth dialogue you have will enrich your thinking. Conversations like this can be uncomfortable for you and the other person. However, this is an excellent opportunity to identify areas of focus and appreciate the value of coaching.

The third layer of the Identify step is to review your list of focus areas again and refine it to focus on one or two areas foundational to your development. As you move to the Design step, consider whether you feel you have the appropriate level and amount of information to design and develop a plan of action to help build the Leadership Attribute.

In Figure 1.4, the physician leader, in collaboration with their coach, identifies and prioritizes just one or two fundamental skills to become a more Effective Communicator. The leader starts thinking more deeply about each one and their focus, thus launching the next step in the GUIDES process: Design.

Design

The purpose of the Design step is to create your professional development plan. In this step, you carry over the fundamental focus areas you prioritized in the Identify step and then specify the actions you will take. The Design step is where you set your goals and how you plan to achieve them, including the actions you plan to take, when you will take them, resources you may need, and the criteria by which you will measure your success, as shown in Figure 1.5. This plan should be fun, exciting, and doable. If your plan is daunting and too time-consuming, it will be much harder to follow through, ultimately slowing or impeding your development. Balance your enthusiasm to rapidly develop your skills

---

Step 3: IDENTIFY your strengths and opportunities.

Spend a few minutes thinking about each of these questions. Record your thoughts and responses.

1. **Which skills do you want to develop further?** *Not jumping in with my perspective or solutions prematurely; asking for explicit permission to share my viewpoint or advice.*

2. **Which skills are foundational?** *Slowing down, listening attentively, and using clarifying and empathetic statements to make people feel heard.*

3. **Which skills are your highest priority?** *Using empathetic statements such as "Wow, I hear you." "This has to be tough for you." and clarifying what was said.*

Figure 1.4   Example of the Identify step.

with the reality of actually being able to achieve your goals. Remember, with the ILM, you will cycle several times through GUIDES and practice new skills until they become habits; therefore, you do not need to pile everything into one iteration or cycle of improvement. Strive to make each cycle manageable so that you can sustain your commitment to professional development over the long term.

Once you have designed your development plan, it is time to implement it in the next step of the GUIDES process: Execute.

Execute

Now that you have spent a significant amount of time thinking and processing how to improve some of your leadership skills, you are ready for action. As Peter Drucker is often attributed with saying, "Ideas don't move the mountains, bulldozers do." Through practice – through learning by doing – you can change ingrained habits that may hinder your leadership development and derail your success. Depending on which skill you are working on, the frequency of practice may change. If you

Step 4: DESIGN your leadership development plan.

What are your development priorities? Record two or three high-priority opportunities and actions.

Area for Development	Developmental Opportunity	Actions to Take	Resources Needed	Target Date	Success Metrics
Effective Communication	*Listening with respect and empathy*	*Use empathetic statements*	*Post-its with prerecorded statements*	*10/15/23*	*Tick sheet can be used in meetings to track number of times I take this action*
Effective Communication	*Listening with respect and empathy*	*Clarify what was said*	*Notebook to take notes to help clarify*	*11/1/23*	*Tick sheet, as above*

Look over your development plan, then consider these questions. Record your thoughts below.

1. **Does this plan address the foundational opportunities identified in your self-assessment, research, and input from others?** *Yes, it helps me practice empathetic communication and clarifying so people feel understood.*

2. **Does your plan take into consideration the personal triggers that could help or hinder your development?** *Yes, I will use a visual cue such as a sticky note to remind me to use empathetic and clarifying statements.*

3. **Is the plan incremental and doable?** *Yes, using sticky notes as a reminder is very doable.*

4. **Are you excited about your plan? Why or why not?** *Yes, it is simple, and I will practice developing a habit.*

Figure 1.5   Example of the Design step.

are working on "Listen with respect and empathy," you may have daily opportunities to practice a new skill. It is critical to add your execution steps (or action plan) to your calendar. Add visual reminders to trigger intentional practice. If you are going into a meeting or a situation where you intend to use newly learned skills, spend a few minutes to get centered, to achieve the right mental state. If you get easily distracted due to stress or excitement and forget to practice, choose a signal to help you stay on track. For some people, it may be sitting on their hands. For others, it may be writing reminders in a notebook. One executive used sticky notes to write out empathetic and clarifying statements which she attached to the computer screen during virtual meetings. Whichever method you use is unimportant as long as it is a method that works for you. Making leadership skills changes is no different than diabetes management or another lifestyle change that requires practice and persistence. It is well known that regular glucose testing and the act of recording the results will improve diabetes control. For new skills to become habits, consistent practice is a must. It is the process of doing – and not the process of thinking – in which your new skill will become part of your leadership DNA. Record specific actions you will take, as shown in Figure 1.6.

The key question in the Execute step is: How will you know if you are improving and becoming a more successful leader? To answer this, let's move to the next step: Self-Reflect.

Self-Reflect

Self-reflection is a practice that requires a few minutes each day or week to focus on your professional development journey. Reflection time has to be planned, deliberate, and purposeful. It is a personal experience. It requires digging deeper and observing our own behaviors from the balcony, not the dance floor, a metaphor coined by Heifetz and Linsky in their book *The Practice of Adaptive Leadership: Tools and Tactics for Changing Your Organization and the World* (2009). What some call "reflection" is often just thinking about the day in a haphazard and random way. We may replay upsetting conversations and think about what we should or should not have said. We may hyper-focus on minute details of the day that may feel urgent but are not critical. We may obsess over a presentation or report, dwelling over details we may have missed. Though reflecting while bike riding or walking the dog is useful, having time blocked on the calendar

---

Step 5: EXECUTE your development plan.

Put your development plan into action! As you proceed with the execution of your plan, spend a few minutes thinking about each of these questions. Record your thoughts and responses.

1. **What circumstances or triggers will signal that "now" is the time to act and practice new behaviors?** *Whenever I am asked a question in a meeting, I will acknowledge the person asking and, if needed, clarify the question to make the person feel heard.*

2. **What specific behavior(s) or action(s) will you try? How far are you willing to push your comfort zone?** *Even if the question is triggering, I will use an empathetic and/or clarifying phrase and will not appear defensive, which is often my natural response.*

3. **How do you know if you are improving and becoming more successful with this attribute and as a leader?** *I will check in with my peers, superiors, and direct reports weekly to see my progress.*

4. **How will you gauge the impact of your actions or behavior changes? What responses will you be watching for?** *I will observe if I am putting people at ease or on the defensive. I will observe how my responses change the temperature in the room.*

Figure 1.6   Example of the Execute step.

---

is better. Use a set of questions like those in Figure 1.7 to guide the reflection process. Adopt and adapt the questions to suit the Leadership Attributes and skills you are honing. Take time to reflect on both personal development and work-related activities to accelerate your growth that will make you stand out as a leader.

Step 6: SELF-REFLECT on your execution of the development plan.

Spend a few minutes at the end of the day and/or week thinking about each of these questions. Record your thoughts and responses.

1. **Was I mindful of my development today/this week? What did I do well? What could I have done better?** *I am glad that out of five meetings today, I was intentional in three of them about slowing down, acknowledging my colleagues, and clarifying what they shared with me.*

2. **How did others respond when I intentionally led in a new way? Were people more (or less) engaged with me as a leader?** *I am not sure yet and will have to check in to find out.*

3. **Was I mindful of my triggers? How did I respond to those?** *In a meeting with the CFO, I got triggered and couldn't focus on her argument. Instead, I tried to convince her of my point of view, and she wasn't tracking with me, appearing unusually tense.*

4. **What will I do differently tomorrow/next week? What should I be watching for?** *Next time, I will ask her questions to understand her perspective better.*

5. **What else do I need to do or learn to further my development of this attribute?** *I should start asking people to reflect on my understanding of their problems so I can see they are connecting with me. I finally understand that relationships are a prerequisite to me getting things done that require cooperation from others.*

Figure 1.7   Example of the Self-Reflect step.

Prepare for Your Leadership Development Journey

Now that we have introduced the ILM and the GUIDES development process and plan, reflect on your leadership journey for a few minutes. Be mindful of your starting point and where you want to go as a leader.

- What are your professional goals?
- What kind of leader do you want to be?
- How would you describe your leadership style (e.g., direct, coaching, autonomous)?
- How would you describe your leader mindset (e.g., beliefs, attitudes, notions)?
- How would you describe an effective leader?
- What worries you the most about (a) this process and (b) your ability to be successful?

You may have concerns about your starting point. This is common. You won't be perfect on day one. Knowing that your vulnerability is real and uncomfortable is vital to your success. You will not always be in control or make the right decisions. Failures in leadership are opportunities for learning, growth, and improvement. This "failure as an opportunity" thinking is a different mindset from your clinical practice. Unlike in clinical practice, there is greater leeway to experiment in business. "Failures" are the golden nuggets for growth.

The ILM helps you develop the necessary mindset for successful leadership. Commit to investing in yourself: actively engage in the activities throughout this book and reflect on your growth. Remember, this is a continuous learning journey; there is no endpoint at which you will one day arrive and declare that the journey is over.

Bibliography

Heifetz, Ronald A., Marty Linsky, and Alexander Grashow. *The Practice of Adaptive Leadership: Tools and Tactics for Changing Your Organization and the World.* Boston, MA: Harvard Business Review Press, 2009.

Chapter 2

Seven Leadership Attributes for Successful Physician Leaders

A true leader has the confidence to stand alone, the courage to make tough decisions, and the compassion to listen to the needs of others.

Douglas MacArthur

The aim of leadership should be to improve the performance of man and machine, to improve quality, to increase output, and simultaneously to bring pride of workmanship to people.

W. Edwards Deming

Introduction

As new writing partners, our first collaborative session was the easiest. Standing by the large, clean whiteboard, we quickly created a list of characteristics of successful leaders, recalling the many people we have worked with and everything we knew that contributed to their success. The whiteboard filled up fast as we both called out and wrote down one characteristic after another. We were challenged later when it came time to select only the essential characteristics to include in this book from

DOI: 10.4324/9780429352355-2

that long list. We ultimately chose seven characteristics and called them Leadership Attributes.

1. Strategic Thinker
2. Effective Communicator
3. Coach
4. Team Builder
5. Change Manager
6. Learner-in-Chief
7. Problem-Solver

These Leadership Attributes are critical to success in today's super-competitive healthcare environment. Excellent social skills, such as emotional intelligence, humility, and approachability, are essential to leadership but are not enough. The seven attributes have technical aspects intertwined with soft skills that drive strategic breakthroughs, organizational learning, and iterative innovation. Fortunately, many physicians have experience and practice with facets of each of the seven attributes through clinical training and practice. Yet, surprisingly, physician leaders may find it difficult to transfer their patient care skills to business interactions and relationships. As you study the seven vital Leadership Attributes, it will become easier to connect what you do in your clinical practice to the business environment.

The term "Leadership Attribute" is meant to collectively encompass the necessary skills, characteristics, and competencies that set great leaders apart. Each attribute is brought to life through case studies, leader profiles, didactic content, reflection questions, and exercises to improve and broaden your grasp of the concepts. Each attribute is further enriched with the contributions of expertise and wisdom of several physician and non-physician leaders who generously shared their leadership lessons and experiences with us through interviews.

Often, attributes are confused with leadership styles such as authoritarian, democratic, participatory, visionary, and laissez-faire. This book intends to focus on something other than leadership styles and instead, the focus is on leaders appropriately flexing their approach based on their assessment of the situation and adjusting as needed to engage, influence, and inspire others. For example, some leadership situations may require an authoritarian style, while others may call for a coaching or visionary style. Just as a physician uses a nuanced approach in caring for patients with distinct medical conditions, a leader should be able to flex their approach to varied business and people situations.

Leadership Attributes are more static. They are ingrained habits that will take effort to change. They can't be easily flexed but can be improved through continuous learning and intentional practice. Therefore, it will be worthwhile to master the seven Leadership Attributes to thrive as a physician leader.

> Janelle Banat, Founder and CEO of Footlamp Consulting, LLC, coached many physicians at all levels of leadership from clinic chiefs to executives. She helped many physician leaders change unproductive behaviors and habits. *Although it is near impossible to remove the old neural pathways resulting in habits we would like to get rid of, it is, thankfully, incredibly easy to create the new neural pathways to the behaviors we desire. With the right technique, attention, and energy on the preferred behaviors, any and all of the old behaviors can be transformed into a new, and better way forward.*

Leadership Attributes

This section briefly introduces each of the seven Leadership Attributes. Subsequent chapters dive deeply into each attribute, providing context and the necessary mindset and Leadership Strategies for success. Each chapter also includes an example of the GUIDES development plan to assist you in completing your own development plan. Appendix 1 contains a template of the GUIDES Framework.

Adopting the Iterative Leadership Model (ILM) and the GUIDES (**G**ather, **U**nderstand, **I**dentify, **D**esign, **E**xecute, and **S**elf-Reflect) Framework to hone the seven Leadership Attributes and Leadership Strategies is shown in Figure 2.1.

Strategic Thinker

Strategic thinkers analyze ambiguous external environments, coalesce various stakeholders around the mission, vision, and values, and focus on the vital few initiatives to drive results and achieve outcome metrics. They create a line of sight between frontline teams and executives, tapping into collective energy and ingenuity to bring to life cutting-edge solutions.

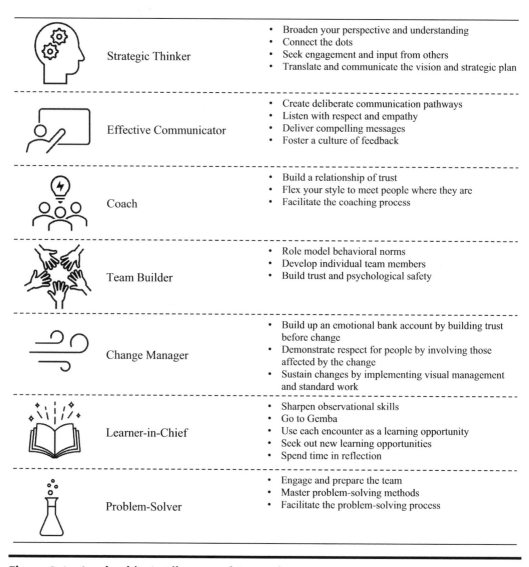

	Strategic Thinker	• Broaden your perspective and understanding • Connect the dots • Seek engagement and input from others • Translate and communicate the vision and strategic plan
	Effective Communicator	• Create deliberate communication pathways • Listen with respect and empathy • Deliver compelling messages • Foster a culture of feedback
	Coach	• Build a relationship of trust • Flex your style to meet people where they are • Facilitate the coaching process
	Team Builder	• Role model behavioral norms • Develop individual team members • Build trust and psychological safety
	Change Manager	• Build up an emotional bank account by building trust before change • Demonstrate respect for people by involving those affected by the change • Sustain changes by implementing visual management and standard work
	Learner-in-Chief	• Sharpen observational skills • Go to Gemba • Use each encounter as a learning opportunity • Seek out new learning opportunities • Spend time in reflection
	Problem-Solver	• Engage and prepare the team • Master problem-solving methods • Facilitate the problem-solving process

Figure 2.1   Leadership Attributes and Strategies.

Identify someone who you think is a great strategic thinker.

■ What makes them stand out?
■ How do they engage others in developing strategy?
■ How do they communicate their vision?
■ How do they connect strategy to operational action plans?

What is your experience with strategic planning? You may have participated in or led the development and execution of a strategic initiative. Or you may have minimal exposure to strategic planning. For new physician leaders, working and thinking at the strategic level can be challenging and uncomfortable. In addition, making strategic decisions can sometimes feel like trying to predict the future. Chapter 3 provides an overview of the strategic planning process, then highlights four Leadership Strategies to develop your strategic thinking skills:

■ Broaden your perspective and understanding.
■ Connect the dots.
■ Seek engagement and input from others.
■ Translate and communicate the vision and strategic plan.

Whether experienced or novice, these are the skills to engage you and your colleagues and teams in the process. In addition, to be an exceptional strategic thinker – to translate strategy into operating plans throughout the business enterprise – one must have first-rate communication skills.

Effective Communicator

Communication skills are the centerpiece of medical education throughout a physician's career. Just as physicians invest significant effort and time in developing effective communication skills, so should physician leaders. There is both an art and a science to effective communication. Getting it right is foundational to your success with all other attributes. Coaching, team building, leading change, creating a learning organization, and problem-solving require effective communication.

Identify someone you consider to be an effective communicator.

■ Why do you think they are effective?
■ What characteristics make them stand out?

Think about your own communication skills.

■ Are you ever frustrated that the information you are communicating doesn't reach your audience as intended?
■ Are the people you are communicating with not understanding or embracing your message?

Perhaps you've asked yourself, "How can I communicate more effectively?" Chapter 4 introduces four Leadership Strategies that will help you excel as an Effective Communicator:

- Create deliberate communication pathways.
- Listen with respect and empathy.
- Deliver compelling messages.
- Foster a culture of feedback.

Starting with a strong foundation in effective communication will help you master other Leadership Attributes. Take coaching, for example.

Coach

Coaching is a critical leadership skill. The impact of leading through coaching is a game changer. Coaching can feel unnatural and even contentious at times. However, coaching sets people up for success and ensures they perform to their full potential. There are many examples when the performance of individuals completely turned around through intentional, direct, and timely coaching. Coaching based on facts (and not assumptions) creates visibility into the leadership behaviors to be refined. Coaching is analogous to providing medical advice to your patients. It should not be threatening or intimidating. Leaders demonstrate respect and caring when they focus on developing others. They build close relationships and personal connections. For them, coaching their direct reports and teams is an integral part of their job. Formal and informal opportunities for coaching are abundant.

Think of someone you consider a gifted coach or mentor.

- Why do you think of them as great?
- What skills and characteristics do they exhibit?
- How do they engage and relate to those they are coaching or mentoring?

Chapter 5 discusses three Leadership Strategies to hone your coaching skills:

1. Build a relationship of trust.
2. Flex your style to meet people where they are.
3. Facilitate the coaching process.

Coaching skills are a prerequisite to mastering team building. Developing individual team players and the team as a cohesive group requires intentional and ad hoc coaching skills.

Team Builder

The most successful organizations develop high-functioning teams led by strong leaders. There is a great deal of literature on high-performing teams.

- How would you describe the best team you were part of?
- What steps did the leader take to develop the high-performing team?

Chapter 6 demonstrates how the ILM and GUIDES Framework support your effort to develop highly effective teams. You will understand your team's current state of performance, envision what a successful, cohesive team looks like, and iterate together to improve continuously as a team. The following Leadership Strategies to strengthen team building are discussed:

- Role model behavioral norms.
- Develop individual team members.
- Build trust and psychological safety.

In this chapter we discuss the phenomenon of physician as the "captain of the ship" that can derail leadership effectiveness. Transitioning from the "I" (lone hero) mentality to the "We" (team) mentality is a vital leap to advance your healthcare leadership journey.

Change Manager

Leaders are often faced with uncertainty, ambiguity, and change; these are regular occurrences that can cause unnecessary anxiety in an organization. Change management is one of the most frequently discussed topics in business publications. Changing behaviors and habits, whether at work with colleagues and teams or in the exam room with patients, requires herculean effort. Only one-third of change initiatives take hold, resulting in wasted human effort and financial resources.

Think of a time when you experienced ambivalence about change.

- What role did leaders play?
- How did leaders help ease tension?
- How did they communicate to the team and the individuals impacted?
- What actions did they take that were most helpful, and what steps could have helped the situation more?

Chapter 7 focuses on practical approaches to change management and exploring parallels with the exam room experience through these Leadership Strategies:

- Build up an emotional bank account by building trust before change.
- Demonstrate respect for people by involving those affected by the change.
- Sustain changes by implementing visual management and standard work.

Learner-in-Chief

Being a Learner-in-Chief is about embracing learning opportunities, especially those that are new and different. For example, while doctors spend a lot of time-consuming an inordinate amount of medical information, they may find leadership and business education boring and some may even think it is irrelevant to their day-to-day activities.

Identify someone you think learns continuously and reinvents themselves as a leader.

- Why do you think of them in that way?
- What do you think they do to remain consistently effective?
- How do they demonstrate a "continuous learner's" mindset?
- Where and how do they seek knowledge to stay ahead of the game?

Learning and self-development do not often make a top ten list of crucial leadership characteristics. Yet, as healthcare undergoes regular and seismic transformations, leaders who prioritize learning create organizations that ultimately are more successful and have a competitive advantage. Leaders can learn in many ways, including:

- Reading business publications, listening to podcasts, and attending conferences.
- Experiential learning by engaging with patients and frontline employees.
- Learning internal or external best practices and benchmarks.
- Personal reflection time to consider what worked and what didn't in leadership situations.

Your effectiveness and ultimate growth in your leadership career requires commitment and a passion for learning. Following Learner-in-Chief strategies will accelerate your self-development and allow you to role model them for your team, peers, and other leaders:

- Sharpen observational skills.
- Go to Gemba (the "actual place," where value is created for the patient or customer).
- Use each encounter as a learning opportunity.
- Seek out new learning opportunities.
- Spend time in reflection.

Problem-Solver

Think of a time when you worked with a team to problem-solve an issue in your organization.

- What process was used?
- How did the discussion start (e.g., by brainstorming solutions or identifying what may have contributed to the problem)?
- Did all the team members contribute to the discussion?
- Did everyone agree on what problem they were trying to solve?

Problem-solving is not a stand-alone attribute but an amalgamation of all other Leadership Attributes. For example, to solve small and large problems, you have to balance being strategic with being tactical, which may feel like walking a tightrope. In addition, your ability to take your team through a structured problem-solving process while leaving room for creativity and innovation requires considerable communication and change management skills. In this space, you will shine as a leader, role modeling the Problem-Solver strategies below as well as those for the previous six Leadership Attributes:

- Engage and prepare the team.
- Master problem-solving methods.
- Facilitate the problem-solving process.

Before you turn the pages of this book to learn more about each of the seven critical Leadership Attributes, please reflect on the following questions:

- What is your reaction to our characterization of these attributes as critical to success?
- How can developing each of the Leadership Attributes help you excel in your role?
- Which of the Leadership Attributes do you feel you have already mastered? Which of the Leadership Attributes will you need to focus on?

As you read the pages of this book, please remember that your professional development is a continuous journey and not a destination. Don't be disappointed if you zigzag or experience temporary setbacks as you learn and develop your leadership acumen.

> *Every day you may make progress. Every step may be fruitful. Yet there will stretch out before you an ever-lengthening, ever-ascending, ever-improving path. You know you will never get to the end of the journey. But this, so far from discouraging, only adds to the joy and glory of the climb.*
>
> **Sir Winston Churchill**

Chapter 3

Strategic Thinker

A strategy is necessary because the future is unpredictable.

Robert Waterman

The best way to predict the future is to create it.

Peter Drucker

Leadership Case Study: Preparing for the Strategic Planning Process

Dr. Catherine Willis re-read the email she had just received from the Chief Executive Officer (CEO). She was excited to learn she would join a leadership team meeting in a few weeks to develop the organization's long-term strategic plan. As the recently appointed senior medical director for the West Region, Catherine had never participated in the organization's strategic planning process. Still, she had several ideas to present that would evolve her leadership role and transform her region. Moreover, she felt certain the leaders who reported to her would also like to contribute their ideas to the strategic plan. The CEO's memo suggested that participants could prepare for the planning process by reviewing the organization's previous strategic plans and current financial performance and looking at regional market conditions and local competition. Catherine thought she could probably locate and review most of the recommended materials.

DOI: 10.4324/9780429352355-3

Armed with ideas for the future and an understanding of the past, she was confident in her ability to contribute to the organization's strategic plan. Yet, to be thoroughly prepared for the first planning session, Catherine wondered if there was anything else she should be paying attention to; she decided to call her leadership coach to ask some questions and learn more.

Introduction

An organizational strategy is a big-picture view of issues that affect the organization as a whole. It represents how the organization intends to thrive and fulfill its mission and vision for a defined time horizon, such as three or five years. In healthcare, the strategy usually focuses on exceptional patient (or customer) experience, geographic or service expansion, financial security, and high-quality care. So how is a strategic plan created? Strategy design and implementation methods vary among organizations. However, what successful organizations have in common is that they follow a defined process with inputs from various stakeholders which is executed diligently within a specified timeframe.

Whether developing an organization's long-term strategy or creating a new medical subspecialty service line, a strategic thinker engages a group of leaders in brainstorming to generate a vision, strategic direction, and plan for future success. This strategic plan reflects intentional choices made with careful deliberation by physicians and administrative leaders at all levels. Ultimately, this plan acts as a map by which the group navigates to its future, with leaders at the helm, making adjustments in response to new or changing internal and external factors. The finished strategic plan is a dynamic document that answers three questions:

1. Where are we now?
2. Where are we going?
3. How will we get there?

Where Are We Now?

This first step includes the assessment of the organization's current strengths and weaknesses and identifies challenges and opportunities in the industry, the market, and the competition. Leaders gather and analyze relevant inputs, such as facts and data about the patient's (or customer's) needs and expectations, market research, industry trends and risks, and financial and capital resource needs. In addition, they perform an environmental assessment such as a SWOT analysis (Strengths, Weaknesses, Opportunities, and Threats), traditionally employed to systematically assess internal strengths and weaknesses and external opportunities and threats. In this step, leaders define the unique value the organization brings to its patients (or customers) within the context of its mission and vision, then evaluate its ability to execute its strategy. This step is akin to a clinician:

- Taking a patient's history (subjective or qualitative data).
- Conducting a physical exam and ordering diagnostic tests (objective or quantitative data).
- Understanding the patient's values and vision for their future health and treatment goals.

Where Are We Going?

In the next step, leaders respond to current conditions. They discuss and debate ideas and options based on their diagnosis of current and future challenges and their strategy to outperform competitors. They choose the best way to grow the business, deal with anticipated market and regulatory forces, and assess the financial and human resources needed to achieve its strategic goals. This step is similar to the assessment part of the physician–patient visit.

Focusing on the few initiatives most likely to achieve the desired outcomes is critical for organizational success. Strategies may fail due to a lack of focus, as organizations spread their human and financial resources too thinly. Just as patients can only change one or two health routines, organizations can only change one or two principal capabilities and sustain them over time.

How Are We Going to Get There?

In the last step, leaders create a first draft of the strategic plan, which is then shared with operational leaders to test for accuracy and completeness of their assessment of challenges, and the priorities and activities identified to meet those challenges. Then, in close collaboration with operational leaders, the strategic plan is translated into operating or implementation action plans.

Sharing, communicating, and "translating" the strategic plan into operational action plans is critical. Operational leaders are expected and entrusted to execute the strategy, so they must clearly understand and advocate for it. Executing the strategic plan is a core responsibility of operational leaders. They are responsible for creating operational action plans with concrete steps, milestones, and targets that reflect and align with the strategy. Their responsibility is then to carry out that plan to achieve the intended results.

Just as physicians continue to iterate patient clinical plans in consultation with patients, executive leaders in close collaboration with operational leaders continue to iterate strategic and operating plans as new inputs come in.

Regardless of the strategic planning process an organization uses, the role and expectations of leaders are the same:

■ Participate in the development of the strategy.
■ Make difficult choices to prioritize the activities to engage in.
■ Translate the strategy into implementation plans.
■ Communicate the plans.
■ Solicit input from others to iterate the strategy.
■ Maintain organizational focus and commitment to execute the strategy.

With an understanding of how strategic and operational plans are developed and the role that leaders play, the next step is delving into the mindset and four Leadership Strategies necessary to lead successfully as a strategic thinker. To bring it closer to home, parallels are drawn between clinical practice and physician leadership. Finally, at the end of the chapter, to help build your strategic thinker muscle, the personalized GUIDES development plan is provided for you to create your own plan.

Take a moment to review your notes in Chapter 2 in response to the question, "Who do you consider to be a great strategic thinker, and why?" Keep this person in mind as you read this chapter.

Physician Leader as Strategic Thinker

What clinical practice strategies do you recognize in the strategic thinker attribute? Though you may be new to the strategy design process as a physician leader, you will recognize similarities in the mindset, approach, and skills used in the exam room as a practicing physician. Mapping a plan for the health and well-being of a patient is similar to designing a roadmap for a healthy organization. Many physicians practice daily in an environment of fast-moving case assessments, evidence-based decisions, and directing the work of care team members. The practice is primarily focused on today: today's patients, today's problems, and today's tasks. The clinical day often involves activities to address patients' immediate concerns. Yet, in addition to these day-to-day transactions, physicians must also focus on long-term health goals and clinical outcomes along with mapping strategies designed to achieve them. In doing so, the practicing physician considers a patient's condition or disease state today ("Where are we now?"), their health goals for the future ("Where are we going?"), and the treatment plan to achieve those goals ("How will we get there?"). Physicians are always thinking ahead, considering how the care plan will impact the patient now, in the short term, and in the long term, throughout the disease course. Both time horizons require creatively engaging patients and crafting a tailored approach to the unique situation. The focus on long-term targets (strategy) while addressing immediate needs (tactics) is similar in both clinical and business practices. Just as practicing physicians create unique treatment plans to ensure patients' long-term health, administrative leaders develop tailored organizational plans to secure long-term viability and success.

Mindset of the Strategic Thinker

Whether practicing physician or administrator, the strategic thinker often finds themself assessing incomplete and ambiguous information and formulating a longer-term plan – for the patient or the organization – that mitigates risks, leverages opportunities, and judiciously applies resources to achieve the goals.

Strategic thinkers usually think many steps ahead about the organization's future, evolving patient needs and expectations, fluctuating markets, and environmental conditions, and how the competition responds. Strategic thinkers' mindset is open-minded and future-focused. They are willing to challenge generally accepted views (including their own), the status quo, and even historical best practices. They catalyze others to pursue innovation, accelerating the organization's ability to excel and improving outcomes and performance. Strategic thinkers are learners; they seek new knowledge and try new ideas. They reimagine the future while keeping their finger on the organization's pulse and the tactical work that is currently underway. They are attuned to the organization's culture and create intentional communication opportunities to bring their teams along on this forward-looking journey. They can paint a clear and exciting vision of the future, engaging the hearts and minds of the people.

> *Leaders who are AMBIGUOUS create followers who are AMBIVALENT.*
>
> **Jack Cochran, MD**

Leadership Strategies for the Strategic Thinker

What advice might Dr. Catherine Willis (introduced at the beginning of this chapter) receive from her leadership coach? Catherine felt confident about the process of strategic planning. However, she wanted reassurance that her approach would prepare her to contribute meaningfully and fulfill her role in her organization's strategic planning process. In coaching leaders like Catherine, we would introduce her to four Leadership Strategies we have observed in effective strategic thinkers:

1. Broaden your perspective and understanding.
2. Connect the dots.
3. Seek engagement and input from others.
4. Translate and communicate the vision and strategic plan.

These Leadership Strategies will help Catherine and other leaders prepare for the strategic planning process in their organization and engage with leadership teams. They will also inform the answers to the questions posed earlier (Where are you now? Where are you going? How will you get there?) and provide techniques for gaining buy-in and communicating the plan to others.

Broaden Your Perspective and Understanding

Defining market differentiation is one outcome of creating and implementing an organizational strategic plan. It is only possible to gauge differentiation by understanding current and emerging patient (or customer) needs, local and regional markets, and the competition. That is why strategic thinkers strive to see the big picture and broaden their perspectives by reading, listening, learning, sharing, and seeking information. They seek opportunities to gain insights about internal and external trends and new business drivers in the industry, imagining what success in healthcare might look like in one, five, or even ten years. They amass a wide assortment of information and consider how their organization – or even a department – should adapt and innovate to achieve differentiation.

COACH'S CORNER: HOW ONE LEADER BROADENS HIS PERSPECTIVE

I coached a leader for several years. He was a successful healthcare executive, considered to have exceptional strategic skills. He stayed current by reading articles about the local and national healthcare market trends. He considered how his organization performed by comparison and what adjustments it needed to make to remain competitive. Although incredibly busy, he regularly connected by phone and email with colleagues and acquaintances outside of the organization. He leveraged his network at conferences, breakfast meetings, dinner meetings, and even while at the gym. He also spent time with people inside his organization in individual conversations and group meetings, sharing what he was hearing and seeking perspective from those caring for patients every day. These inputs contributed to his broadened perspective and gave him invaluable insight into the views and attitudes of the individuals inside the organization.

A leader's approach to broadening their understanding is a foundational skill for the strategic thinker. Nevertheless, this idea can make some leaders uncomfortable, as they may have been successfully relying on their current playbook for many years. It can feel risky to put that aside and be open to a different approach, and it may prompt questions for leaders, such as:

■ How do I know this approach will work?
■ Does this mean my previous way of thinking was wrong?
■ What will my colleagues think if I put out different ideas than I have previously?

These are natural questions but don't shy away from the challenge of broadening your thinking. This can be a pivotal moment in evolving your strategic thinking mindset.

> *A strategic thinker is able to think conceptually: "What do you want the organization to look like? What are you seeing that healthcare is doing right?" Another question you may have thought of is: "In the busy-ness of my day, where will I find the time to regularly engage in the activities to keep abreast of market and industry trends and innovations?" As a leader, managing your time is critical to your success. Getting bogged down with fire-fighting – jumping from one crisis to the next all day long – means that you will not have the capacity or mental energy to operate at the strategic level. Firefighting isn't necessarily bad; it is often an unavoidable and normal part of the work. We are not advocating for leaders to be detached from realities on the ground – quite the opposite. There are times when leaders will need to be more tactical and less strategic; however, as you advance in your leadership career, your focus should naturally shift toward strategy and coaching and developing others to carry out the strategy. Therefore, as a leader, you must balance strategy with daily operations so you are not consumed with managing the urgent minutiae and thus miss opportunities to see the critical connections between the organization's core work and the bigger picture.*

> **Barbara Ladon**, *Managing Director, CB Vision*

COACH'S CORNER: THE FIREFIGHTING LEADER

While consulting for several years with the leadership team of a cancer care clinic, a specific coaching focal point was to help them think more strategically and learn how to balance long-term focus with daily operations. The chief nursing officer said one day, "I won't be happy if I'm not fire-fighting every day. This is how I add value, and I enjoy solving problems for people. This is why I come to work."

Remember, leaders set direction (vision) and adjust the course (the strategy) based on the conditions and realities inside and outside the organization. Strategic thinkers bring value to the organization when they spend more time in what Stephen Covey categorized as "Quadrant

II," not urgent but important activities (2013). Managing your time is up to you. No one can do it for you. Table 3.1 presents best practices for avoiding firefighting.

Table 3.1   Best Practices for Avoiding Firefighting

Trap	Firefighting daily urgent problems leaves no time to focus on long-term strategic issues.
Best Practices	As you progress on your leadership ladder, spend more and more time addressing long-term issues, not urgent issues. Carve out time on your calendar for strategic thinking.
Questions to Ponder	■ How much time do I spend thinking about and planning for the future versus time spent firefighting? ■ What gets in my way of spending more time thinking about the future and the strategy of my organization or department?

Connect the Dots

Recall the successful healthcare executive introduced in the previous section. He knew all the activities meant to broaden his perspective were core to his success as a leader and critical to his organization's future. He ensured he had time to reflect on what he was hearing and learning from others and took time to consider what it meant to his organization, what innovations it might explore, and what new opportunities might be worth pursuing. He was connecting the dots. Connecting the dots is the second Leadership Strategy. Much like the dot-to-dot puzzles that kids solve – carefully penciling a line from one numbered dot to the next until the picture is finally revealed – practicing physicians "connect the dots" to diagnose a patient's health problem. Physicians connect the patient's symptoms, appearance, vital signs, and diagnostic test results to arrive at a "picture" of the patient's condition. Connecting disparate pieces of information to arrive at a decision or solve a problem is just as important in strategic thinking. As a physician leader, solving problems, making decisions, and developing organizational strategy are strengthened when you connect the dots and see the whole picture. Imagine holding a wide-angle lens to see the broadest view of the current situation and the context surrounding it. From that perspective, a strategic thinker can:

■ Look for relationships among multiple variables.
■ Consider past, current, and expected future performance, trends, and goals.
■ Estimate the impact of decisions on the organization's ability to thrive.

Making connections between the informational inputs positions the strategic thinker to assess the current situation accurately, answer the question "Where are we now?", and feed the generation of ideas for the organization's strategic plan. Then, in collaboration with others on the leadership team, you are ready for the question, "Where are we going?" This question is answered by linking the organization's purpose with its capabilities and narrowing the list of activities that will exploit its strengths, differentiate itself in the market, and produce value for its patients (or customers) and its people. Finally, in drafting the first version of the strategic plan's broad descriptive goals, choices can be made about the organization's priorities and aspirations and how it will close the gap between where it is now and where it wants to go.

By now, you have probably realized that strategic thinking is not limited to the annual process of strategic planning. Adopting a strategic mindset, practicing strategic thinking daily, and making connections to strategy in myriad activities strengthen your ability to plan long term while being flexible enough to adjust in the short term. For example, you may find yourself in a group problem-solving session where you have an opportunity to explain how this problem impacts overall organizational or department targets. Or you could be coaching a team member and have the chance to share with them how they can help support a change management effort going on in another part of the organization. In a reply to an email string, you may take the opportunity to reference how the topic fits in with an upcoming organizational initiative. These are just a few examples of how taking the time to "connect the dots" advances the organization's ultimate success. Table 3.2 presents best practices for connecting the dots.

Table 3.2 Best Practices for Connecting the Dots

Trap	Missing opportunities to highlight connections between various organizational activities and strategic imperatives.
Best Practices	Create a line of sight for frontline leaders and teams so they can see a direct connection between local and organization-wide goals.
Questions to Ponder	■ How does my team's work today connect to and influence the organization's strategic short-term targets and long-term goals? ■ How do I align my department's goals with that of my colleagues, so we can jointly drive organizational strategy?

Seek Engagement and Input from Others

Seeking engagement and input from others is critical in the strategic planning process. This Leadership Strategy requires considerable finesse and skill in order to:

- Build support for the plan.
- Surface gaps in thinking.
- Elicit new ideas and innovative approaches.
- Demonstrate respect for the expertise of the people closest to work.

Seeking engagement and input is not a consensus-building activity, and it will result in some tension and even conflict as difficult choices about organizational priorities need to be made. Not all ideas will be included in the strategic plan. Remember that you share a draft of the strategic plan in the interest of transparency and dialogue, so be ready for difficult conversations about the priorities. Invite feedback and input and be open to hearing new ideas and criticism.

> *We can't afford to do everything people identify as important. Brainstorming is the first step, followed by working collaboratively to identify top priorities. Then, communication is key. To be effective, people need clear feedback on what (policies or programs) have been selected and why. Let people know which ideas you can commit*

resources and leadership to. Tell people what you can and cannot do in a first round or budget cycle, but absolutely put them on the list for later consideration.

Barbara Ladon, *Managing Director, CB Vision*

Be humble in acknowledging that you do not have all the answers. Participation from others with diverging opinions will improve the next iteration of the strategy. How can you be effective in encouraging productive participation and discourse? We have four ideas:

1. Take time to educate and coach participants.
2. Ask engaging questions to prompt discussion.
3. Remain open-minded.
4. Close the loop with participants.

Educate and Coach

Discussions about strategy at the organizational or departmental level open up opportunities to teach and coach participants. Leverage these opportunities to share relevant information, such as the approach to the strategic planning process, how market intelligence was incorporated into the strategic plan, or how the day-to-day work connects to the goals, vision, and mission. If you aren't an expert on these topics, consider partnering with another leader who is so you can learn along with the others. Consider these golden opportunities to help develop your team and to advance the organization's strategy. Finally, actively look for opportunities to connect strategy to the daily work of frontline leaders, physicians, and staff.

Ask Engaging Questions

One of your objectives is to ask others to check the thinking process of the leadership team that drafted the strategic plan. When sharing the plan with others, ask questions to determine if the current state assessment is accurate and complete. Ask whether the activities and ideas presented will produce the intended results. Ask about the resources needed to carry out the activities. Ask what contributions participants could make toward the goals. Engage in a back-and-forth conversation and ask probing questions to clarify and ensure your understanding of the input and feedback.

Be Open-Minded

Being open-minded in the strategic planning process may seem obvious, but it is not always as easy as it sounds. In your leadership role, you have invested time and effort to develop the strategy and plan, participated in reviewing market data, set a long-term vision, and established annual goals and targets. When intimately involved in the process, you naturally become committed and attached to the outputs, making it hard to bear having them questioned or critiqued. Do your best to go into team discussions with a curious and open mind, willing to hear things you and other leaders may not have considered. Many pleasant surprises can surface when you enter the dialogue with an open, curious mindset, ready and eager to learn how others think. People need to feel that the plan is created for them, with them, and by them.

Close the Loop

What will you do with the input, feedback, and possible challenges you get to the strategic plan? You will bring it back to your leadership team for consideration. Some inputs you and your colleagues receive may be appropriate for your strategic-level discussions; some may be too detailed or tactical. Regardless, follow up with teams and individuals to close the communication loop and explain how their input was incorporated (or not) into the strategic plan and why. Acknowledge and respect the contributors and their contributions; demonstrate the value you place on their ideas and engagement in shaping the organization's path forward. Table 3.3 presents best practices for seeking engagement and input from others.

   After a series of back-and-forth conversations with colleagues and leaders, and further refinement of the strategic plan and its subsequent finalization, it is time to share it more broadly, especially with the leaders and teams responsible for carrying it out.

Translate and Share the Vision and Strategic Plan

In this final Leadership Strategy, actualizing the strategic plan becomes paramount, specifically, how to make it a reality across the organization and keep it alive beyond the initial roll-out. Let's begin by defining the phrase "translate the vision." Recall that the strategic plan contains broad,

Table 3.3   Best Practices for Seeking Engagement and Input from Others

Trap	Premature attachment to the plan while it is still being iterated.
Best Practices	The core strategy team engages in conversation with middle-level leaders, tossing ideas for tactics and metrics back and forth and incorporating input.
Questions to Ponder	■ What structured process should I use to facilitate preliminary strategy discussions with the next-level leaders? How will I incorporate their feedback? ■ How will I prevent groupthink? How will I elicit direct and unabashed feedback?

descriptive goals, objectives, and activities. A strategic plan is merely a map providing guidance to achieve the vision.

Translating is the process of articulating the destination, the intended route to get to the destination, the time it will take, and what (resources) will be needed to get there. The plan becomes relevant for departmental and frontline leaders when teams and individuals see their work reflected in it:

■ What are they expected to do differently?
■ What are they accountable for?
■ How will their work be measured?
■ How will their work contribute to the larger goals?

Typically, an action plan or operational plan is created by detailing the activities the department or team will engage in, a timeline for the activities, measurable targets, and the financial and human resources needed. The action plan is derived from and aligned with the strategic plan. Creating the action plan should not be a new task; it should already be underway. Think back on the previous Leadership Strategy, Seek Engagement and Input, where initial conversations about the activities, resources, targets, and results started. All the techniques presented in the Seek Engagement and Input section are just as helpful when you draft and negotiate action plans. Continue to model respectful communication and leadership behaviors:

■ Educating and coaching.
■ Asking questions.
■ Listening to ideas and criticism with an open mind and following up as needed.

Using these techniques grounds people as to where the organization is, where it is headed, and how they will contribute to achieving the vision by translating the strategic plan into concrete operational initiatives.

Bringing the plan to life means engaging hearts and motivating people to think beyond today's tasks and enlisting participation from those impacted by the plan's activities, ensuring everyone knows how they will contribute to fulfilling the organization's long-term vision and making the plan successful. Leaders are responsible for keeping the organizational focus on the plan's implementation and avoiding distractions, finding that balance between continuing to achieve organizational excellence today while also building its future.

Reflect on these questions as you consider how you will do this:

■ How will you persuasively tell the story of the organization's plan so that all staff can "see" the vision and understand how their work contributes to achieving it?
■ How will you engage others to gain their buy-in for the plan?
■ How will you get them excited about the future they get to build?
■ What challenges do you anticipate, and how might you mitigate them?

For each of these questions, think about the needs of your audience and the message you want to convey. Each audience will have its own information needs and communication preferences. The message must be compelling so your audience will listen to and understand the organization's vision, plan, and what it means for them. Formal and informal ways to deliver the message include written communications, town hall forums, staff meetings, huddles, and ad hoc conversations. Regardless of the delivery method, the message starts with you:

■ Be excited about the vision and plan you are sharing.
■ Be confident in the organization's direction and its leaders executing the plan.
■ Project enthusiasm and confidence.
■ Openly address concerns; use them to help refine your messaging in the future.
■ Invite participants to join you in sharing the vision and ask them what they need to support it.
■ Ask for their ideas on how to engage others in implementing the plan.
■ Find out what barriers they anticipate and how to overcome them.

Table 3.4   Best Practices for Communicating the Vision and Strategic Plan

Trap	Under-communicating the new strategy, initiatives, and targets.
Best Practices	■ Create a comprehensive cascading communication plan to make vision and strategy accessible to everyone in the organization. ■ Consider opportunities for bidirectional communication. ■ Over-communicate, over-communicate, over-communicate.
Questions to Ponder	■ How will I frame my communications so that everyone easily understands the plan? ■ How will I make the message "accessible"? (Consider using plain language and limiting jargon.)

People want to be involved, valued, and contributing to meaningful and impactful work. Translate and share the strategy with everyone in the organization to ensure the plans will be executed and the goals achieved. Table 3.4 presents best practices for communicating the vision and strategic plan.

Leadership Strategies: Bringing It All Together

What do these Leadership Strategies look like in action? A few years ago, one of the authors was privileged to provide strategic planning consultation to a large health system. Their goals were to design and implement a reliable and repeatable process for annual strategic planning and build the leadership team's strategic planning capabilities.

COACH'S CORNER: LEADERS COACHING LEADERS

The CEO was talented and skilled at thinking ahead, staying abreast of industry trends, connecting all the dots, and using it all to build the vision of where her organization might go in the future. The CEO also had the ability to share her vision with physicians, managers, and staff, effectively communicating and "translating" the opportunities she was seeing in such a way that others could also see them. She was planting these seeds, incrementally moving everyone's thinking forward and influencing their decisions all year long. In addition, she used every opportunity to share and test her vision with others and solicit their reaction, so momentum and support were already building internally when the formal strategic planning process began.

In coaching the CEO, we focused primarily on helping her sharpen her thinking, especially her assessment of the organization and how the current situation fit with her vision. This level of coaching support also helped prepare her for her role in guiding the leadership team, beginning with their readiness to participate in strategic conversations. She drafted several questions to help engage the team in the process, including:

- What is our vision in the next three to five years, focusing first on our patients, then our physicians and teams?
- What do we want our patients to say about us? What is their vision for providing healthcare to them, and how can we achieve that?
- What are our clinical quality goals?
- What type of environment do we want to have for our teams? How can we be the employer of choice in our community?
- What are our financial goals? Will these goals help us grow and expand our exceptional patient care and patient loyalty?
- What reputation do we want to have in our community?

Going through this questioning process with the CEO and her leadership team was eye-opening. Not surprisingly, some leaders posed the questions back to her and said they looked to her for these answers. Some leaders didn't know where to begin in trying to respond to the questions, while others provided responses resulting in rich dialogue that pushed everyone to think differently. The CEO encouraged every leader in the organization to contribute to its vision and strategy. From their responses, she had a much better idea of her leadership team's thinking and the level of mentoring and coaching she would need to help them through this process. This CEO's leadership exemplifies many vital qualities of a strategic thinker: visionary, communicator, listener, team builder, and collaborator.

Exceptional strategic thinkers can project the future, connect it to the present, navigate through stormy waters, and adjust the course as necessary – always staying attuned to internal and external inputs.

The GUIDES Framework and the Strategic Thinker

Let's return to the fictional Dr. Catherine Willis introduced in the Leadership Case Study at the beginning of this chapter. Many new physician leaders like Dr. Willis may not be:

- Experienced with accessing industry competition and benchmarks.
- Natural at thinking strategically, seeing the big picture, and connecting the dots.
- Comfortable making major decisions or taking action with limited information.
- Patient enough to engage others in the back-and-forth process of strategy iteration.
- Able to translate and communicate the vision and strategic plan in a compelling way.

As Dr. Willis turns to her executive coach to work through the four Leadership Strategies and GUIDES Framework to devise a personal Strategic Thinker development plan, the coach asks Dr. Willis the following questions to understand her leadership mindset, her grasp of the strategy design process in her organization, and her role as a leader in that process. In doing so, Dr. Willis realizes that while she does not immediately know every answer, she now knows what she must work on to prepare herself to contribute to the strategic planning process.

- How is the strategy developed in your organization?
- How is the competitive landscape analyzed?
- What is your role in developing the strategy in your organization?
- What are leaders expected to do before, during, and after the strategic planning process?
- How will you "connect the dots" and bring all the different inputs into a single view and find the emerging picture?
- How and when do other teams get engaged in the process?
- What is your role in engaging others in the process and sharing the vision?
- How will you solicit input from others and incorporate it into your thinking?

■ How will you translate and communicate the strategy/plan to others? How can you make the strategy or plan accessible and relevant to others?

This concludes our exploration of the four Leadership Strategies: (1) broaden your perspective and understanding, (2) connect the dots, (3) seek engagement and input from others, and (4) translate and communicate the vision and strategic plan. In Chapter 2 we asked you to think of someone you consider to be a great strategic thinker. To what extent do they embody and demonstrate the four Leadership Strategies?

Next, access and print the GUIDES Development Plan template in Appendix 1 and create a development plan to improve your strategic thinking skills. See Figure 3.1 as an example of honing the Leadership Strategy "Seeking engagement and input from others."

GUIDES Development Plan – Strategic Thinker

Step 1: GATHER inputs to evaluate your skills gaps and opportunities for development.

1. Record your own assessment of your degree of confidence in these skills.

To what extent are you confident in your ability to:	Not at all	Somewhat	Great deal
Broaden your perspective and understanding		x	
Connect the dots		x	
Seek engagement and input from others	x		
Translate and communicate the strategic plan		x	

Figure 3.1 Example of GUIDES Development Plan for Strategic Thinker.

2. **Reflect on your answers to the questions above. Record your additional thoughts.** *After reading this chapter, I know I must focus on the "Seek engagement and input from others" strategy while working on the other three strategies.*

3. **Ask for feedback from others (e.g., trusted colleagues, your coach, or direct reports) on the skills, and take notes.** *My coach helped me better understand that I need to "Broaden my perspective" by getting background information on prior strategic work in my company and understanding internal strengths and weaknesses as well as the competitive landscape.*

4. **What does your additional research tell you about this attribute?** *Many strategies don't get implemented due to poor communication, resulting in employees not understanding or implementing the strategy.*

Step 2: UNDERSTAND and interpret the data you collected.

The following questions help you understand and interpret the data you collected in the GATHER step. Spend a few minutes thinking about these questions. Record your thoughts and responses.

1. **What did you learn from your self-assessment?** *I tend to underestimate the time and effort needed to communicate new initiatives and get constructive feedback from my teams.*

2. **How did you interpret feedback from others (e.g., trusted colleagues, your coach, or reports)? Were you surprised? Did their feedback match your self-assessment?** *I get attached to the decisions or solutions I've developed with others, and I find myself taking other's input and feedback personally.*

3. **What were your key takeaways from the research? Were you surprised by anything you learned?** *The strategic plan must be*

Figure 3.1 (Continued)

focused and clear. It should be discussed in multiple venues. The process of strategy development must be built into my leadership routines.

Step 3: IDENTIFY your strengths and opportunities.

Spend a few minutes thinking about each of these questions. Record your thoughts and responses.

1. **Which skills do you want to develop further?** *Presenting strategy effectively to leaders who are not part of the design, then iterating the strategy based on their constructive feedback.*

2. **Which skills are foundational?** *"Connecting the dots" for people who need to develop operational plans from the strategy, showing how their day-to-day work contributes to the company vision.*

3. **Which skills are your highest priority?** *Getting buy-in into the strategy so everyone becomes an owner of operational strategy execution.*

Step 4: DESIGN your leadership development plan.

What are your development priorities? Record two or three high-priority opportunities and actions.

Area for Development	Developmental Opportunity	Actions to Take	Resources Needed	Target Date	Success Metrics
Strategic Thinker	*Seek engagement and input from others*	*Conduct 1:1 and group meetings*	*Ask my assistant to schedule*	*1/1/24*	*Complete all meetings.* *Close the loop with all meeting participants.* *Complete a Reflection exercise.*

Figure 3.1   (Continued)

Look over your development plan, then consider these questions. Record your thoughts below.

1. **Does this plan address the foundational opportunities identified in your self-assessment, research, and input from others?** *This plan will help me practice effective communication to seek understanding and accept feedback.*

2. **Does your plan take into consideration the personal triggers that could help or hinder your development?** *Yes, I cringe from feedback and take it personally when decisions I am attached to need to be changed.*

3. **Is the plan incremental and doable?** *Yes, I am focusing on my ability to seek understanding and solicit input from various stakeholders in the organization.*

4. **Are you excited about your plan? Why or why not?** *Yes. It allows me to work on my triggers of shutting down or becoming defensive with feedback.*

Step 5: EXECUTE your development plan.

Put your development plan into action! As you proceed with the execution of your plan, spend a few minutes thinking about each of these questions. Record your thoughts and responses.

1. **What circumstances or triggers will signal that "now" is the time to act and practice new behaviors?** *The scheduled meetings will trigger me to prepare for them.*

2. **What specific behavior(s) or action(s) will you try? How far are you willing to push your comfort zone?** *I will ask direct questions, encouraging people to poke holes in the drafted strategy.*

Figure 3.1   (Continued)

3. **How do you know if you are improving and becoming more successful with this attribute and as a leader?** *I will reflect if I got triggered or became defensive when receiving input and feedback.*

4. **How will you gauge the impact of your actions or behavior changes? What responses will you be watching for?** *Do people remain open? Do they enthusiastically share their ideas? Or, do they close up?*

Step 6: SELF-REFLECT on your execution of the development plan.

Spend a few minutes at the end of the day and/or week thinking about each of these questions. Record your thoughts and responses.

1. **Was I mindful of my development today/this week? What did I do well? What could I have done better?** *I did well in my 1:1 meetings this week. In the group meetings, I became tense.*

2. **How did others respond when I intentionally led in a new way? Were people more (or less) engaged with me as a leader?** *I am not sure and have to check in to find out.*

3. **Was I mindful of my triggers? How did I respond to those?** *Yes, I was paying attention. When I got tense during the group meeting, I took a few breaths, wrote down comments, and invited questions for me.*

4. **What will I do differently tomorrow/next week? What should I be watching for?** *I will spend more time explaining the strategy using plain language but also asking teams how the new plans connect with their current work.*

5. **What else do I need to do or learn to further my development of this attribute?** *I need to have a colleague with me in some of the meetings so they can observe me in action and provide me with feedback and coaching.*

Figure 3.1 (Continued)

Bibliography

Covey, Stephen R. *The 7 Habits of Highly Effective People: Powerful Lessons in Personal Change*, 25th anniversary edition. New York: Simon & Schuster, 2013.

Chapter 4

Effective Communicator

The single biggest problem in communication is the illusion that it has taken place.

George Bernard Shaw

A primary function of language, besides conveying information, is to motivate, to influence each other's behavior.

William R. Miller and Stephen Rollnick

Leadership Case Study: Too Many Communications

Dr. Marcus Franklin slumped in his office chair, exhausted and perplexed. After a long day of back-to-back meetings with multiple physician groups and administrative teams, he struggled to understand how so many interactions could have gone so badly. Stepping into the Chief of Surgical Services role a few months ago, he was determined to communicate better with his department members than his predecessor. But instead, people had been telling him that they couldn't keep up with all the emails he sent; they were tired of receiving so many surveys asking for their opinions; they ignored most of the quality and financial reports and journal articles that he stacked in their offices; and lastly, they wished he would help them determine what was most important. Finally, today during one of the monthly check-ins, one physician angrily exclaimed, "You are smothering

DOI: 10.4324/9780429352355-4

all of us with too many emails, updates, memos, reports, surveys, and whatnot!"

As he finished eating the remains of his lunch, Dr. Franklin gloomily realized that all his efforts to change the culture in the organization through increased communication and information sharing backfired.

Dr. Franklin had started with good intentions; as a new leader, he wanted his team to feel included and informed; he wanted them to know their opinion mattered and that he genuinely cared about their well-being. He vowed to keep people abreast of organizational priorities, provide updates about new services, share the results of process improvement efforts, and regularly seek everyone's input in the business's day-to-day operations. After just three months in his new role, he had received more feedback than he could process, but it all seemed to point to one problem: he was not communicating effectively. Dr. Franklin slowly drove home, barely keeping pace with other cars on the freeway while mulling over everything he had heard. By the time he reached his driveway, he realized he needed to rethink his communication strategy.

Introduction

Communication is used to persuade, inform, acknowledge, ask, and entertain. We communicate all the time with the people around us. As we are bombarded with information from television, websites, books, presentations, meetings, movies, and mobile devices, think about what makes some messages stand out and others fade away. What makes information relevant and memorable?

In the workplace, demonstrating the art and science of effective communication is one of the top determinants of professional success. Leaders' effectiveness is judged to a large extent by their ability to connect with people both formally and informally. Yet, given the firestorm of information bombarding people daily, leaders are forced to compete for audience attention. As a result, leaders must strive to make their messages compelling and memorable, striking all the right notes for content, tone, delivery, and style. Leaders also benefit from listening carefully to messages from people they work with and hearing about problems, improvements, and business opportunities as early as possible. The payoff for effective communication is fewer misunderstandings and disruptions and increased productivity and morale.

Some of my early leadership roles were with physicians who were very business savvy and very direct in their communication style. While being direct worked well in that smaller group, in a larger group with a broader range of administrative and business skill sets, being overly direct can come across as confrontational. This goes back to the idea of listening. I not only needed to understand what someone was saying but make sure they "felt heard." I spend a lot more time listening. People presenting information to me and others have typically done their "homework" and have a high skill set in their area, and I can make better decisions by doing all I can to understand what they are bringing to other leaders and me. Listening to my colleagues who serve as front-line physicians in other departments or other areas of our company is critical for understanding the barriers we put in front of our patients and physicians.

Mitch Peterson, *MD, Family Physician and Past Chair of the Board, The Polyclinic*

With an understanding of how critical communication skills are for leadership success, let's delve into the mindset and four Leadership Strategies of an effective communicator. Parallels are drawn between clinical practice and physician leadership to better clarify concepts. At the end of the chapter, to help build your effective communication muscle, an example of the GUIDES development plan is provided to ease you into creating your own personalized GUIDES development plan.

Take a moment to review your notes in Chapter 2 in response to the question, "Who do you consider to be an effective communicator, and why?" Keep this person in mind throughout this chapter.

Physician Leader as Effective Communicator

What is your responsibility for conveying and receiving information as a physician leader? Do you filter out the noise so your team and colleagues can focus on the most relevant, essential, and well-packaged communications? Do you tailor your communication style to fit different audiences and situations? Do you encourage open communication and feedback?

Physicians typically control the environment and much of the flow of information in interactions with patients and their families. Staff, patients, and family members perceive physicians as experts and often defer to their authority in the conversation. Additionally, although physicians may actively work to combat the physician–patient power differential, the pace, content, and direction of a conversation are often controlled by the clinician rather than the person seeking care.

In contrast, an effective communication style at the leadership level is collaborative and less autonomous or directive. The exchange of ideas, weighing options, and decision-making processes occur cooperatively among business leaders, including cross-functional clinical and administrative partners. Given key stakeholders' views, positions, and influences, this cross-functional team comes together as experts in their respective fields to negotiate win–win decisions.

COACH'S CORNER: THE FOUR HABITS MODEL OF PHYSICIAN–PATIENT COMMUNICATION

As a practicing physician, I learned about Kaiser Permanente's Four Habits Model of physician–patient communication, first published in *The Permanente Journal* more than 20 years ago by Richard Frankel, PhD, and Terry Stein, MD. They believed physicians could improve their communication style with appropriate coaching, and the coaching model they developed is still in use at Kaiser Permanente and many other healthcare organizations. The Four Habits Model focuses on essential communication skills designed to build trust and foster an open dialogue centered on a patient's values and beliefs, such as quickly creating rapport with the patient, active listening, expressing empathy, collaborative decision-making, and demonstrating cultural sensitivity. The Four Habits Model provides the structure for physicians to lead conversations with patients and their families, inviting them to engage in the dialogue as equal participants. The Four Habits Model focuses on four essential skills:

1. "Investing in the beginning" by quickly creating rapport with the patient, eliciting their concerns, and planning the visit with the patient.
2. "Eliciting the patient's perspective" by asking the patient for their ideas regarding their medical concerns, eliciting specific requests, and exploring the impact of medical problems on the patient's life.

3. "Demonstrating empathy" by opening up to the patient's emotions, making empathetic statements, and demonstrating empathy nonverbally.

4. "Investing in the end" by delivering the diagnosis, providing education, involving the patient in decision-making, and completing the visit by summarizing and eliciting additional questions (Frankel & Stein, 1999).

This model relies on listening skills, asking open-ended questions, expressing empathetic statements, using verbal and nonverbal communication, engaging in shared decision-making, and demonstrating cultural sensitivity. These same communication skills are effective outside of the physician–patient relationship, and over the years, I have often thought about the applicability of this model to leadership communications.

Clinicians focus on effective patient communication in medical training and throughout their careers. They often receive direct feedback from preceptors' observations (in training) or patient surveys (in practice). This feedback guides their self-improvement in empathetic listening, unbiased questioning, respectful coaching, and collaborative treatment design. Fortunately, many of the communication skills physicians practice with patients will serve them well in leadership positions.

Mindset of the Effective Communicator

Buttressing one's communication skills with those defined in the Four Habits Model is essential but insufficient without also strengthening the underlying mindset of an effective communicator. Effective communicators demonstrate respect for others. They invest in listening empathetically, without judgment, to demonstrate they value others' views and ideas. Curious leaders invite feedback. They are intentional about eliciting diverse perspectives. They create a culture and environment of empowerment and inclusiveness, conveying information to others clearly and directly across various communication channels while hearing and internalizing what others have to share.

Leadership Strategies for the Effective Communicator

Most leaders are inundated with information; they generally have many incoming lines of communication, whereby messages get "pushed" to them by those above them in the organizational hierarchy or from other functional departments, while at the same time, they push their own messages to colleagues and direct reports. Few leaders, including the hypothetical Dr. Marcus Franklin, introduced at the beginning of this chapter, create an intentional strategy and process for receiving and sending information. Though you may not be able to staunch the flow of messages delivered to you from above, you are entirely in charge of reducing the volume and refining the quality of messages you forward to the people who report to you. In fact, you will want to take an intentional and strategic approach to managing communications, building a precise communication pipeline that delivers accurate, diverse, and timely information.

The business section of any bookstore is filled with many good titles promoting improved communication skills. There is nothing wrong with their focus on the technical components of communication: writing, presenting, and speaking skills. Our focus is on the four Leadership Strategies that complement the technical skills and will take your leadership to a new level:

1. Create deliberate communication pathways.
2. Listen with respect and empathy.
3. Deliver compelling messages.
4. Foster a culture of feedback.

Create Deliberate Communication Pathways

Your level and role in the organization will necessitate unique communication strategies. These strategies will not be static but will change over time as you, your team, and your organization change and grow with internal and external inputs.

To have your finger on the pulse of the organization, you should establish communication pathways designed to be bi-directional to allow reliable information flows between the organization's executive leaders and you, and between you and your direct reports.

For example, you can introduce opportunities for bi-directional communication using team and leadership huddles that connect every layer of your organizational structure and occur on a patterned schedule that aligns with the needed speed of information sharing. Huddles are brief meetings that often happen in front of the huddle or visual board. Happening once or twice daily, they serve several purposes: urgent information-sharing, escalation of safety concerns up the chain, on-the-fly problem-solving, and "just do it" daily improvements. The primary goal of huddles is to identify and solve problems in real time at the local and enterprise-wide levels. The secondary purpose is learning, team building, and change management. Many hospitals have daily safety and problem-solving huddles, while non-clinical parts of the healthcare organization have weekly information-sharing and problem-solving huddles.

AUTHOR'S REFLECTIONS: EFFECTIVE HUDDLES AT INTERMOUNTAIN HEALTH

One of the most effective enterprise-wide huddles I ever witnessed took place at Intermountain Health. NEJM *Catalyst* published an article about tiered escalation huddles there. Within a 75-minute turnaround time, information travels through six tiers – from the frontline teams to the CEO – of the system with multiple hospitals and medical groups. By identifying critical knowledge and problems in patient flow, access, and safety and breaking through layers of bureaucracy, enterprise-wide changes take place within hours or days compared to months or years.

In addition to the communication infrastructure, pay attention to the timing, sequence, and especially content of your messaging. The content of the information flow and your role as a leader in translating the messages between various parts of the organization is just as critical as the communication structure you build. Consider this simple, straightforward example to illustrate the concept of bi-directional communication pathways.

Let's assume you receive a strategy update from the Chief Operating Officer (COO) via a prerecorded video on the first Monday of each month. You receive key performance reports from the Finance and Quality departments on the second Monday of each month. What are some strategies for sharing this information in a timely manner while ensuring the recipients know what is most important? What do recipients need to do differently? What avenues exist to ask questions and provide feedback?

You may choose to share the updates and reports in their entirety, just as they were sent to you; however, it may be more helpful to direct the recipients to information that is most important or relevant to your team, providing a digest. For example, annotate performance metrics that align with your team's current improvement efforts; draw attention to the progress the team is making or the gap yet to be closed. Help the team focus on specific content that will be discussed in the upcoming weekly (or monthly) team meeting. You could specifically direct your team to the five-minute mark in the COO's video update or to the second chart in the Quality report, then invite dialogue about them in the team meeting to uncover barriers that get in the way of achieving team and organizational goals and elicit suggestions for solving problems. Doing so helps the team focus on relevant strategic goals and commit to the processes that will improve performance and patient care. With this strategy, you now have your team's feedback for your next round of leadership discussions, highlighting the actions your team is taking to improve key metrics and escalating the operational problems and barriers that get in the way of progress.

In this example, information flows from organizational leaders to frontline teams, with you translating how their daily work connects to the company's strategy and mission. You share information with your team in an intentional way, and in return, frontline teams communicate their progress, problems, and issues up the chain of command.

You may install other communication pathways to ensure you get maximum input from your team, such as meeting individually with your team members on a regular basis and observing their work processes to understand workflow problems. You may talk informally with patients or clients to appreciate their care delivery experience. Chapter 3 emphasized seeking input from others on the organization's strategic goals. Though these can be ad hoc conversations, the established communication pathways discussed here are also sources of gathering and testing new ideas and identifying market opportunities. Your frequent and intentional conversations with your direct reports are fuel for achieving both local and organizational strategies, but you must be willing to seek them out and listen with an open mind. Table 4.1 presents best practices for building intentional communication pathways.

Table 4.1 Best Practices for Building Intentional Communication Pathways

Trap	Leaders rely on ad hoc information flows.
Best Practices	Create an intentional communication path between executives and frontline teams with a daily or weekly cadence to allow bi-directional information flow.
Questions to Ponder	■ How do I ensure that my message has reached every intended audience member?

It can be a big task to get someone to a different place, to either think or act differently. I carve out time on my schedule almost every week to talk about the issues that are getting in the way. I begin by asking different questions, and try to get them to see things in a different way. It could be three-, six-, or nine months before they begin to open up. All of that is building trust, and you just have to spend the time to build trust.

Larry Gray, *MSBA, Managing Director,*
Gray Dynamics LLC

Listen with Respect and Empathy

Foundational to respectful and empathetic communication is learning how to listen and how to read the audience's needs. Larry Gray, MSBA, Managing Director, Gray Dynamics LLC, believes, "From a leadership standpoint, in today's world, listening is the most important quality."

As a physician, you likely came across studies that discuss the criticality of listening skills in the accurate diagnostics of medical conditions, the likelihood of adherence to physician recommendations, and the success of treatment outcomes. A 2018 *Journal of Internal Medicine* article (Singh et al., 2019) reported that in clinical practice, physicians listen to their patients for an average of 11 seconds – and sometimes as few as three seconds – before interrupting their narrative. As a result, patients often shut down and do not share additional clinical details that are critically important for diagnostic accuracy. The study additionally reported that physicians ask patients about their goals and expectations for a visit less than half the time. Physicians may be more focused on addressing their own agenda, choosing to tackle what they think the patient needs and not what the patient prefers to focus on. Not surprisingly, many patients leave feeling frustrated and not listened to, while the physician comes away from the same visit thinking it was a successful encounter because all of the medical problems were addressed. Recall a personal experience when, as a patient, you felt rushed and unheard. How likely were you to follow up on the treatment plan?

COACH'S CORNER: LEARNING TO LISTEN

Early in my leadership journey, I truly lacked the ability to listen. It was my Achilles' heel, my biggest personal weakness. I enjoyed it when others listened to me, and I pretended to listen to them, yet all the while, all I could do was think of my response. My mind was racing ahead with the ideas and advice I planned to dispense. Upon reflection, I realized that I exhibited the same behaviors with my patients. I was getting high satisfaction scores from patients in all areas except one: "I felt listened to." Learning to listen for the sake of the other person is something I continue to work on to this day. I actively practice not interrupting and just taking information in without judgment or opinion. It isn't always easy, so I remind myself of the wise words I heard years ago: "Listening is not waiting to talk." I repeat it often, and when I want to jump in before the other person has had a chance for self-expression, I tell myself:

- *The time and place will come for me to share my expertise.*
- *If I interrupt, I will lose my chance to build trust with this person.*
- *Listening builds relationships ... and relationships spark change.*

As my listening skills improved, so did my patient satisfaction scores and leadership evaluations. Now I find that listening saves time during patient visits and business meetings. It helps uncover problems faster and makes change management easier.

As a leader, can you remember a situation when you needed a listening ear just to enable your processing of a problem or concern, and instead, your boss provided unsolicited advice? Stop and think about how it made you feel. What would have been more helpful? If your boss restated and clarified your concerns, would it feel different? Would you prefer to be asked additional questions so you can arrive at the solution on your own versus being given the answers? Hearing the needs of others, both as a physician and a leader, empowering others to solve problems or at least co-design future changes is imperative. How many great ideas are not shared with leaders because of feelings or perceptions that leaders are not sincerely interested in hearing what people have to say? How often are patient safety concerns or service issues not raised only to become large problems later? Do not miss these opportunities to learn about challenges, opportunities, and successes by conveying the impression you aren't interested or by being distracted.

> *The most important skill I used in leadership is the clinical skill of listening and validating with active listening, while summarizing a person's concerns and suggestions for improvement. I would advise a new leader that not every problem needs to be solved. Most importantly, physicians need to feel heard but often don't expect their specific solution to be enacted. One of my most important lessons was simply realizing the value of listening and acknowledging a person's concerns.*
> **Christopher Pepin**, MD, MD[2]

If you are already great when it comes to actively listening to your patients, then you are in an excellent position to apply your exam room skills to your administrative and leadership interactions. Respectful and empathetic communicators are open and attentive to the ideas and opinions of others. They are committed to understanding people's perspectives and will ask questions until they achieve sufficient clarity. They effortlessly restate or paraphrase what others have said. They can put themselves in others' shoes and emerge with a better understanding of the situation and the person's motivation.

Commit to being an open, respectful, attentive, and empathetic listener of others' ideas and opinions. Feeling listened to and understood is of utmost importance to your patients, direct reports, supervisors, peers, and team alike. Table 4.2 presents best practices for respectful listening.

Deliver Compelling Messages

Over the course of your career, you will have plenty of opportunities to present information to small and large audiences. Your communications may inspire or educate; they may announce the launch of new products or provide project updates to stakeholders. Whether written, spoken, or visual, ensure your messages have a clear purpose, meet the audience's needs, and inspire them to solve a problem, make a decision, or take action. Every message competes for the audience's attention and must quickly engage their hearts and minds. How can you frame your message so they want

Table 4.2 Best Practices for Respectful Listening

Trap	Listening with the intent to jump in with your own opinion or solution.
Best Practices	■ Listen attentively, focused on the other person. Elicit their agenda early in the conversation. ■ Give the other person time and space to express their thoughts. ■ Minimize interruptions.
Questions to Ponder	■ What tone of voice, body language, and empathetic statements do I use when listening to concerns or feedback from my direct reports, colleagues, or other leaders?

to hear, see, or read what is coming next? The most compelling messages begin by creating an emotional connection with the audience.

Like clinical meetings that start with a case presentation, business communications could start with a patient or customer story, detailing behaviors, emotions, and feelings. Healthcare delivery serves up an infinite number of patient stories from which to choose: formal and informal complaints, reported errors and near misses, and process and flow issues surfaced by physicians and clinical staff. Behind each complaint, error, and near miss is a story with human characters: patients, spouses, children, parents, and friends. Storytelling engages the audience emotionally, draws immediate attention to affected parties, and creates a call for action. Lisa Cron, in her book *Wired for Story*, points to neuroscience research confirming that, "Our brain is hardwired to respond to the story … Story is what makes us human not metaphorically but literally" (2012). Storytelling is crucial to human evolution.

Sharing a real patient or customer story when launching a process or system improvement makes influencing others to embrace the proposed changes easier. Patient stories explain the "why" behind the change and create the feeling of immediacy for improvement, change, or action. Storytelling aims to immerse the audience in your message, much like the "hook" a writer uses to draw the reader into their narrative.

In addition to storytelling, visualizing presented information helps your audience to pay attention, grasp the situation, and form conclusions. Visualizing supporting information, whether trial results, proofs of concept, or other facts and data, through pictures, diagrams, graphs, tables, videos, and animation, makes complex messages more accessible to the audience. When used effectively, visuals improve audience engagement, comprehension, and retention.

As the saying goes, "A picture is worth a thousand words." A lot of data and textual information is encountered in medicine and business. Embedding data and long stretches of text in presentations and other communications can bore the intended audience. This is easily noticeable with dense PowerPoint content that causes the audience's eyes glaze over or completely check out. Why do visual images keep the audience's attention and trigger a higher level of information recall? Why do visual images compel people to act?

Research from Prezi (n.d.) shows that

> *our visual memory is much stronger than our ability to recall both spoken and written text – a phenomenon known as the picture superiority effect … When you pair your ideas with visuals – photographs, illustrations, or even simple icons – your audience will have a much easier time remembering them.*

A study published by co-researchers at the University of Minnesota and the 3M Corporation found that when information is presented visually, people are 43% more likely to act on the information (Vogel et al., 2019). Cole N. Knaflic, author of *Storytelling with Data: A Data Visualization Guide for Business Professionals*, believes that to effectively deliver your message, use story visualization through simple graphs or images, minimize words on slides and in communications, and remove any superfluous textual or graphic elements (2015).

Ensure your messages are compelling. Pay attention to any power differential and cultural differences between you and your audience. Your goal is to not only say the right thing but to ensure the clarity of the message while setting the right tone and mood. When presenting in person or via video, be aware of your facial expression and body language – and their impact on others – especially when you feel tired, irritated, impatient, or hungry. You may inadvertently frown, demonstrating displeasure with what is being discussed when your intention is the opposite. Due to the power differential perceived by others as you advance in the organization, you may be considered unapproachable because of your title or position. A relaxed tone of voice and non-threatening nonverbal cues will create a calm atmosphere that will prevent a stress reaction in your teams.

Table 4.3 Best Practices for Delivering Compelling Messages

Trap	The message is not culturally attuned, too verbose, or not focused on the audience and desired outcome.
Best Practices	■ Present your case from the patient's or customer's perspective. Make your audience feel their pain, discomfort, and distress to create an emotional connection. ■ Visualize your data and text. ■ Be culturally sensitive.
Questions to Ponder	■ Do I know who my audience is and what I want them to do with the presented information? ■ Do I use storytelling and visualization to present my message in as few words as possible? ■ Am I aware of the power differential between me and my audience? How can I mitigate it?

Fear – even if triggered unintentionally – will nullify the effectiveness of any message. To muddle things further, communication may differ greatly between cultures. Diverse workplaces, such as our healthcare clinics, require heightened cultural sensitivity. As physicians, we often strive to understand cultural differences in order to be more effective with patients. As leaders, to create compelling messages, we should be attuned to cultural differences as well. Table 4.3 presents best practices for delivering compelling messages.

AUTHOR'S REFLECTION: "DON'T CROWD ME"

When I moved from New York to Denver, I worked closely with several clinical pharmacists as a chief and physician in my new practice. Over time, I sensed that our relationship was tense as if there was an impenetrable barrier between us every time we communicated. I enlisted the help of the pharmacy chief to sit down and mediate a conversation with us. After we exchanged some niceties, I acknowledged the elephant in the room. "I have been working with you for several months, and I greatly appreciate all you do for our patients," I said. "I do feel at times that there is some tension when we interact. I am not sure if I am doing something wrong when we talk that contributes to this." I paused and waited for their response. One clinical pharmacist spoke hesitantly, "Doctor, every time you talk with us, you are always in our space. You talk fast, and it feels intense. It feels intimidating." Was I ever surprised by this response! I always considered myself to be an effective communicator: easygoing, sociable, interactive, and pleasant. Maybe I was too direct sometimes, but was I also intense and intimidating? As the saying goes, "perception is reality," so I had to think hard about the feedback I had invited and received.

Cultures vary on what is considered acceptable body language, conversational energy, and interpersonal space. In Belarus, where I grew up, the distance between people in conversation was shorter. What I knew to be normal in Belarus was perceived as an invasion of "personal space" by my clinical pharmacy colleagues in Denver. What was considered normal when it came to the intensity and energy of the conversation in New York, bustling with immigrants from all over the world, was coming off as rude and intimidating in Denver. As a physician leader, I had to be aware of the energy (positive, neutral, or negative) I brought to the room through my facial expressions, tone of voice, and body language. I had to pay close attention to how my nonverbal communications affected the people around me.

Foster a Culture of Feedback

Leaders communicate with their colleagues and direct reports to share information, inspire action, and set expectations for performance and behavior. Another aspect of leadership is receiving and delivering constructive feedback to improve performance and outcomes. Before giving feedback to others, spend time understanding how you process feedback given to you.

AUTHOR'S REFLECTION: LEARNING TO GIVE AND RECEIVE FEEDBACK

Early in my clinical and leadership journeys, I struggled to receive feedback. I often found myself defensive, hyperinflating negative comments and disregarding all the positive comments I received. I often focused on the messenger, not the message, finding excuses for my derailers. Similarly, I noticed my reports tensing up when I shared their opportunities for improvement with them. To help me overcome my fear of receiving and giving feedback, I made it part of my standard leadership routine to regularly ask for feedback from my direct reports, colleagues, and superiors. I had to train myself to listen without defensiveness, taking note of ineffective and unproductive leadership behaviors I exhibited. Initially, it was an intensely painful experience, but with the repetitive exposure, just like with allergens, I became sensitized and started incorporating feedback into my leadership improvement plan. Asking for feedback, especially from my direct reports, brought an unexpected change. My reports started to ask for feedback without me initiating the conversation.

Delivering feedback, though well-intentioned, may feel unnatural and even confrontational at times. When faced with a behavioral or performance issue, many leaders do not address it directly, waiting and hoping the situation will resolve itself. This rarely happens, as avoidance does not solve problems. Small problems often snowball over time and become an insurmountable mountain of challenges. Providing feedback – an act of honest communication – sets people up for success and allows them to perform at their full potential. Your feedback to a direct report can reinforce their demonstration of the effective use of skills and positive outcomes; your feedback can also help build skills and change behaviors when they are not meeting expectations. Without feedback, your team lacks guidance and has no basis for future growth or development, which may imperil achieving the organization's goals.

> *Doctors are so achievement-oriented that I make a practice of calling out good behaviors. So I try to bring them in and give feedback. I'll say, "You know, I noticed in the meeting that you deliberately stopped yourself from dominating the conversation even though I know you know a lot about the topic. I saw you do that and I just want to say I really appreciated that." And that person will remember that and it helps to move the change behavior along. Or, I'll say, "I saw you controlling your temper. And that really helped. Did you see how that*

helped facilitate the discussion?" I try to give them that feedback and let them know they are improving.
Nanette Santoro, *MD, Professor and E. Stewart Taylor Chair, Department of Obstetrics and Gynecology, University of Colorado*

Though constructive feedback may have a negative connotation, as a leader, taking ownership of the development of your people is a positive demonstration of respect and caring. Reflecting honestly on the intent and the purpose of feedback is critical. Is feedback given to help the other person succeed or to get them in trouble? Weaponizing feedback, which unfortunately is not that uncommon, leads to a culture of fear and hiding problems that, more often than not, drive poor outcomes. Feedback must be timely, concise, and based on facts, not assumptions. Additionally, it should be based on performance goals and expectations that were transparently communicated previously. Taking time for a thorough investigation and getting everyone's perspective helps you to not jump to conclusions you may regret later. Focusing on the situation and/or observable behavior without labeling or judging a person makes feedback less threatening. Additionally, a close personal relationship between two parties in the feedback exchange is critical for the feedback to lead to improvement and growth. Feedback outside of a trusting and supporting relationship often backfires. Humble, curious, and authentic leaders are focused on developing others. They build close relationships and personal connections. For them, developing their direct reports and teams is a considerable responsibility.

In fostering a culture of feedback, leaders recognize that improving their own leadership skills depends on the honest communication they receive from colleagues, executives, and direct reports. Creating an environment conducive to feedback is often impeded by "a culture of politeness" when any language affecting self-esteem is discouraged or "a culture of excellence in which the institution's reputation" inhibits constructive feedback (Ramani et al., 2018). Building a culture of graciously giving and accepting feedback requires positive intent from feedback givers and a perception of psychological safety from feedback receivers. Leaders can help build this culture by modeling their own openness and willingness to receive constructive feedback. Opening the door of bi-directional feedback allows others to step through and engage in honest communication with you. In the interest of ensuring the best care delivery and health outcomes for the

Table 4.4 Best Practices for Fostering a Culture of Feedback

Trap	Leaders expect staff to read their minds. Goals and expectations are not clearly stated. When performance feedback is called for, they stall or obfuscate.
Best Practices	■ Be very clear about goals and performance expectations. Ensure appropriate training. ■ When performance is missing the mark, respectfully give specific and timely feedback based on facts, not assumptions.
Questions to Ponder	■ Does the person receiving feedback understand success goals and expectations? Have they received adequate training to be successful? ■ Is my feedback based on facts (and not assumptions) that were well researched?

patients you serve, feedback must flow both ways. Table 4.4 presents best practices for fostering a culture of feedback.

Leadership Strategies: Bringing It All Together

In the high-intensity healthcare environment, when we are barraged with unending information, effective communicators ask the following questions to stay focused on getting their message across:

- How do I guarantee that my message reaches the intended audience?
- How do I engage others to pay attention to my message?
- How do I ensure the message is understood and not taken out of context or misconstrued?

As we discussed in the chapter, creating deliberate communication pathways is critical for the message to reach the intended audience. Sharing the message through storytelling and visualization while paying attention to the power differential and cultural differences will make it stand out. Continuously checking for understanding of the message and welcoming clarifying questions ensures that the communication is perceived as intended.

In addition, especially in high-stakes communications, the audience must be given the opportunity to study and question the supporting information, including data and facts upon which decisions are made. Their willingness to proceed with the solution or recommendation is contingent upon their understanding of the leader's assessment and the evidence presented. When possible, leaders solicit input from the audience, listen to their opinions and points of view, address their concerns and questions, and incorporate their input.

Great leaders are open to changing the message based on feedback or new ideas. Most people are likely to embrace new ideas and proposals if they can put their fingerprints on the process or decision. It is similar to shared decision-making in medicine. Patients are more open to guidance if their opinion is heard, their point of view is incorporated into the plan, and their concerns are addressed. Effective communicators employ two-way conversation to clarify the message and ensure it is heard in its entirety. Regardless of the type of communication, its delivery and style should be clear, concise, and accessible.

The GUIDES Framework and the Effective Communicator

Let's return to the fictional Dr. Marcus Franklin mentioned at the beginning of this chapter. Many physician leaders like Dr. Franklin have good intentions but inadvertently:

■ Overwhelm their teams with a large amount of information coming from multiple sources.
■ Assume that everyone learns and processes information in a similar fashion.
■ Neglect to consider individual or team communication preferences.
■ Miss the opportunity to design their communication by learning through feedback.

Dr. Franklin turns to his executive coach to work through the four Leadership Strategies and the GUIDES Framework to devise a personal Effective Communicator development plan. The coach asks Dr. Franklin questions to understand his leadership mindset and his understanding of various communications strategies:

- How do you approach the design of your communication strategy?
- What communication pathways do you find effective in your organization and why?
- Do you take individual communication preferences into account, and if not, why?
- How do you go about receiving timely feedback on your communication effectiveness?
- In one-on-one interactions, what percentage of time do you listen versus talk? Does the percentage change if it is your colleague, direct report, or supervisor?
- Can you share an example of a difficult conversation that went well?
- Can you discuss a situation when constructive feedback backfired?
- How do you make it compelling when you are asked to deliver a difficult message to your team?

This chapter explored the four Leadership Strategies: (1) create deliberate communication pathways, (2) listen with respect and empathy, (3) deliver compelling messages, and (4) foster a culture of feedback. In Chapter 2, we asked you to think of someone you consider to be an effective communicator. To what extent do you think they embody and demonstrate the four Leadership Strategies? What other skills or characteristics do they exhibit that make them effective?

Now, access and print the GUIDES Development Plan template in Appendix 1 and create a development plan to assess and improve your communication skills. See Figure 4.1 as an example of a plan to improve the strategy "Fostering a culture of feedback."

GUIDES Development Plan – Effective Communicator

Step 1: GATHER inputs to evaluate your skills gaps and opportunities for development.

1. **Record your own assessment of your degree of confidence in these skills.**

To what extent are you confident in your ability to:	Not at all	Somewhat	Great deal
Create deliberate communication pathways		x	
Listen with respect and empathy		x	
Delivering compelling messages		x	
Foster a culture of feedback	x		

2. **Reflect on your answers to the questions above. Record your additional thoughts.** *After reading this chapter, I know I must focus on "Foster a culture of feedback" while also working on the other three strategies. I wonder what "culture of feedback" means to my peers, my team? I worry about them asking me questions like: "How is this different from our existing culture? What does it mean to me? What are you going to do different?" What if I stumble in my response? As I reflect, I think I'm a bit afraid I won't know how to go about this.*

3. **Ask for feedback from others (e.g., trusted colleagues, your coach, or direct reports) on the skills, and take notes.** *I met with my whole team and individual team members to ask them for honest feedback on my performance in four areas of effective communication, diving deeper into how to create a culture of giving and receiving feedback. I also asked them what developing a culture of feedback means to them.*

Figure 4.1   Example of GUIDES Development Plan for Effective Communicator.

4. **What does your additional research tell you about this attribute?** *A culture of politeness or a culture of reputational excellence often impedes a culture of feedback. Now I need to understand how this fits in with not only my development but also my peers and team.*

Step 2: UNDERSTAND and interpret the data you collected.

The following questions help you understand and interpret the data you collected in the GATHER step. Spend a few minutes thinking about these questions. Record your thoughts and responses.

1. **What did you learn from your self-assessment?** *I hardly ask for feedback or give feedback. I need to get solid in my own thinking about "culture of feedback."*

2. **How did you interpret feedback from others (e.g., trusted colleagues, your coach, or reports)? Were you surprised? Did their feedback match your self-assessment?** *I construct my communication based on what I think works best and not on what others think. I love reading a lot of information and crystallizing what matters most to me and I assume others do the same. I don't take time to learn from others what their preferences are for conveying information. I also learned there are various views on what a culture of feedback means. In some cases, people even seemed confused by the terminology.*

3. **What were your key takeaways from the research? Were you surprised by anything you learned?** *I learned about the concept of "face" or perceived image of self. I have to be careful that the feedback I give doesn't make people lose "face."*

Figure 4.1 (Continued)

Step 3: IDENTIFY your strengths and opportunities.

Spend a few minutes thinking about each of these questions. Record your thoughts and responses.

1. **Which skills do you want to develop further?** *Becoming receptive to and comfortable with receiving feedback, so I don't get defensive outwardly or inwardly.*

2. **Which skills are foundational?** *Regularly asking for feedback, not waiting for special circumstances. Do plus/delta in every meeting to check what went well and what can be better next time. Ask for in-depth feedback in scheduled one-on-one meetings.*

3. **Which skills are your highest priority?** *Asking for feedback, internalizing it without defensiveness, and creating a specific and doable plan to address any shortcomings.*

Step 4: DESIGN your leadership development plan.

What are your development priorities? Record two or three high-priority opportunities and actions.

Area for Development	Developmental Opportunity	Actions to Take	Resources Needed	Target Date	Success Metrics
Effective Communicator	*Fostering a culture of feedback*	*Learn how my team thinks about culture of feedback*	*Various – Include in existing forums; survey; 1:1 meetings*	*1/31/24*	*Have a thorough understanding of what this means to my team – a document that outlines their viewpoints.*
Effective Communicator	*Fostering a culture of feedback*	*Conduct 1:1 meetings*	*Outlook calendar*	*3/31/24*	*Monitor the "Culture of Inclusiveness" metric on Physician Satisfaction Survey*
Effective Communicator	*Fostering a culture of feedback*	*Group meetings*	*Teams calendar*	*5/31/24*	*Same as above*

Figure 4.1 (Continued)

Look over your development plan, then consider these questions. Record your thoughts below.

1. **Does this plan address the foundational opportunities identified in your self-assessment, research, and input from others?** *Yes, I can ask and give feedback, targeting communication in 1:1 meetings. I can co-design an effective communication strategy that takes individual and team preferences into account. Simultaneously, I can start to learn from my team what culture of feedback means to them and start to get their ideas.*

2. **Does your plan take into consideration the personal triggers that could help or hinder your development?** *I can get easily defensive with feedback, just like many of my team members, so making it a routine part of every meeting or interaction will demystify it and hopefully make it non-threatening.*

3. **Is the plan incremental and doable?** *I think so. I have to remember that I learn incrementally and therefore, need a plan that is incremental.*

4. **Are you excited about your plan? Why or why not?** *I am excited. I truly believe this plan will be foundational in our future successes. I'm a bit nervous and excited about taking an incremental approach. I've always tried to do too much too fast which usually doesn't go well but I've never tried a different way. This will definitely be a learning experience for me in several different ways. That's exciting.*

Step 5: EXECUTE your development plan.

Put your development plan into action! As you proceed with the execution of your plan, spend a few minutes thinking about each of these questions. Record your thoughts and responses.

1. **What circumstances or triggers will signal that "now" is the time to act and practice new behaviors?** *I can start by adding feedback as part of every meeting agenda including in my 1:1 meetings.*

Figure 4.1   (Continued)

2. **What specific behavior(s) or action(s) will you try? How far are you willing to push your comfort zone?** *I will ask others to give me feedback. I will incorporate that feedback into my conversations with my coach/trusted colleague and into my development plans.*

3. **How do you know if you are improving and becoming more successful with this attribute and as a leader?** *Checking in once a month with my colleagues and team members to share what I'm learning about myself and reinforcing our culture of feedback. I will take that opportunity to ask them how I'm doing.*

4. **How will you gauge the impact of your actions or behavior changes? What responses will you be watching for?** *Nonverbal cues during meetings in addition to direct inquiries and solicitation of feedback about my actions and behaviors in the area of communication effectiveness.*

Step 6: SELF-REFLECT on your execution of the development plan.

Spend a few minutes at the end of the day and/or week thinking about each of these questions. Record your thoughts and responses.

1. **Was I mindful of my development today/this week? What did I do well? What could I have done better?** *I asked for feedback in half of the meetings this week and will aim for at least 75% next week. I also started asking people what culture of feedback means to them.*

2. **How did others respond when I intentionally led in a new way? Were people more (or less) engaged with me as a leader?** *Some people were excited, but others looked guarded. Some people were confused and others didn't seem to notice any change.*

3. **Was I mindful of my triggers? How did I respond to those?** *Yes, I noticed that comments about me asking the team to read books to learn about having a culture of feedback triggered me as I was surprised to hear comments that they "just don't learn from books."*

Figure 4.1 (Continued)

4. **What will I do differently tomorrow/next week? What should I be watching for?** *I have to reassess my communication strategy when I am asked to deliver information about decisions such as organizational restructuring, in which the team wasn't asked for their input.*

5. **What else do I need to do or learn to further my development of this attribute?** *I will reach out to an experienced leader to get guidance on how to relay information that wasn't appropriate for soliciting input from my team. Next month, I will ask my boss to check in with my direct reports on my progress as an effective communicator focusing on feedback.*

Figure 4.1 (Continued)

Bibliography

Axtell, Paul. "Make Your Meetings a Safe Space for Honest Conversation." *Harvard Business Review* (April 11, 2019). https://hbr.org/2019/04/make-your-meetings-a-safe-space-for-honest-conversation

Bryant, Adam. "How to Run a More Effective Meeting." *The New York Times*, 2017. www.nytimes.com/guides/business/how-to-run-an-effective-meeting

Cron, Lisa. *Wired for Story: The Writer's Guide to Using Brain Science to Hook Readers from the Very First Sentence*, 1st ed. New York: Ten Speed Press, 2012.

Feloni, Richard. "Google Chair Eric Schmidt's 8 Rules for Running a Great Meeting." *Business Insider* (September 30, 2014). www.businessinsider.com/googles-rules-for-a-great-meeting-2014-9

Frankel, Richard, and Terry Stein. "Getting the Most Out of the Clinical Encounter: The Four Habits Model." *The Permanente Journal* 3, no. 3 (August 1, 1999): 79–88. www.thepermanentejournal.org/doi/epdf/10.7812/TPP/99.949

Knaflic, Cole Nussbaumer. *Storytelling with Data: A Data Visualization Guide for Business Professionals*. Hoboken, NJ: Wiley, 2015.

Prezi. "The Science of Effective Presentations." (n.d.). www.wilmu.edu/edtech/documents/the-science-of-effective-presenations---prezi-vs-powerpoint.pdf

Ramani, Subha, Karen D. Könings, Karen V. Mann, Emily E. Pisarski, and Cees P.M. van der Vleuten. "About Politeness, Face, and Feedback: Exploring Resident and Faculty Perceptions of How Institutional Feedback Culture Influences Feedback

Practices." *Academic Medicine* 93, no. 9 (2018): 1348–1358. https://journals. lww.com/academicmedicine/Fulltext/2018/09000/About_Politeness,_Face,_ and_Feedback__Exploring.29.aspx

Reitz, Megan, and John Higgins. "Managers, You're More Intimidating Than You Think." Harvard Business Review (July 18, 2019). https://hbr.org/2019/07/ managers-youre-more-intimidating-than-you-think

Singh Ospina, Naykky, Kari A. Phillips, Rene Rodriguez-Gutierrez, Ana Castaneda-Guarderas, Michael R. Gionfriddo, Megan E. Branda, and Victor M. Montori. "Eliciting the Patient's Agenda – Secondary Analysis of Recorded Clinical Encounters." *Journal of General Internal Medicine* 34, no. 1 (January 2019): 36–40. https://doi.org/10.1007/s11606-018-4540-5

Vogel, D. R., G. W. Dickson, and J. A. Lehman. "Persuasion and the Role of Visual Presentation Support: The UM/3M Study." Accessed August 7, 2019. http://misrc. umn.edu/workingpapers/fullpapers/1986/8611.pdf

Vozza, Stephanie. "How 12 Companies Make Meetings Memorable, Effective, And Short." *Fast Company* (July 28, 2015). www.fastcompany.com/3048815/how-12-companies-make-meetings-memorable-effective-and-short

Wertheim, Edward G. *"The Importance of Effective Communication."* Northeastern University, 1999. https://ysrinfo.files.wordpress.com/2012/06/effectivecommuni cation5.pdf

Chapter 5

Coach

The essence of coaching is helping leaders get unstuck from their dilemmas and assisting them in transferring their learning into results for the organization.

Mary Beth O'Neill, *Executive Coach and Author*

At the heart of coaching lies the idea of empowering people by facilitating self-directed learning, personal growth and improved performance.

Jonathan Passmore, *Professional Executive Coach*

Leadership Case Study: Recognizing the Need for Coaching

Dr. Consuela Alvarez knew she had 20/20 vision for spotting qualified and talented potential physician leaders; in her first year as the Chief Medical Officer, she identified and promoted three outstanding physicians into leadership roles throughout the organization. All three picks were doing well, learning and growing in their new leadership positions. Lately, though, she observed skill gaps in each new leader. For example, Dr. George had trouble delivering performance feedback to a struggling physician. And reports of Dr. Alexander's poor facilitation of the previous month's staff meeting were still circulating among his colleagues. And just this morning, Dr. Angel reported being unsuccessful in getting a medical specialty department to adopt a new operational process.

DOI: 10.4324/9780429352355-5

Consuela wondered what responsibility she had for recognizing the leadership skill gaps in her physician leaders sooner. What could she have done differently when these talented individuals took on their new roles? What actions should she take now to develop her physician leaders' skills to improve their feedback, facilitation, and change management skills?

Introduction

Professional athletes have coaches. Executives have coaches. Actors have coaches. Ordinary people hire business, life, spiritual, and financial coaches. In your role as a leader, you are a performance coach charged with developing the skills, mindset, and behaviors valued by your organization. This responsibility is not always articulated overtly to new leaders, but it is an obligation critical to the leaders' success and that of the organization. Your team needs your leadership and coaching to perform at the top of their game, to feel encouraged and supported, to be inspired and motivated to excel, and to realize where they can improve.

Professional coaches may invest years of intense study in learning coaching techniques, passing tests to earn coaching certifications, then building substantial practices and client lists. However, physician leaders, like the fictional Dr. Alvarez at the beginning of the chapter, are not full-time professional coaches and typically do not intend to become one. The focus of this chapter is on the essentials of the art of coaching and people development so that you are comfortable stepping into the coaching role and can inspire and model the same standards, behaviors, and skills that you ask of your people.

Coaching is defined broadly as the process used to close the gap between where one is now and where one wants to be. Coaches help people make small and large changes, challenging them to go further than they would typically go on their own to maximize their potential. As a leader, you are automatically a coach, even if you do not realize it. Therefore, you will want to take a well-thought-out approach to coaching others. This chapter discusses the mindset, Leadership Strategies, and processes for developing your coaching skills using the GUIDES Framework. It is not our intent that you will be an expert coach by the end of the chapter, but instead you will begin to develop a coach's mindset and accept the responsibility you have as a leader to develop and coach those with whom you work.

Physician Leader as Coach

The best leaders know that most interactions at work are coaching opportunities. Coaching shapes thinking, builds relationships, advances the work, and strengthens the organizational culture. However, it can be daunting to think of every interaction as a coaching moment. Does that mean you must show up to work every day prepared to engage in a formal coaching session with every person you encounter, ready to help them develop new skills or challenge them to be more effective at work? That feels overwhelming. Yet it is very similar to the day-to-day interactions in the clinic. Practicing physicians conduct multiple coaching sessions with patients throughout the day. With each patient, the physician encourages them to invest in themselves. Physicians help patients see the gap between the current state of their health and the improved future one. To support patients in achieving their health goals, physicians look at them holistically, considering the whole person. It is no different as a leader; they will always influence those around them whether they intend it or not. Being intentional about every leadership interaction, just like every patient interaction, helps ensure that teams function optimally.

Physician leaders can role model to others how to coach their staff, which in turn improves the work environment and patient experience. Though most of this chapter will focus on purposeful coaching that requires a significant time commitment, we also share an example below demonstrating how timely, short bursts of coaching can help clinical teams provide better patient care.

COACH'S CORNER: COACHING TO IMPROVE PROCESSES

A few years ago, physicians in one healthcare organization felt overwhelmed by the number of electronic messages they received each day from patients. Physicians want their patients to receive timely responses and be completely satisfied with them and the organization. Physicians wondered if medical assistants could help decrease the physician workload and provide better service to patients by screening and handling role-appropriate and straightforward patient queries such as "Where can I get my physical therapy?" and "Can you give me the address for the endocrine office?"

The training department took the lead in preparing an online training course for medical assistants and physicians, laying out the new workflows. Months after the training, neither medical assistants nor physicians changed their practice. Physicians were disappointed and, at times, openly upset that no progress was made. The medical assistants were also frustrated because the new practices weren't working well. As a result, the department's leaders next encouraged physicians, nurses, and medical assistants to try real-time coaching. For the next several months, physicians printed select patient messages and used them in one-on-one conversations with their clinical staff to describe what they expected in response to the patient query; they clarified which message types were appropriate for staff handling and explained how to address and fulfill the patient's needs. Then, the team iterated the workflow, documented the message handling process steps, implemented a problem-solving (or escalation) system, and refined the communication flows necessary for spreading the new workflow department-wide. With clear expectations and one-on-one coaching, staff could perform at a higher level, freeing physicians to focus on physician-level care.

What we want from a physician leader is what we want from a physician. We want leaders to be compassionate with their colleagues, their trainees, their mentees. As someone in charge of clinician career development, I applied what I had hoped were my best attributes as a physician: taking care of people by "taking a complete history," finding out about their past issues and current issues. I tried to see them holistically. To help people progress in their careers, they needed to take me into their confidence, they needed to trust me, and I needed to make them feel trusted.
Harley A. Rotbart, *MD, Professor and Vice Chair Emeritus, Department of Pediatrics, University of Colorado School of Medicine*

Mindset of the Coach

Think about a time when you've been coached at work or on a sports field. What was it like to be coached and given suggestions for improvement? Were you open and willing to hear the suggestions? Did you dread it? Did you internalize what you were hearing? Did you wonder if the recommendations actually applied to you and your situation? When you are about to coach someone, it helps to remember what it feels like to be coached.

What mindset and qualities are the most essential for a coach? In our experience, the best coaches are curious and open to possibilities and the unknown. Together with their coachee, they are willing to explore and discover the path forward rather than dictate it. To be of value to your coachee, you must demonstrate faith and confidence that the coachee will improve and achieve their goals. Like a good physician, a coach considers the whole person and not just the immediate problem to be solved. They listen and pay attention to all dimensions of a person: physical, mental, and spiritual. How you "show up" as a coach is vital to a successful coaching session.

Coaches adeptly step back from a situation, hear and understand all perspectives, ask questions, and provide insights that improve the direction and quality of the work. To establish credibility and build trusting relationships, physician leaders, when coaching, must bring curiosity, humility, and authenticity to interactions with their coachee.

COACH'S CORNER: MY FAVORITE COACH

Several years ago, I met Lisa Williams, my coach assigned to me in the Master of Business Operational Excellence program at the Ohio State University, via a virtual meeting. Today, virtual meetings and coaching sessions are common but a few years back, this was not a usual practice, and I anxiously awaited our first video call. Speaking with each other for the first time was enlightening. In the first several sessions, Lisa focused on getting to know me as a human being and a person and understanding my interests, goals, and ideas. She was curious about my leadership mindset, style, and behaviors. Lisa's coaching style centered on asking questions, then role modeling the practices of deep listening and reflection. She focused our conversations on the thinking process behind my leadership decisions, always probing and gently pushing me out of my comfort zone.

Right from the beginning, I felt Lisa had my interests and welfare at heart. She was there to make me a better leader, spark my curiosity to lead differently, and identify and tackle my derailers without making me feel defensive. Her style disarmed me. Her humility and curiosity helped us develop an intense emotional bond that I had not felt with my previous mentors or supervisors. Our coaching sessions were free of politics and competition. I craved our time together, waiting impatiently for our next meeting so I could share my leadership struggles and get her advice on how to overcome my personal and professional challenges. I am a better leader today because of Lisa's coaching. In particular, her role-modeling behaviors, such as asking and not telling, and listening intently before offering advice, helped me overcome my command-and-control, fire-fighting leadership tendencies that had been ingrained in me with my medical training.

Leadership Strategies for the Coach

Your coaching style and demeanor will likely change as you adapt to various situations, dynamics, and problems, similar to how practicing physicians may adjust their style to fit their patients' needs. As a coach, your ability to project a welcoming and safe environment should remain constant through every encounter, where ideas are shared, and honest conversation occurs without feelings of defensiveness or hesitation. In addition, a successful coach quickly yet patiently builds a relationship of trust, is adept at flexing their coaching style, and skillfully facilitates the coaching process. Let's explore each of these Leadership Strategies in more detail:

- Build a relationship of trust.
- Flex your style to meet people where they are.
- Facilitate the coaching process.

Build a Relationship of Trust

It is difficult to coach someone with whom you have not established a relationship of trust. You can demonstrate all the skills and characteristics of a good coach, but they won't matter without the respect and confidence of those you are coaching. Coachees will not open up, expose their vulnerabilities, or share things they would ordinarily disclose if you haven't established a rapport or emotional connection. Building a trusting relationship takes time, energy, and the utmost discretion.

> *I've been continually impressed over the years by how much work it takes to maintain a sense of trust with people I am leading and how easy it is to lose some of that trust. Clear, consistent, compassionate communication is really key to maintaining that trust. I am always thinking about how I communicate with everyone else. Did I convey the proper message and tone? Was I respectful? Did I take all the relevant facts and opinions into account? Effective leading is largely about making people feel cared for. This has never been truer than in our current environment!*
>
> **M. Sean Rogers**, *MD, MBA, Regional Medical Director, Optum CA*

Building a close work relationship and a personal connection with a coachee starts with small acts of kindness and appreciation informed by a deeper understanding of the coachee's life in and outside of work. Learn about the coachee's background, where they came from, and how their upbringing influenced who they are now as a person, a leader, and a colleague. What interests and hobbies are they passionate about? What are their challenges and fears? Are they taking care of an elderly parent who is in and out of the hospital? Is their kid struggling at school? Remind yourself to see your coachees as fellow human beings who show up daily at work to perform, improve, and succeed. If they are not doing well in your eyes, pause before judging their effectiveness. Before coaching, learn what internal and external factors affect their work successes and failures. Take time to get to know them on a deeply personal level and form an emotional connection before attempting to change their behavior. This emotional bond will create space for your coachees to share their own insight on how they are doing at work and what help and support they may need from you to help them improve, resulting in a more personalized coaching experience. Many post-Covid-19 jobs and teams function remotely. Building personal connections is definitely more challenging now, but not impossible. It does require intentional effort to schedule "get to know each other meetings" that are not focused on work-related agendas or dedicating a part of some meetings to learning about your coachees' life outside of work. Table 5.1 presents best practices for building relationships of trust.

Table 5.1 Best Practices for Building Relationships of Trust

Trap	Engaging in coaching before there is trust and a personal connection.
Best Practices	Be intentional in getting to know your coachee on a deeply personal level: background, goals, and hobbies. Share your own story.
Questions to Ponder	■ Do I know what makes my coachee tick? How will I find out? ■ What questions can I ask my coachee to build a trusting relationship? What stories do I feel comfortable sharing about me?

COACH'S CORNER: BUILDING CLOSE COACHING RELATIONSHIPS

Early in my career, I worked with internal medicine residents who trained in the hospital and the ambulatory clinic in the inner city. Several of them were foreign medical school graduates who, though coming from privileged backgrounds, struggled clinically and personally, mostly due to cultural differences. They lacked insight into the complicated lives of the patients they cared for. They were quickly labeled as poor performers, unlikely to succeed in their medical training. As a fellow-immigrant, I struggled to adapt to a new culture myself when I was younger, but I was fortunate to be immersed in the diverse New York City landscape during my years in college and medical school. This multicultural environment taught me to be sensitive to people from different backgrounds by getting to know them better as people, seeing beyond differences, and finding the commonalities. Just as I was helped by many people on my immigration journey, I was committed to others' success, whether at work or in the community. I made the decision to help struggling medical residents succeed and graduate. As such, I focused on building close personal relationships with them. First, I learned to relate to and appreciate their background and challenges, then I could start guiding them on better interactions with patients, leaders, and colleagues. Our emotional closeness disarmed them. It allowed for more direct coaching as time progressed. Their defensiveness melted, and improvement accelerated. They all graduated from the residency program and went on to competitive fellowships. To this day, we stay in touch.

Table 5.2   Best Practices for Flexing Your Coaching Style

Trap	Cookie cutter coaching style that doesn't meet people where they are.
Best Practices	Take time to understand coachee's readiness to be coached as well as their preferred setting and style of coaching.
Questions to Ponder	■ Have I sufficiently assessed my coachee's willingness to be coached and change their behaviors with feedback? If not, what are my next steps? ■ How will I structure coaching, taking my coachee's readiness and preferences into account?

Flex Your Style

An effective coach adjusts their style so the coachee can listen openly and receive the message without feeling defensive or inferior. A good coach finds ways to make the experience comfortable, open, and safe. It is imperative that the coachee feel motivated, assured, positive, and enlightened. Successful coaching requires you to meet the coachee where they are; you have to start at their comfort level and let them describe what is needed from the coaching experience. This may mean working with them on things other than what you think they should. That's okay because this helps establish a relationship of mutual respect and trust. Patience is a key characteristic of a good coach. Proceed at the pace of the one you are coaching. Table 5.2 presents best practices for flexing your coaching style.

COACH'S CORNER: ESTABLISHING NEW COACHING RELATIONSHIPS

When I go into a new coaching relationship with a physician or an executive leader, my first rule of thumb is to listen and be cognizant of the coachee's attitude and head space. I listen to the words, what is spoken, and also what is not shared. I "listen" to the body language and degree of comfort or discomfort. I listen to the energy in their tone of voice. Am I hearing excitement? Curiosity? Dread? Or a "Let's get this over with" tone? The second rule when going into a new coaching relationship is to be patient and take the coaching experience at a pace at which the coachee is comfortable. This doesn't mean I won't focus on the coaching opportunities or won't push the coachee outside of their comfort zone, or avoid providing constructive feedback. It just means I will adjust the pace to allow the coaching relationship to form and build.

Let's apply these concepts to preparing for a new coaching relationship. How do you know where to start and what to focus on first? How do you assess the coachee's readiness to be coached? Coaching is not a cookie-cutter endeavor; it is a very individualized and often personal experience for the coachee. Let's demonstrate what it means to "meet people where they are" by describing a variety of coaching experiences.

In this first vignette, the coachee was a new medical director in a large hospital. He had almost 20 years of tenure with the organization, having worked there since residency. He took great pride in having "grown up" in the system to now become one of its top clinical leaders. Part of the requirement of any new leader in this system was to have an executive coach for the first year. During the first coaching session, when I asked him what he hoped to get from these sessions, he responded by saying, "I just need to check this box for the next year, but I'm sure I'll get something of value from it." Needless to say, my approach with this new leader took a different path than moving directly into formal coaching. Over the next few sessions, I asked him to share what was going well in his new role and what wasn't. The focus was not on him but on the circumstances. It took a few months, but eventually the conversation moved from the circumstances to how his actions and behaviors contributed to the circumstances (both positively and negatively). In order to help this new leader, I had to meet him where he was, and it was clear in the beginning that he was not ready at all to talk about himself.

In this second vignette, the coachee was a physician leader who served in a governance role with the board of directors. This physician had been in leadership for many years but never served in a governance capacity. In the first coaching session, she quickly said, "This shouldn't take long, I just need you to tell me what to do and not do in this new governance role." I appreciated her candor and interest in learning but recognized the need to adjust my approach so she would stay engaged in the process, knowing that our coaching sessions would take longer and be more introspective than she could initially appreciate. Meeting this leader where she was meant identifying the clear, tangible steps she could take that would give her the immediate gratification she needed to stay engaged. It also gave me opportunities to highlight personal opportunities for improvement for her to consider as she learned this new role.

Meeting people where they are means considering the personal preferences of the coachee. For example, a coachee might prefer to have coaching sessions while walking outside, feeling that physical movement allowed them to be more open and creative in their thinking. Another leader I coached preferred to have coaching sessions at the whiteboard because making the conversation visible took some of the personal emotion out of the session. It allowed them to "see" the issues and be more creative in designing solutions and seeing developmental opportunities.

Facilitate the Coaching Process

Coaching can occur as a formal session or as an ad hoc encounter. For example, Dr. Alvarez, the fictional Chief Medical Officer profiled at the beginning of this chapter, may choose to engage each of her new physician leaders in formal coaching sessions to help them become better skilled at delivering performance feedback, meeting facilitation, and change management. Let's explore the formal coaching environment and process in more depth.

The formal coaching process broadly follows five steps.

1. Establish the coach/coachee partnership.
2. Prepare for the coaching session.
3. Engage in one-on-one coaching sessions.
4. Evaluate results and progress.
5. Reflect on your role as a coach.

Establish the Coach/Coachee Partnership

The first step is for the coach and the coachee to recognize the need for coaching and identify the skill, behavior, or performance gap. Get agreement that this is an important gap to close and determine whether the coachee has the motivation and energy to close the gap. As a coach, you must understand the coachee's willingness to be coached and their mindset and readiness for closing the gap. You must be able to use their starting point as your starting point in the coaching process in order to move them forward from there. "Contract" with the coachee to ensure you are both on the same page for the likely coaching duration, set expectations for the coaching relationship, determine process, establish goals, and agree on rules of engagement (e.g., how the coachee prefers to receive feedback).

Prepare for the Coaching Session

You may spend up to 60 minutes preparing for a coaching session. During this time, reflect on and review your notes from any previous sessions; review past assignments given to the coachee for completion; prepare an agenda with items that you would like to cover (although you should not necessarily share your agenda with the coachee); and finally, prepare yourself mentally for the coaching session and ensure you are in the right frame of mind for coaching. It is a disservice to your coachee if you cannot be fully attentive to the coachee and engaged in the session.

Engage in One-on-One Coaching Sessions

Just as a physician begins their assessment of a patient's health upon meeting in the exam room, a coach begins to assess their coachee's attitude and mindset at the outset of the coaching session. Be prepared to adjust your approach and style based on your assessment of the coachee's "coming in" attitude. Then, use your initial coaching time with the coachee to first ask clarifying questions and check your understanding of the gap or problem. Be prepared to let the coachee express or vent their thoughts and feelings. Refrain from offering advice. You may ask questions such as:

- What is the issue? Please summarize what the problem is.
- What would happen if this problem were to stay the same and never change?

▪ What have you already tried to address the issue?

Now that you and your coachee have explored the problem, you can move to the next phase and generate a vision for what it would look like to no longer have the problem. You may ask the coachee questions such as:

▪ If this were no longer a problem, what would you see, hear, and feel?
▪ What is standing in the way of achieving that ideal vision?

Next, you can move toward making a plan and taking action. You may ask the coachee:

▪ What are some of the actions that you could take to close the gap?
▪ How will you judge which options to pursue?
▪ What are some early signs you might see to indicate things are getting better?
▪ Which option seems most viable right now?
▪ What is your first step? When will you take it?

Finally, ask the coachee to commit to their own accountability for the coaching process and the results. Ask them for the best way to hold them accountable. Arrange check-in dates and determine the process for follow-up.

COACH'S CORNER: COACHEE ASSIGNMENTS

Coaches frequently give assignments to their coachees – activities to complete outside of the coaching session – as a means for them to practice new behaviors. Assignments constantly test their commitment to the coaching process and their desire for change and positive results. Here are a few of the assignments given to coachees over the years in my role as an executive coach:

▪ Research some ideas or strategies to help you close the performance or skills gap. In one case, I asked a coachee to research "reputation management" to find strategies for repairing a damaged professional reputation. Then, I asked that we role-play, and the coachee coached me on what they had learned.

- Track the number of times you exhibit an undesirable behavior in a meeting. I asked a coachee to make a tick mark at the top of the page in their notebook to indicate each time they spoke up in a meeting, as they endeavored to reduce their speaking time and allow others to speak up. Similarly, I asked one coachee to time how many minutes they spoke during a meeting and then reflect on whether their comments advanced the dialogue.

- One physician leader often received feedback that they were not approachable, and staff members were sometimes afraid to ask them questions. The coaching assignment was to "check their expression at the door" by taking selfie pictures as they arrived at work. The assignment was to keep taking pictures until they were satisfied that their expression exuded openness, confidence, and warmth.

- Some leaders only focus on their coaching when the next coaching session is near. With these individuals, I often ask for them to send me examples – real examples – of how they are executing their plans in the interim period between sessions. I may even require them to send me a certain number of examples (depending on their development plan). This allows informal coaching between sessions because I respond with curious questions or tips. This also provides a level of accountability that some coachees need.

- Self-reflection is always a coaching assignment. Depending on the coachee, the assignment can be structured with specific questions the coachee should answer. In other cases, it can be more informal. This assignment is a critical step for every coach/coachee relationship.

Evaluate Results and Progress

In subsequent coaching sessions, you and your coachee will focus on the results of their actions and the progress they are making toward their vision. Acknowledge to the coachee the improvements you see as they learn and grow. Your responsibilities in these sessions also include giving assignments that will push the coachee outside of their comfort zone and providing honest feedback to them about their progress. And you are checking on their commitments to the coaching process and their improvement plan. Ensure that you keep the responsibility for change with the coachee. It is not the coach's role to "own" the changes needed for improvement.

Reflect on Your Role as a Coach

Following the session, spend some time reflecting on your coaching. Ask yourself:

- Was I fully present in the coaching session? Did I listen? Was I focused?
- If the session did not go well, ask: How could I have prevented the session from derailing?
- Did I push appropriately?
- Did I check out too early?

Be sure you are "present" throughout the entire coaching session. Assume a neutral posture, remove or set aside visual distractions, such as a cell phone or file folder, and maintain direct eye contact. In each encounter, you should also pay attention to the cues that tell you how you are being received in the interaction: Did the coachee's posture change after your previous question or comment? Did their tone of voice change? Consider using silence in the session to give the coachee time to think. Remain self-aware, reflect on how your actions and words are coming across, and adjust accordingly in the moment if you can. Table 5.3 presents best practices for facilitating the coaching process.

Leadership Strategies: Bringing It All Together

This chapter focused on making coaching interactions coachee-focused by "meeting people where they are" and flexing your style as a coach to build trust with the coachee. A formal five-step coaching process to structure

Table 5.3   Best Practices for Facilitating the Coaching Process

Trap	Not being "present" or focused when coaching.
Best Practices	Stay self-aware throughout the coaching session. Observe how your words and actions are being received.
Questions to Ponder	■ What verbal and nonverbal queues will I be watching for to assess whether my message is being received as intended? ■ What went well with my coaching approach today? What should I try to improve next time?

your coaching sessions and to close the skills gaps between where one is now and where one wants to be was also described. As this chapter wraps up, let's return to the fictional Dr. Consuela Alvarez, introduced at the beginning of this chapter. She has opportunities to leverage her interactions with her physician leaders by turning everyday interactions into coaching opportunities. She can observe her leaders engaging in their roles and providing helpful feedback. Also, the skills gaps that she observes in them are skills that she can model for them. Role modeling is a powerful learning tool, bringing concepts to life for the coachee to study. Recently, a physician leader, focused on improving his meeting facilitation skills, led his colleagues in a discussion to get agreement on the following quarter's after-hours on-call schedule. The meeting started out a bit tense because it was during the summer months when several were planning to take vacations, and another physician would be out on maternity leave. The physician leader could have continued the meeting and forced decisions. Instead, he took the time to have each person talk about and agree first on what problem they were trying to solve and secondly, what guiding principles they would use together to solve this challenging situation. It took time and patience, but after nearly two hours, they had a call schedule they could all agree to and a set of guiding principles they could support and adhere to long term as a team. In this example, the physician leader facilitated the meeting while also modeling solid leadership, essentially coaching the rest of the team in problem-solving.

COACH'S CORNER: MY FAVORITE COACHEE

Hanah and I met for our first coaching session in December 2016. Even in that first meeting, I could see that Hanah was a go-getter, action-oriented, ready to pursue her goals with a level of rigor and persistence that I had not seen before. She knew what she wanted and wouldn't stop until she got there. I admired her right away but knew that she had a few things to learn about leadership. Later that day, I remember telling my husband that Hanah Polotsky was going to force me to step up my game as a coach – in a good and challenging way!

Hanah and I met weekly by telephone for coaching sessions, and I visited her practice twice during the following year. I got to know Hanah on a deeply personal level; her life journey fascinated me. I had insights into where she came from as a person and a leader and why she approached leadership the way she did.

It didn't take me long to realize that Hanah wanted the "playbook" for being a physician leader. She needed to know how to reach the goal so that she could go after it – not an uncommon approach for clinicians. As I invested in many coaching sessions to develop a close relationship with Hanah, I was ready to have a more direct conversation.

One day, we discussed one challenging situation in her clinic. Hanah expressed some frustration when I mentioned that it was critical to understand what her team thought about the problem before jumping to solutions. She replied: "I am skeptical that our staff understands how to solve this issue." As we continued to talk through the problem, I wondered out loud if she involved her patients in solving their medical problems. "I surely do, we call it shared decision-making. Though I ultimately decide which medication or test to do, I absolutely solicit patient input. Otherwise, they just wouldn't follow through on my treatment plan." At that moment, Hanah had a breakthrough realization that she should apply her clinical approach to her leadership.

> *Oh, I get it now. Leading a team is not about me being the sole decision-maker just to get to the results promptly. It's about taking time and coaching my team on how to solve problems together. This is a new way of thinking for me.*

That was a critical reflection point not only for Hanah's MBOE project but for her overall leadership growth. This moment drastically changed her leadership trajectory.

Every successful leader has or has had a coach. The best leaders are committed equally to their own development and to the development of others. If you do not have a coach, consider asking your dyad partner or a skilled and trusted colleague to support you in developing your coaching abilities.

The field of coaching exploded in the last few decades. This book can't do justice to the topic of coaching, so learn from experts if you become passionate about coaching after reading this chapter.

The GUIDES Framework and the Coach

Let's return to the fictional Dr. Consuela Alvarez, introduced at the beginning of this chapter. She called her executive coach and asked, "I wonder if I should have invested more time earlier in coaching my leaders. I am noticing some gaps and wonder if they could have been prevented." Her coach reassured her, "We are all on learning journeys. Let's not look back on what could have been done but let's look forward." She asked Consuela:

■ How would you proceed with helping direct reports – new physician leaders – to close their skills gaps?
■ Would you consider coaching each of the three leaders personally and establishing regular coaching sessions with them, following the five-step process?
■ Should you enlist the help of your organization's professional leadership coaches to handle the coaching process with each physician leader?

"You may want to individualize your approach going forward. Once you establish a close one-on-one coach/coachee partnership, negotiate with them about what coaching process would work best."

Dr. Alvarez thought for a few minutes and committed to leveraging everyday interactions with her leaders as opportunities to coach. She could observe her leaders engaging in their roles, solicit their perspectives, and provide timely and situationally appropriate coaching. Also, she could role model the desired skills she wants her direct reports to adopt, as role modeling is a powerful teaching tool.

This concludes the exploration of the three Leadership Strategies: (1) build a relationship of trust, (2) flex your style to meet people where they are, and (3) facilitate the coaching process.

In Chapter 2, we asked you to think of someone you consider a great coach. As you consider them now, to what extent do you think they embody and demonstrate the three Leadership Strategies we have discussed? What other coaching skills or characteristics do they exhibit that make them effective?

Now, access and print the GUIDES Development Plan template in Appendix 1 and create a development plan to improve your coaching skills. See Figure 5.1 as an example of honing the Leadership Strategy "Facilitate the coaching process."

GUIDES Development Plan – Coach

Step 1: GATHER inputs to evaluate your skills gaps and opportunities for development.

1. **Record your own assessment of your degree of confidence in these skills.**

To what extent are you confident in your ability to:	Not at all	Somewhat	Great deal
Build a relationship of trust			x
Flex your style to meet people where they are		x	
Facilitate the coaching process	x		

2. **Reflect on your answers to the questions above. Record your additional thoughts.** *After reading this chapter, I know I must focus on "Facilitate the coaching process" strategy while continuing to work on "flexing my style." I'm nervous about facilitating a coaching process when I still need coaching myself. I'm not an expert in this.*

3. **Ask for feedback from others (e.g., trusted colleagues, your coach, or direct reports) on the skills, and take notes.** *My coach helped me better understand that I need to have a more structured approach to coaching with intentional preparation and reflection.*

4. **What does your additional research tell you about this attribute?** *It may help to do an in-session reflection with the coachee, checking how they find my facilitation and what changes might be helpful. I also learned that different people prefer various coaching approaches.*

Figure 5.1 Example of GUIDES Development Plan for Coach.

Step 2: UNDERSTAND and interpret the data you collected.

The following questions help you understand and interpret the data you collected in the GATHER step. Spend a few minutes thinking about these questions. Record your thoughts and responses.

1. **What did you learn from your self-assessment?** *I often facilitate based on my gut instinct, not by preparing adequately, which can make my coaching sessions feel unstructured and lacking focus.*

2. **How did you interpret feedback from others (e.g., trusted colleagues, your coach, or reports)? Were you surprised? Did their feedback match your self-assessment?** *Without preparation, a structured coaching process, and built-in reflection, my coaching doesn't feel like it's adding value. Some people even said that I was "winging it" and not taking it seriously. I shouldn't have been surprised by this given my actions.*

3. **What were your key takeaways from the research? Were you surprised by anything you learned?** *Intentional reflection with your coachee can help align coaching goals and continuously improve the coaching experience. Having a structured approach to coaching helps build trust and communicates the importance of helping the coachee.*

Step 3: IDENTIFY your strengths and opportunities.

Spend a few minutes thinking about each of these questions. Record your thoughts and responses.

1. **Which skills do you want to develop further?** *Structured facilitation.*

2. **Which skills are foundational?** *Reflection both during the session with the coachee as well as self-reflection after the session.*

Figure 5.1   (Continued)

3. Which skills are your highest priority? *Use reflection to prepare for the next coaching session.*

Step 4: DESIGN your leadership development plan.

What are your development priorities? Record two or three high-priority opportunities and actions.

Area for Development	Developmental Opportunity	Actions to Take	Resources Needed	Target Date	Success Metrics
Coach	*Facilitate the coaching process*	*Develop structured approach for each coaching session*	*Time: block time each week for this specific task*	*9/1/23*	*Keep all time blocks for this task and do not miss or reschedule*
Coach	*Facilitate the coaching process*	*Schedule 1:1 coaching sessions*	*Ask my assistant to schedule, rearranging other meetings if necessary*	*10/1/23*	*Coachee survey and feedback*

Look over your development plan, then consider these questions. Record your thoughts below.

1. Does this plan address the foundational opportunities identified in your self-assessment, research, and input from others? *This plan will help me practice structured coaching and hopefully increase my confidence level in facilitating this process.*

2. Does your plan take into consideration the personal triggers that could help or hinder your development? *Yes, I can get easily distracted and unfocused if I don't have notes and coaching agenda written out.*

Figure 5.1 (Continued)

3. Is the plan incremental and doable? *Yes. I will focus on only one development strategy at a time. In keeping my time commitments, I should have plenty of opportunities to prepare and practice.*

4. Are you excited about your plan? Why or why not? *Totally excited, as planning and being intentional will greatly improve my coaching skills and confidence level. I am hopeful it will help build more trust with my colleagues and team.*

Step 5: EXECUTE your development plan.

Put your development plan into action! As you proceed with the execution of your plan, spend a few minutes thinking about each of these questions. Record your thoughts and responses.

1. What circumstances or triggers will signal that "now" is the time to act and practice new behaviors? *I will build coaching preparation time into my schedule, rearranging other meetings if necessary to demonstrate the importance.*

2. What specific behavior(s) or action(s) will you try? How far are you willing to push your comfort zone? *Keeping my commitments for preparation (which will be a challenge given everything that is going on in the organization). Following a structured coaching process and not shooting from the hip.*

3. How do you know if you are improving and becoming more successful with this attribute and as a leader? *I will continue to check in and reflect with my coachees. My own comfort level will also be an indicator for me personally.*

4. How will you gauge the impact of your actions or behavior changes? What responses will you be watching for? *I will be watching for the response to my facilitation changes and ultimately the performance of those I coach.*

Figure 5.1   (Continued)

Step 6: SELF-REFLECT on your execution of the development plan.

Spend a few minutes at the end of the day and/or week thinking about each of these questions. Record your thoughts and responses.

1. **Was I mindful of my development today/this week? What did I do well? What could I have done better?** *I did well in three of the coaching sessions but in one, I got derailed and skipped reflection entirely.*

2. **How did others respond when I intentionally led in a new way? Were people more (or less) engaged with me as a leader?** *The people I coached were more engaged and open to change. Asking them to reflect on my coaching somehow triggered them to be more open themselves.*

3. **Was I mindful of my triggers? How did I respond to those?** *I tried to pay attention to the coaching session agenda to keep me on track.*

4. **What will I do differently tomorrow/next week? What should I be watching for?** *Based on my after-session reflection, I will prep right away for the next week's coaching session, incorporating what needs to be improved, while it's still fresh in my mind.*

5. **What else do I need to do or learn to further my development of this attribute?** *I should check with my coach to learn additional coaching techniques based on how my coachees respond to a more structured facilitation approach.*

Figure 5.1 (Continued)

Chapter 6

Team Builder

Leadership isn't about the title. It's about how you treat people, how you work with people, and how you value what they bring to the table. We all bring something; we all help each other.

Debbie Zuege, *Chief Nursing Officer Kaiser Permanente Colorado (Retired)*

Every team must be made up of people with different roles, strengths, temperaments, and perspectives. They must always be open to criticism and they must always be on the alert against groupthink.

Rabbi Lord Jonathan Sacks

Leadership Case Study: The Stellar Team

Dr. Sarah Steele was elated. Her team had just finished presenting a proposal for improving infection control audit results in their medical center. The proposal itself was stellar. It analyzed the current performance gap and demonstrated how their recommended solutions would close it. It also outlined the role of physician leaders in implementing and sustaining the recommended changes. It was evident that each team member had contributed to the final product, and Dr. Steele could sense the team's enthusiasm for the work. They had worked well together over the last six weeks; they tackled a challenging organizational problem yet appeared before her today as though they had all just returned from summer camp,

DOI: 10.4324/9780429352355-6

exuding joy, excitement, and enthusiasm. What had happened in the last six weeks to bring about such a significant change to this team's performance? Was it their coming together to solve a seemingly impossible, complex problem and finding such an elegant solution? This team, after all, had not had many successes this year, which was why Dr. Steele had invested so much time coaching each individual and the entire team over the past few months while keeping clear expectations, objectives, and deliverables front and center. Perhaps the team's presentation today was the result of her focused efforts.

Introduction

When you encounter a group of people working effectively together, you can bet that it has a leader who invested time and energy to intentionally develop the team. Not only has the leader focused on the team as a whole, but the leader has also invested coaching time and energy into each individual member of the team. The payoff is a group of individuals who trust, respect, and support one another; they operate under the principles of openness and authenticity, exceed performance expectations, and can perform well together whether or not the leader is present. A team that is encouraged and expected to perform at a high level will find its rhythm in any setting and deliver productive outcomes. It is an esprit de corps that transcends individual interests and contributions so that teams can do their best and most creative and innovative work.

> *The team is the star, never an individual player.*
>
> **John Wooden**

Teams are the lifeblood of organizations, and whether big or small, organizations can only succeed with strong teams. Do not allow your teams to develop haphazardly. Be intentional. Understand team development theories and harness the power of your teams for the benefit of the organization and, more importantly, for the benefit of the patients you serve. Let's delve into a team builder's mindset and three Leadership Strategies. To bring it closer to home, parallels are drawn between clinical practice and physician leadership. At the end of the chapter, to strengthen your team builder muscle, an example of the GUIDES Development Plan is provided to ease you in creating your development plan.

Take a moment to review your notes in Chapter 2 in response to the question, "Who do you consider to be a masterful team builder, and why?" Keep this person in mind throughout this chapter.

Physician Leader as Team Builder

Practicing physicians invest in developing trusting and open relationships with patients. Without trust and a safe clinical space, patients are unlikely to take medical advice to heart, perhaps nodding in agreement with little likelihood of engaging in or sustaining changes long term. Patients have families and other supportive persons in their lives. Great physicians often engage patient families as a part of the treatment team to develop accurate diagnoses and achieve successful clinical outcomes. Studies show that patients who are surrounded by others with healthy habits are likely to embrace healthy habits as well. What habits and behaviors the people on your patient's team (family, friends, and physicians) role model matters.

This important concept of modeling behaviors to influence others is also applicable to leaders. Leaders build relationships with colleagues and teams one person at a time while simultaneously creating a psychologically safe learning environment that fosters an effective team dynamic. Regardless of the team's formal structure – whether it is a group of colleagues developing organizational strategy, one's direct reports solving an operational problem, or even an ad hoc collection of people who have come together to improve a process – bringing out the very best in the team and leading them to collaboration and action is critical. If the environment is tense or unfriendly, team members will absorb the negative, psychologically unsafe dynamic, affecting their interactions with one another. In contrast, when leaders are cheerful and positive and coaching their staff, they can achieve high performance and drive better outcomes.

What do successful leaders do that allows their teams to deliver the best work and achieve business goals? Leaders demonstrate authenticity and humility in asking for the team's thoughts and ideas rather than providing solutions. They cultivate an open, judgment-free environment where ideas can be exchanged freely. To inspire the team's best thinking and creativity, the leader provides sufficient background and context for the issue or problem, sets the direction for the team when needed, and then allows the team the time and space to work together to achieve the agreed-upon and clear objectives.

Respect for people as a prerequisite of building trust is critical at work yet is sometimes overlooked. One can't build trust without respect. The Golden Rule appears in many religions and in many sources and dates back to Confucius.

> *Don't do unto others what you don't want done unto you.*
> **Confucius**

There are many examples of when a lack of respect destroys trust or makes it impossible to develop trust. For example:

- Dressing down people in front of others.
- Sharing details of private conversations.
- Discussing others when they are not present.
- Belittling someone's background, looks, education, etc.

It is not unusual to spend years building trust, only to have it destroyed in one act of disrespect. As a leader, being aware of what to do to build trust is crucial.

Mindset of the Team Builder

There is both science and art in successful team building and development. To begin, leaders must consider their current mindset. Though curriculums are now changing, many practicing physicians received years of medical training preparing them to be heroes, working independently and assuming control of all clinical activities and decisions. While this approach is necessary for some medical situations, the hero mindset is counter to that of an effective team builder.

> *Physicians are knowledge workers. They're highly motivated to do the right thing for the patient. They enjoy or want to enjoy a high degree of autonomy, and they can be less collaborative than others. And that's a direct outcome of how people get selected to go to medical school. It's competitive and ingrained in you: you're a standalone person. The need to do everything yourself is ingrained in residency. "If you don't check on the task yourself, assume nobody checked on it." How many times did you hear that? And so the idea that you have to do everything yourself is*

something you have to shed. To be a leader, you have to trust, delegate, and not micromanage because nobody wants to be micromanaged. Give people very clear roles, understand what they're really good at, and then let them go. Let them make mistakes; let them come back and figure it out.

   Jenny Bajaj, MD, *Chief Medical Officer UCHealth Medical Group*

Smart team builders check their egos at the door and, with vulnerability and humility, ask the team to take the lead in solving problems and deciding a course of action. Surrounded by a group of smart people, it only makes sense that the leader would first solicit the team's expertise by tapping into their collective energy, then coaching and asking questions to push their thinking further while generating the excitement and commitment necessary to carry out the agreed-upon actions. The "return" on this intentional investment of time and effort in individuals and teams is paid back each time the team gathers and actively solves problems, supports one another, provides candid feedback, participates in productive conflict, and shares accountability for results.

Thinking in this way can seem antithetical to everything you have been trained to believe in your professional career. Acting as the ship's captain and assuming all control and responsibility may be hard to change and even harder to consistently demonstrate in your leadership behaviors. Start by realizing that you do not have all the answers. With your unwavering support and guidance, your team will experiment and iterate to solve dilemmas you wouldn't or shouldn't try to manage alone. Unlearning this command-and-control leadership style is a real challenge for physician leaders.

Most of the physicians I knew over the years had a style of being independent or autonomous: never make a mistake; always get the right answer; the buck stops with me; and I'm the captain of the ship. It comes in various forms, and that, in my view, is a real obstacle to effective physician leadership because, without exception, over the almost 40 years that I was in different venues of practice, the really autonomous physician leaders tended to be the autocratic ones. They didn't tend to collaborate. They have that mindset: "I'm here to solve the problems and make things right." They didn't delegate well. You've got to get out of that mindset if you're going to be a really effective physician leader.

   W. Gray Houlton, *MD, Medical Director of Risk Management and Patient Safety (Retired), Colorado Permanente Medical Group*

A "captain of the ship" or "lone hero" leadership style discourages team building, leaving leaders exasperated and overloaded with unending work demands. Teams under this type of leadership will not feel psychologically safe. And without psychological safety, as we learn next, the teams will not reach their potential. Shedding the hero mindset demonstrates to the team that the leader is willing to go first and willing to change themselves before expecting others to change. Role modeling this critical mindset shift signals teams to be open-minded, flexible, and not stuck in their ways.

Leadership Strategies for the Team Builder

The success of Dr. Sarah Steele's team, introduced at the beginning of the chapter, working together to improve infection control audit results, did not come about instantaneously or without effort. Dr. Steele engaged and developed her cross-functional team by leveraging three Leadership Strategies:

1. Role model behavioral norms.
2. Develop individual team members.
3. Build trust and psychological safety.

Role Model Behavioral Norms

As a leader, you are a role model. How you carry and present yourself can create either a positive team atmosphere of openness, discovery, and the free flow of ideas or, conversely, a negative vibe that shuts off innovative thinking, suppresses creativity, and undercuts ingenuity. Choose to intentionally role model the qualities you want your team members to embody, especially:

- Trust and respect.
- Open and transparent communication.
- Continuous learning.
- Experimentation without fear of failure.
- Openness to feedback.

Trust and Respect

Role model relationships of trust and respect. Whenever possible, please get to know team members on a deeply personal level; find out what is happening inside and outside of work and what makes them tick. Build them up, praising them frequently. Listen to your team's perspective and learn from their experience. Identify the company's historians and the informal leaders on your team and tap into their collective wisdom to make decisions. Demonstrate confidence in your team to deliver results without micromanaging every step of the way. Keep commitments and deliver on promises, whether large or small, such as returning phone calls promptly, keeping appointments, and following up when you say you will. Keeping commitments builds trust and demonstrates that you, the leader, value and respect the individuals and the team.

> *Fortunately, I already had a fair degree of leadership experience prior to taking on this new role. However, it did take a solid 12–18 months to become really familiar with the people, processes, and complex business arrangements. During that time, I consciously backed off on change management and focused on developing strong working relationships with my colleagues and team. That effort has paid off, as I now have the knowledge and the buy-in from my team to be an effective leader. I can make good decisions quickly and have enough trust from the team for them to follow my lead.*
>
> **M. Sean Rogers**, *MD, MBA, Regional Medical Director, Optum CA*

Open and Transparent Communication

Role model open, respectful, and transparent communication. As discussed in Chapter 4, effective communication is mission-critical for your leadership success. Communicate in ways that meet the needs and preferences of your team; give your team a line of sight into your thinking and help them see the big picture. Transparency regarding goals, challenges, and opportunities will provide the necessary local and organization-wide perspective needed to achieve results.

> *I learned communication is critically important in bringing along a team. You really can't over-communicate. Sometimes even a*

two-sentence email recognizing a challenge exists and explaining a fix is in the works is what members of the team need. Also, when big issues were in development within the department, I looped in senior leadership and administration to keep them from being surprised and behind the eight ball when problems or issues were developing.

Craig Pepin, *MD, Practice Lead, Gastroenterology, The Polyclinic*

Continuous Learning

Role model continuous learning (discussed in depth in Chapter 8). Incrementally push your teams out of their comfort zone, encouraging them to learn from other individuals, teams, organizations, and literature. Demonstrate humility by acknowledging that you do not have all the answers. Answers matter, but the process of learning and getting the answers together is of real value. It is in the process of growing together as a team that you help them develop independent and creative thinking.

Experimentation Without Fear of Failure

Role model experimentation without fear of failure (discussed in depth in Chapter 9). For a practicing physician, a prevailing sentiment is that "failure is not an option." For a physician leader, however, growth and development without failure is impractical, unrealistic, and counter to the ability to mature as a leader. Too many physician leaders can become paralyzed, waiting for a perfect solution that is failure-proof. Instead, engage in quick iterative experimentation; you will get meaningful results faster than waiting for the perfect process or plan to be developed and executed.

Perfection and precision are needed in clinical medicine. Good enough, not perfection, is needed in business. Fail fast and learn quickly. Come up with a pilot. This is good enough, try that and iterate as you go.

Imelda Dacones, *MD, FACP, Optum Washington Market President*

"Progress, not perfection" is a common refrain in organizational leadership. In his book *Chief Joy Officer*, author Richard Sheridan cleverly notes, "We are witnessing a shift from a brain-based to a mind-set-based economy … organizations that learn to adapt and change rapidly will be the most likely to thrive." Sheridan encourages "making mistakes faster" because this accelerates learning, and learning leads to improvement. "Organizations must have systems for trying new, uncomfortable things, failing quickly, and learning and growing" (2018). If you create an environment for ideation, visualization, and brainstorming, where each team member's thinking builds off another's without fear of failure, they will undoubtedly generate unexpected and breakthrough outcomes while becoming a stronger team.

Openness to Feedback

Role model openness to feedback. Nothing will close off your team to sharing feedback faster than your defensiveness. Defensiveness is a fatal leadership flaw. No, it will not kill you, but your leadership career may have a short trajectory unless you can overcome it. It is an obstacle to learning, coaching, problem-solving, strategic thinking, and innovation. If you are not genuinely open to feedback, you limit your ability to embrace failure and iterative experimentation, giving little space for self or team improvement and growth. If you are not open to feedback, your team and colleagues may walk on eggshells around you, and you will live in a self-created bubble divorced from reality. Table 6.1 presents best practices for modeling behavioral norms.

Table 6.1   Best Practices for Modeling Behavioral Norms

Trap	Expecting your team to exhibit behaviors that you are not role modeling.
Best Practices	■ Develop team norms and expectations collaboratively with your team. ■ Role model agreed upon team behaviors. Solicit team feedback to verify your leadership behaviors are congruent with team norms.
Questions to Ponder	■ How will I role model building trust? ■ Do I have recent examples of open and transparent communication? ■ What strategies can I use to ensure I am open to feedback?

Develop Individual Team Members

As a leader and team builder, you should regularly engage each team member to understand their skills, interests, and challenges. When conducted consistently and thoughtfully, these engagement conversations can help the leader match skills and development opportunities with a team member's desire for such a challenge. By listening to each team member and investing in their personal growth and professional skills building, you develop trust and confidence while improving their work performance. You have an opportunity to promote your individual team members' emotional well-being and set expectations for them to excel in their work.

> *When I took over the job 17 years ago as the Vice Chair for Academic Affairs, it was my job to develop physicians' careers. I saw my junior colleagues, the people who I was trying to coach … as my patients. They would come into my office, and they had a chief complaint, "I would like to be promoted." Or, "I would like to get tenure." Or, "I need to decide whether I'm going to take this position at another institution; what would you advise?" That's their chief complaint. So they each came in with a chief complaint. And it was my job as a leader to treat them as I would have a patient. So I will take a history from them: "So tell me about yourself?" It was like screening a new patient. And the ones who came back repeatedly were like my chronic patients. I tried to treat them the way I would treat patients in my clinic, who I've known for years. I did everything to understand my colleagues, my mentees, the way I try to understand the families and the kids who came to see me as a pediatrician. As a pediatrician, I have a very holistic approach: I will take care of the patient, parents, and grandparents if they are there. In some ways, that was very helpful in a leadership role with fellow physicians, to try and see them holistically, and not just people in their work lives but people with personal lives and real stories.*
>
> **Harley A. Rotbart**, *MD, Professor and Vice Chair Emeritus, Department of Pediatrics, University of Colorado School of Medicine*

Your one-on-one relationship with a team member can set them up for success or failure. As a leader and team builder, you can set high expectations and encourage team members to believe they can do better. Manzoni and Barsoux (2007) discuss the "Pygmalion effect" (high expectations drive high performance) and the "Golem effect" (low expectations drive low performance) in their book *The Set-Up-To-Fail Syndrome.*

When there is a performance issue, bosses think that the performance problem persists despite their best efforts. We are saying that in many cases the problem persists because of their best efforts. Bosses are producing their own misery, and often creating their own poor performers!

COACH'S CORNER: OVERCOMING THE PYGMALION AND GOLEM EFFECTS

The "Pygmalion" and "Golem" effects resonated with me in my physician–patient interactions. Unconsciously, I tailored my diabetes advice based on how I perceived my patients. If patients appeared "sophisticated," that is, they were employed, dressed well, and spoke eloquently, I expected them to do better, and I pushed them harder with my advice. The opposite happened if my patients were jobless, appeared disheveled, and led what I judged to be discombobulated lives. "How can I expect much from this patient?" I thought. Soon I realized what I perceived as the potential for treatment success or failure was my personal hubris and had zero relationship to the diabetes outcomes. I acknowledged my unconscious bias and developed a standardized approach with the same high expectations for all my patients. I was very surprised when many patients who, in the past, I secretly suspected would fail in their battle with diabetes control actually succeeded beyond my expectations. My patients internalized my high expectations, and with physician support, they were set up for success and not failure.

When I first joined the organization, I began meeting one-on-one with all my regional direct reports. The purpose of these meetings was to get to know them a bit (and for them to get to know me) as well as to probe into their daily challenges. I developed a questionnaire that was designed to get into some detail about things that were going well, as well as pain points. It specifically inquired about burnout and asked a key question – if you could change one thing in your work environment, what would it be? These sessions were critically important because they allowed me the opportunity to identify some problem areas and, in some cases, apply a relatively quick fix. They felt heard and listened to (something they hadn't felt in a long time), and I was able to earn their trust. I use weekly meetings with the clinical leads to review various performance metrics but also to assist in their leadership development, with topics such as how to have difficult conversations, leveraging emotional intelligence, etc.

M. Sean Rogers, *MD, MBA, Regional Medical Director, Optum CA*

Great leaders will spend quality time with individual team members to:

- Learn their ideas and aspirations.
- Coach and develop them for future success.
- Support them during challenging times.
- Celebrate accomplishments.

No matter how large an organization, it is still a collection of people – with all that entails in terms of potential for creativity and compassion as well as human frailties. From my Continuous Process Improvement training, I understood the importance of creating supportive structures, using data, and monitoring outcomes. However, even when doing all of that, if one wants to achieve the best outcome, you really need to pay attention to the individuals on the team – what are their concerns, what is driving them – so they can perform at their best.

Mitch Peterson, *MD, Family Physician and Past Chair of the Board, The Polyclinic*

People often don't recognize their own talents. Great leaders can see the potential, traits, and behaviors that will make their people succeed. Similarly, leaders coach team members, honestly and directly, around personal derailers in a work environment. Setting high – but not impossible – targets for achievement while simultaneously assisting them in getting there, helps team members overcome insecurities and obstacles, and embrace opportunities for growth. In this way, leadership can mirror parenting. Setting high expectations and investing in your team members' success by creating a caring, nurturing, supportive environment sets them

Table 6.2 Best Practices for Developing Individual Team Members

Trap	Not dedicating time to develop team members.
Best Practices	■ Understand personal and career development goals of individuals on your team. ■ Assess their current expertise and performance and identify any gaps. ■ Co-design a plan of action, including coaching, to close the gaps and achieve their aspirations.
Questions to Ponder	■ How will I assess the aspirations of my team members? ■ What can I standardize in my approach to an individual's development, and what should be customized?

up for achievement beyond what they believe is possible. Table 6.2 presents best practices for developing individual team members.

Build Trust and Psychological Safety

Think about the circumstances when you are at your best. When are you at your peak performance? Are you surrounded by new people or people you have known for a long time? Do you feel a sense of connection and trust? What emotional state are you in? Are you focused, relaxed, and engaged? Do you have a sense of exhilaration? Success at work depends on numerous factors, but your emotional state defines your likelihood to succeed. Your relationships with others have a tremendous influence on your performance. Interactions with your leaders and team members influence your thinking and create emotions that can positively or negatively affect your physical being and work performance. A good team builder understands how their interactions and emotions impact the team and performance.

Be real, vulnerable, curious, and open-minded. Be yourself. Consider Pete Carroll, the head coach for the Seattle Seahawks football team since 2010. Some head coaches always have their "game face" on. They adopt a look that is neutral, serious, determined, or grumpy regardless of the action on the field and the points on the scoreboard. They may think this is how they must present themselves to their fans and the opposing team. With Pete Carroll, if he is grumpy, you know it. If he is happy, you see it. If he is excited, it is all over his face. His team follows him and believes in him because he is real and not afraid to be vulnerable. He shows his emotions which helps him build goodwill among his team.

As a practicing physician, you are trained to understand thought–emotion–physical connections better than anyone. Physicians know how fear and stress hormones can wreak havoc on one's mind and body. You can set your team up for success by nurturing trust and psychological safety – or for failure by creating a stressful, political, and competitive team dynamic. Healthy tension, stress, and competition stimulate imagination and improve productivity, while unhealthy tension, stress, and competition depress creativity and paralyze performance. Amy Edmonson pioneered the idea of psychological safety in her 1996 article in the *Journal of Applied Behavioral Science*, "Learning from Mistakes Is Easier Said Than Done: Group and Organizational Influences on the Detection and Correction of Human Error." In her research, Edmondson expected to find that teams with a deep sense of psychological safety would have fewer medication administration errors than teams without psychological safety. Instead, teams who practiced open dialogue and group problem-solving reported higher medication administration errors. Their sense of psychological safety prompted them to report more errors and then rapidly improve workflows and communication to prevent future harm and increase patient safety. Other teams likely experienced just as many (or more) errors but failed to report them due to a fear of punishment. According to Edmonson, psychological safety "is a shared belief, held by a team, that the group is a safe place to take risks. It is a sense of confidence that the team will not embarrass, reject, or punish someone for speaking up" (2004).

Edmondson discusses fear and team performance in her book *The Fearless Organization*. "The free exchange of ideas, concerns, or questions is routinely hindered by interpersonal fear far more often than managers realize. This fear cannot be directly seen." The silence due to this fear robs teams of many innovative ideas and solutions to problems they are already experiencing. In healthcare, this fear results in a perpetuating system where process blunders may cost patients' lives. In medicine, it is common to hear that an environment that encourages a "speak-up" or "just culture" must be created. Both terms describe a culture where team members feel safe reporting and escalating near-misses, sharing that knowledge across the organization to prevent future patient harm. It is not an exaggeration to say that the fear of speaking up in medicine can result in poor patient outcomes, while psychological safety helps teams anticipate and avoid harm. Fear interferes with learning and thinking. Edmondson states, "It's hard for people to do their best work when they are afraid. As a result, how psychologically safe a person feels strongly shapes the propensity to engage in learning behaviors, such as information sharing, asking for help, or experimenting" (2019).

As a leader and team builder, creating a safe environment is key. But what does this mean? Does psychological safety mean creating a kumbaya atmosphere where team members always agree with each other? No, quite the opposite. Psychologically safe teams feel comfortable directly engaging in productive or constructive conflict, discussing their ideas and issues even when they may disagree. Creating a safe environment circumvents triangulation, political behaviors, and "behind your back" discussions that can undermine the team and its performance. Psychological safety is not about consensus. It is about listening, hearing each other's thinking, and then exploring win–win solutions. It is about respectfully holding each other accountable to obligations and agreed-upon decisions. It is about elevating the performance of not only each team member but the team as a whole. As a new leader, you may encounter a psychologically safe or unsafe culture. In an open, positive, safe culture, people are free to share ideas, are not afraid to be wrong, and enthusiastically play off each other's contributions.

Creating safe meeting spaces is the first place to start creating a psychologically safe culture, as they provide the opportunity to facilitate team learning and growth. People want to have their ideas heard. They like to be part of finding solutions to complex problems. Model behaviors that you expect your team members to exhibit. Share your challenges and learnings from failures without hesitation. Encourage open dialogue and respectful disagreement with your ideas.

Be personable. Make sure that your verbal and nonverbal cues are congruent. Do not let your team sense insincerity. People can sense when someone is projecting false emotions or pretending to be someone they are not. Author Patrick Lencioni famously described in his book *Getting Naked: A Business Fable About Shedding the Three Fears That Sabotage Client Loyalty*, as being vulnerable with your team. He suggests getting rid of the "fear of being embarrassed", as this fear is rooted in pride. Though no one likes to publicly make mistakes, endure scrutiny, or be embarrassed by asking questions and making suggestions that may turn out to be laughably wrong, vulnerable leaders do not "hold back their ideas, hide their mistakes, or edit themselves to save face" (2010).

Storytelling

Getting to know each other on a personal level is the fastest way to establish respect and trust among the team members. Before you get to work on conducting behavior styles or personality type exercises, learn each other's story. Uncover and shed the preconceived notions and biases you bring into a new relationship. Intentionally or unintentionally, you gravitate toward people who look or think like you. Get through the clutter of prior experiences and stereotypes with storytelling. Storytelling is one of the most powerful communication tools. You are always immersed in patient stories in your work as a physician. No patient story is the same. They are unique and always full of surprises, with unpredictable turns of events. As a leader or team member, learning your colleagues' stories will naturally bring out empathy and build relationships.

Are you willing to share your story?

Ice Breakers

Many leaders incorporate simple techniques to learn about the team. For example, include short ice breakers in your meetings; leverage these opportunities to engage informally, learning new things about each other:

- Start your next virtual meeting by asking everyone to drop an image into the "Chat" feature that portrays how they feel today. Ask for volunteers to explain why they chose their image.
- Facilitate a quick round-robin conversation, asking everyone to name the one app on their phones that they could never delete.
- For mature teams with high trust, you may ask participants to share a challenging life experience and how they grew from it.

One of the authors asked her team to share one fact about themselves that no one knew. A successful nurse with a family shared that she had been in a car accident that left her with a full-leg prosthesis. A doctor shared that she was adopted and had never met her biological parents. As a child, another nurse was in an African refugee camp and miraculously reunited with his family. By the end of the team-building meeting, many people shed tears learning about each other. The team was never the same after this exercise; they became a tight-knit group, seeing each other as family and not strangers. As people share their personal stories of divorce, health scares, or even near-death experiences, they are more fully seen, and judgments are left behind.

Establishing and adhering to team norms (agreed-upon behaviors) is another mechanism for building a strong team. Google's "Project Aristotle" explored what makes teams at Google effective. First, they clearly distinguished work groups (groups with little interdependence between participants who only get together to share information) from teams (highly interdependent groups of people who work closely together to problem-solve). Team effectiveness was evaluated both qualitatively and quantitatively by executives, team leaders, and team members who judged performance (e.g., product launches or sales) against quarterly metrics. Researchers assessed group dynamics, skill sets, personality traits, and emotional intelligence. After a deep dive into the numerous studies on team dynamics, they found little agreement and reproducibility; the research was inconclusive, with some articles arguing that great teams have the right balance of personality types while others championed the team's diversity (re:Work, 2020). As Charles Duhigg ably chronicled in his book *Smarter, Faster, Better*, after hours of conducting double-blind interviews, followed by extensive statistical analysis of 180 teams' engagement data, researchers did not uncover any correlation between personality types, backgrounds, or skills. Team composition had no effect on team performance. What stood out as one of the critical factors in teams' effectiveness were their norms of behavior. It didn't matter who was on the team but rather how the team members interacted with each other. Psychological safety, dependability, role clarity, work meaning, and impact are the elements that play a large role in the success of any team. "The right norms could raise the collective intelligence of mediocre thinkers. The wrong norms could hobble a group made up of people who, on their own, were all exceptionally bright" (Duhigg, 2016). Table 6.3 presents best practices for investing in team building.

Leadership Strategies: Bringing It All Together

The Team Builder attribute builds upon the Effective Communicator and Coach attributes discussed in Chapters 4 and 5. The leader's role is to

Table 6.3 Best Practices for Investing in Team Building

Trap	Not investing in intentional team building or establishing group norms and behavioral agreements.
Best Practices	■ Be deliberate in fostering trust and psychologically safe team dynamics. ■ Inspire team members to learn each other's stories. Help them discover each other's work styles and personality types. ■ Develop group norms. Encourage productive conflict.
Questions to Ponder	■ Am I intentional about building group norms that foster psychological safety? ■ How does my team respond and perform as I make myself more vulnerable with them? ■ How can I show my feelings and emotions so my team can relate to me as a real person who is not perfect, but is always striving to improve?

create a vibrant team with agreed-upon group norms, a vehicle that allows collective wisdom to bubble up. Leaders depend on their teams and encourage team members to lean on one another. They simultaneously develop individual team members while nurturing a collective brain trust, knowing that group expertise and mastery are infinitely bigger and better than the sum of individual contributors' knowledge and efforts.

Exceptional team builders role model the behavioral norms they want to see in their teams. They show enthusiasm for their teams; they honor the ideas the team brings forward, no matter how "out there" they may seem. It is up to the team leader to explore the ideas, probe them, and challenge them in the spirit of discovery. Leaders foster a learning environment and set up individual team members for success, not failure. They create a psychologically safe atmosphere that drives the group's critical thinking, constructive conflict, innovation, and discovery.

For this to happen, physician leaders must change their mindset from "lone hero" or "captain of the ship" internalized during medical training to that of a team player and team leader. This mindset shift is necessary for success in the healthcare business environment.

> *The traditional mindset of modern medicine is, at least in the United States, that the physician is the captain. You're supposed to be the*

smartest, you know everything. People are supposed to carry out your orders and not question them. You're solely responsible and ultimately accountable for everything, right? Think about it: Can you think of any other leadership role where that's actually true? Probably not. You're completely dependent upon the people you work with to carry out their roles and report to you or tell you what's happening. There's automatic deference to a physician in a clinical team that doesn't allow you to learn and practice leadership skills or get to the next leadership level. You're not the smartest person in the room and you are not the single decision-maker. So there is an unlearning that needs to occur. You need to unlearn how to operate in that environment, and that has to come from a position of humility.

Justin Chang, *MD, President, CirrusMD*
Provider Network

The GUIDES Framework and the Team Builder

Many new physician leaders are mastering team-building skills, often through trial and error. They may be uncomfortable with:

- Holding back their own ideas and solutions and instead letting the team develop theirs.
- Trusting the team to make independent decisions.
- Depending on the team to execute plans.
- Soliciting feedback without becoming defensive.
- Coaching individuals on unproductive behaviors.

Let's return to the fictional Dr. Sarah Steel introduced in the Leadership Case Study at the beginning of this chapter to discover the path she followed to become a successful team builder. Dr. Steel had met with her coach when she transitioned into her new role as Chief Quality Officer. She knew from her prior leadership transitions that the first 90 days on the job were critical to her credibility and that building a strong, independent team would be the cornerstone of her success. "How can I improve my team building skills?" she asked her executive coach. Her coach shared three Leadership Strategies essential to building an effective team. They discussed Sarah's mindset and which of the strategies were not intuitive to her. Then her coach suggested observing another team in action and assessing their effectiveness: "Use the following questions. Focus on the subtle and not-so-subtle signals to see if the team is working well together. Journal what you see. We will discuss it next time."

■ Do team members assume positive intent in their interactions with each other?
■ Does it feel safe for someone to disagree?
■ Does the team engage in candid and respectful conflict?
■ Are alternative views met with respect?
■ What advice or coaching would you give the team leader to develop a more cohesive team?

When Dr. Steel met with her executive coach a week later, she shared her journaled observations. Her coach suggested:

> *Conduct the same assessment with your own team. What are your observations? What do you think are your next steps to building your team's performance? Test these ideas with several individuals on your team; ask them for their thoughts on how well the team performs and what action steps would help the team improve. Encourage their candid thoughts, thank them for helping you, then reflect on their input and actively and visibly execute your action plan.*

Dr. Steel spent several months following the coach's guidance and working with her team. The result was evident, and her investment in developing her team members individually and as a group clearly paid off.

This concludes the exploration of the three Leadership Strategies: (1) role model behavioral norms, (2) develop individual team members, and (3) build trust and psychological safety. In Chapter 2, you were asked to think of someone you consider to be an effective Team Builder. To what extent do you think they embody and demonstrate the three Leadership Strategies? What other skills or characteristics do they exhibit that make them effective? Now, access and print the GUIDES Development Plan template in Appendix 1 and create a development plan to assess and improve your team-building skills. See Figure 6.1 as an example of a plan to improve the strategy "Role model behavioral norms."

GUIDES Development Plan – Team Builder

Step 1: GATHER inputs to evaluate your skills gaps and opportunities for development.

1. **Record your own assessment of your degree of confidence in these skills.**

To what extent are you confident in your ability to:	Not at all	Somewhat	Great deal
Role model behavioral norms	x		
Develop individual team members		x	
Build trust and psychological safety			x

2. **Reflect on your answers to the questions above. Record your additional thoughts.** *Wow, role modeling more effective team behaviors may be challenging for me. I tend to be an introvert, and sharing my personal life and developing close relationships with people is uncomfortable for me.*

3. **Ask for feedback from others (e.g., trusted colleagues, your coach, or direct reports) on the skills, and take notes.** *Many find me aloof, and hard to read what I am thinking or planning.*

4. **What does your additional research tell you about this attribute?** *People tend to mimic the positive and negative traits of their role models. It is important to be trustworthy and honest, lead with integrity, and make decisions based on ethical principles.*

Step 2: UNDERSTAND and interpret the data you collected.

The following questions help you understand and interpret the data you collected in the GATHER step. Spend a few minutes thinking about these questions. Record your thoughts and responses.

Figure 6.1   Example of GUIDES Development Plan for Team Builder.

1. **What did you learn from your self-assessment?** *Since people don't see how I arrive at my decisions due to my tendency to not share much, they can't see if my decisions are based on team agreements or company strategy, for example. I need to remember what I learned about creating a culture of feedback.*

2. **How did you interpret feedback from others (e.g., trusted colleagues, your coach, or reports)? Were you surprised? Did their feedback match your self-assessment?** *I need to be intentional about how I show up in meetings. I need to share the "why" behind my decisions and not be afraid to share my thinking, I want the team to feel comfortable in challenging my assumptions, reasoning, and approach to decision-making.*

3. **What were your key takeaways from the research? Were you surprised by anything you learned?** *If I role model the behaviors I expect from my team, they will likely mimic that behavior. So if I deliver on promises, they will. If I say what I mean and do what I say, they will too.*

Step 3: IDENTIFY your strengths and opportunities.

Spend a few minutes thinking about each of these questions. Record your thoughts and responses.

1. **Which skills do you want to develop further?** *I need to start my day by thinking how I can role model honesty and trust, for example, or open communication. At the end of the day, I should reflect on how I showed up at work today – did I role model the behaviors I expect from my team?*

2. **Which skills are foundational?** *Demonstrating respect for people in each interaction, such as attentively listening or giving direct and honest feedback to others. I have to remember the Golden Rule.*

Figure 6.1 (Continued)

3. Which skills are your highest priority? *Building trust through honest and transparent communication, especially with my decision-making rationale (e.g., the "why" behind my decisions).*

Step 4: DESIGN your leadership development plan.

What are your development priorities? Record two or three high-priority opportunities and actions.

Area for Development	Developmental Opportunity	Actions to Take	Resources Needed	Target Date	Success Metrics
Team Builder	*Role model behavioral norms*	*Role model transparency in the decision-making process*	*Reflection time; team survey; allocate time for feedback from team members*	*6/1/24*	*Team Survey: incremental improvement in team feedback*

Look over your development plan, then consider these questions. Record your thoughts below.

1. Does this plan address the foundational opportunities identified in your self-assessment, research, and input from others? *Yes, it gets down to being transparent with others about my thinking and how suggestions from others may influence my decisions.*

2. Does your plan take into consideration the personal triggers that could help or hinder your development? *I am not comfortable being vulnerable hence it takes effort for me to be transparent and share what I am thinking. I will be more intentional to get myself into a "sharing" mindset before each meeting.*

3. Is the plan incremental and doable? *Yes, I can practice sharing how I think and make decisions while also incorporating opportunities to hear from the team.*

Figure 6.1 (Continued)

4. Are you excited about your plan? Why or why not? *Not so much, as I prefer to keep my decisions closely held, but that can be quite disengaging for my team. This also makes me nervous because of my introverted personality.*

Step 5: EXECUTE your development plan.

Put your development plan into action! As you proceed with the execution of your plan, spend a few minutes thinking about each of these questions. Record your thoughts and responses.

1. What circumstances or triggers will signal that "now" is the time to act and practice new behaviors? *I will talk to my team, explain that I am working on decision-making transparency, and give them permission to probe with questions.*

2. What specific behavior(s) or action(s) will you try? How far are you willing to push your comfort zone? *Talking out loud so others can hear what I am thinking and how I am approaching my decisions. Taking time to pause for questions and input.*

3. How do you know if you are improving and becoming more successful with this attribute and as a leader? *I will check in with my team and have a question on the team survey regarding the leader's transparency and decision-making.*

4. How will you gauge the impact of your actions or behavior changes? What responses will you be watching for? *I will observe if the team is more comfortable sharing their thinking, asking me questions, and if they give me feedback on my behavior.*

Step 6: SELF-REFLECT on your execution of the development plan.

Spend a few minutes at the end of the day and/or week thinking about each of these questions. Record your thoughts and responses.

Figure 6.1   (Continued)

1. **Was I mindful of my development today/this week? What did I do well? What could I have done better?** *In some meetings, I did better than in others. I got defensive when I couldn't explain very well the "why" behind the hot topic of schedule changes.*

2. **How did others respond when I intentionally led in a new way? Were people more (or less) engaged with me as a leader?** *I think I need more time for my own improvement. Some team members are becoming more comfortable asking me questions and sharing their own thinking, while others are still mum.*

3. **Was I mindful of my triggers? How did I respond to those?** *I truly tried to overcome my discomfort in sharing. I don't like feeling vulnerable.*

4. **What will I do differently tomorrow/next week? What should I be watching for?** *I will be more focused on thinking through what I will share and the "why."*

5. **What else do I need to do or learn to further my development of this attribute?** *I may want my coach to attend a few team meetings with me to give me direct feedback after.*

Figure 6.1 (Continued)

Bibliography

Duhigg, Charles. *Smarter Faster Better: The Transformative Power of Real Productivity.* New York: Random House, 2016.

Edmondson, Amy C. "Learning from Mistakes Is Easier Said Than Done: Group and Organizational Influences on the Detection and Correction of Human Error." *The Journal of Applied Behavioral Science* 40, no. 1 (March 2004): 66–90. https://doi.org/10.1177/0021886304263849

Edmondson, Amy C. *The Fearless Organization: Creating Psychological Safety in the Workplace for Learning, Innovation, and Growth.* Hoboken, NJ: John Wiley, 2019.

Lencioni, Patrick. *Getting Naked: A Business Fable About Shedding the Three Fears That Sabotage Client Loyalty.* San Francisco: Jossey-Bass, 2010.

Manzoni, Jean-Francois, and Jean-Louis Barsoux. *Set-up-to-Fail Syndrome: Overcoming the Undertow of Expectations.* Boston: Harvard Business School Publishing, 2007.

re:Work, "Guide: Identify What Makes a Great Manager." Accessed July 26, 2020. https://rework.withgoogle.com/guides/managers-identify-what-makes-a-great-manager/steps/learn-about-googles-manager-research/

Sheridan, Richard. *Chief Joy Officer: How Great Leaders Elevate Human Energy and Eliminate Fear.* New York: Portfolio, 2018.

Whitbourne, Susan Krauss. "We All Need Role Models to Motivate and Inspire Us." Psychology Today (November 19, 2013). www.psychologytoday.com/us/blog/fulfillment-at-any-age/201311/we-all-need-role-models-to-motivate-and-inspire-us

Chapter 7

Change Manager

It is not necessary to change. Survival is not mandatory.

W. E. Deming

Our ability to manage change hinges on our ability to manage ourselves, including our fears and anxieties.

April Rinne, *Author, Speaker, and Change Navigator*

Leadership Case Study: Resistance to Change in the Midwest

Dr. Jenny Chang was recently appointed to oversee the integration of rural private practices into a national insurance company's health plan. Her years of extensive experience working for the company undoubtedly led to this coveted position. With her kids grown, taking this job, traveling all over the country, and meeting new people seemed like a grand adventure. She looked forward to helping physicians transition from their financially struggling primary care practices to a new model with a competitive pay-for-performance incentive program. Jenny studied the integration plan, researched integration best practices around the country, and created materials to introduce physicians to the payment model. She was well prepared for a successful change effort and felt ready to lead this work. She set off to visit a few practices in the Midwest.

DOI: 10.4324/9780429352355-7

Her time at each physician's practice was very structured. She first met with leadership team members and then delivered a presentation to physicians that clearly laid out all of the expectations, metrics, and milestones. To her surprise, she was met with quiet politeness and few questions. The tepid reception didn't concern her, though, because she knew she was offering a win–win proposition to the physicians. Not only were physicians being offered higher salaries they would also have more time with each patient to ensure that all of their concerns and disease states were addressed. Who wouldn't appreciate this type of change? However, not long after she visited the practices, the Vice President of Integration received telephone calls from several of the clinic leaders. Physicians were up in arms following her visits. They found Jenny to be arrogant, not relatable and pushing for tremendous change that felt overwhelming and not well thought through.

Jenny was shocked. Never in her career had she encountered such resistance. After 30 years in her prior position, she felt she knew everyone and everything. In her new role, everyone and everything was new to her. She had to reset and learn how to intentionally lead a successful change effort, even if the change she brought would improve things for everyone impacted.

Introduction

As the fictional story of Dr. Chang demonstrates, implementing change before building relationships can backfire even if the change is positive. Often, when change is introduced abruptly without sufficient preparation, communication, or understanding of the "why" behind it, it can feel to people that you, as a leader in the organization, are inflicting pain or injury. It is not physical pain but more psychological, yet still painful nonetheless. Mind and body respond to change – for some people, even if positive – like it would respond to any acute stress. Anxiety or fear of the unknown may prevent rational thinking, understanding of the situation, and acceptance of the personal or work process adjustment. Make change processes as people-focused as possible. An empathetic approach that addresses the emotional aspects of change helps overcome resistance. Change is change, and many people yearn for a human connection before opening their hearts and minds to new possibilities.

But why is organizational change, such as the successful deployment of new practice standards or workflows, so fraught with challenges? In business, change is the catalyst that ensures an organization's long-term relevance and, often, its survival. However, even as problems surface in healthcare, changes to workflow, strategy, or processes are frequently met with resistance or indifference (Ashkenas, 2013). Healthcare change efforts are short-lived and seldom sustained (Wiltsey Stirman et al., 2012). What can leaders, as change managers, do to ensure that solutions designed to address problems, such as not meeting quality targets, or experiencing a declining market share, are implemented successfully?

> *Leading change in an organization is about taking your team to the very end of where they're comfortable and then pushing one step over, because if you stop at that point, where they're comfortable, that's not change. Leading change is about envisioning and articulating a future state, a future vision, and holding to it ... not being bound by it, but not letting it be stopped by the naysayers. Your job as a leader is to get your team from here to there, but you set the ultimate goal about where you're going. Leading the team is about figuring out how they will get there, how fast they will get there, and what they do to get there. But you are solely responsible at the end of the day for setting the vision.*
>
> **Justin Chang**, *MD, President, CirrusMD*
> *Provider Network*

Change is experienced at three levels within organizations: the organization, the team, and the individual. All three levels are equally important in the change management process. Paying attention to just one and not the others during times of change is erroneous and risks failure. In this chapter we focus on organization and individual-level change, while Chapter 6 addresses team-level structures. Macro-level changes are Big Changes, such as offering patients a new specialty service, implementing a new staff scheduling system, or redesigning organizational structure. These organizational transformations are successfully implemented only when staff embrace the new normal on a micro-level, consisting of the Little Changes that affect the team and individuals. Thus, Big Changes are a collection of Little Changes (see Figure 7.1). Successful change implementation and sustainability rely on the ability of leaders to accurately assess the current state, break down Big Changes into Little Changes, then guide people through the team and individual-level changes that affect them.

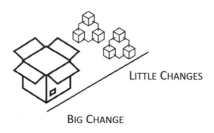

Figure 7.1   Big change is a collection of little changes.

Effective change managers deconstruct, or unpack, the Big Change, then communicate and implement the Little Changes.

COACH'S CORNER: A SMALL CHANGE EXPERIENCED AS A BIG CHANGE

A healthcare organization needed to make an accounting change, splitting all of its employees into two separate legal entities. Clinical staff were placed in one entity, while non-clinical staff were placed in another. Because this change in accounting practices had to be made immediately, a thoughtful change and communication process was overlooked, resulting in enormous confusion for both staff and physicians. When they next logged in to the organization's computer network, they were prompted to select the entity with which they were now associated. Confusion erupted. People asked, "Did our company change?" "Was there something concocted in secret that I don't know about?" "Am I going to have a job in the new company?"

Though the leadership team making the accounting decision certainly did not intend to mislead or hide the change, the reality was that people were confused and angered by the lack of transparent communication, creating fertile ground for rumors and fear. On reflection, the leadership team realized that what appeared to be a small change to them was perceived as a Big Change to staff. All changes, big and small, require broad and specific communication strategies.

This chapter provides the tools to successfully lead and sustain change on macro–and micro-levels, beginning with mindset and Leadership Strategies. Seminal change models that help individuals, teams, and organizations prepare for, implement, and sustain Big and Little Changes are reviewed.

The change management skills physicians use with patients are translated and applied to leadership change management efforts.

Physician Leader as Change Manager

Physicians' medical education is relatively standardized as ACGME, an accreditation agency for graduate medical training, oversees most training requirements. All physicians learn that risk factors such as tobacco and alcohol use, obesity, poor nutrition, inactivity, and stress contribute to many diseases. So, with most things being equal, why are some doctors successful in helping their patients achieve sustainable changes in lifestyle and habits, while other doctors – similarly trained, experienced, and knowledgeable – are not?

Excellent clinicians invest time in understanding where a patient comes from and their capacity for change as they tailor a treatment regimen. A patient may know they can only comply with taking their medications once a day, but to please their doctor and unless asked, may never voice an objection to a more complex regimen. Unrealistic physician expectations only set patients up for failure. Patients, like team members, intend to change, but this doesn't always translate into action. Clinical leaders with limited management experience may think leading change means directing people to "just do it" and expecting colleagues to "fall into line" (2019).

Physicians act as change managers with their patients in clinical practice. Similarly, leaders act as change managers with their constituents in the organization. In both situations, the change manager leads the introduction, implementation, and sustainability of new (or improved) behaviors, initiatives, workflows, technology, and organizational policies and structures. Exceptional change managers go beyond simply telling people what to do differently and passively observing the outcomes. Skilled change managers, just like masterful clinicians, are intentional and deliberate in all aspects of the change effort, knowing that success rests almost completely on engaging people throughout the entire process. Through engagement, the leader creates an environment that motivates people to actively participate in changing behaviors and mindsets.

AUTHOR'S REFLECTION: AN OVERZEALOUS CHANGE

My first failure as a new physician leader left me feeling defeated and puzzled. Shortly after starting my role as Chief of Internal Medicine, energized and inspired to improve how clinic teams interacted, I sent a memo to my team describing the new "daily huddles" initiative. Over the years, I had become self-assured and comfortable as a physician in clinical practice, confident in the leadership I demonstrated with my clinical team. This overconfidence led to my decision to form a new "daily huddle" by combining two Internal Medicine teams. The East and West teams were physically separated only by two sets of doors, so it seemed pretty logical and straightforward that two huddles should be combined. Culturally, however, they were distinct and disconnected. They existed in two separate worlds with almost no interaction between staff and physicians from both sides.

On launch day, I expected all physicians to attend the new daily huddle and be enthusiastic about the check-in as a team. But only a handful of physicians trickled in. Moreover, the few team members who did show up seemed utterly disengaged. Deflated, I managed to muddle through my prepared remarks and cut the huddle short.

Thoughts of frustration were circling in my head: "These doctors do not respect me. Maybe they think I am too inexperienced to lead." Then as I calmed down, I wondered: "Why aren't these doctors willing to come 10 minutes earlier to interact with their colleagues and staff, which would make their clinic run smoother?" Further, as an extreme extrovert who recently moved from the east coast, I saw a combined morning huddle as a perfect opportunity to socialize with clinicians whose paths wouldn't ordinarily cross due to the physical layout of the clinic. Unfortunately, at the time, I had little insight into how other people in the clinic saw things.

To understand the "why" behind their resistance, I met with each physician individually to learn how they felt about the clinic, in general, and this change in particular. Spending time with each physician, I learned about their daily pain points – the problems that keep them from optimally functioning. Many of them mentioned the incredible amount of non-physician administrative work they had performed and how late they stayed after clinic hours to respond to messages in their electronic inboxes. They had no time or interest in socializing or developing relationships with their colleagues; they felt they were already spending too much time at work and not enough time at home with their families. Unexpectedly, as I spent time one-on-one time with physicians, I opened a window into their personal lives. I learned about their passions in and out of work. In addition, I began to understand that their initial lack of "buy-in" and what appeared to be an apathetic reaction was due to the lack of a personal connection and ownership in the decision-making process.

Ultimately, the two clinic teams devised a schedule that would allow them to huddle quickly at the beginning of each clinic session and problem-solve common issues. Once they understood my rationale (the "why") for combining the teams, their engagement in the process increased, as did their attendance at the huddle.

This leadership moment was not a failure but an opportunity for me to reflect and learn how to lead change. As a result, I learned four important lessons that have stayed with me to this day and are foundational to my transformation as a leader: (1) do not take it personally if people do not like what you are proposing; (2) build a personal connection with people you want to influence; (3) help people understand the "why" from their perspective; and (4) get those affected by change involved in designing it.

Seminal Change Management Models

Numerous change models have been developed and studied over time. They all address common facets of change. Unsurprisingly, these models often focus on life's biggest challenges and borrow heavily from the field of human psychology. Change models have similarities and differences. Collectively, they help you understand various facets of change. Mastering these models and intentionally leading change will ensure your work is not dismissed as yet another flavor-of-the-month change effort. We explore three categories of change models: Enterprise Transformation, Individual Adjustment, and Effective Change Manager.

Implementing organization (or macro) level changes benefits from employing a change framework such as Beer's Critical Path, Kotter's Leading Change Model, and the Prosci ADKAR Model. Each focuses on effective approaches to enterprise-wide change, reorganization, or transformation and has several principles in common:

■ Creating and communicating the future, to-be vision.
■ Ensuring leaders are committed change managers.
■ Empowering frontline employees.
■ Anchoring change with new systems, skills, and behaviors.

At the individual employee or micro-level, several psychological models clarify how people process or accept the changes that affect their day-to-day lives. These include Kubler-Ross Grief, Bridges' Transition, and Kurt Lewin's Unfreeze-Change-Refreeze, models which focus on an individual's progression from one phase or zone of change to the next, typically moving from letting go of the old way, engaging in some fashion with the new way, and finally accepting the new way and making it the new normal.

The final category of change models necessary for effective change managers focuses on the people skills needed to lead change, including Stephen Covey's 7 Habits, Miller and Rollnick's Motivational Interviewing, and Egan's Skilled Helper Model. All three models teach invaluable people skills needed to overcome psychological disruptions brought about by the fear of the unknown and changing of the status quo. At this level, the interactions between leaders and employees are surprisingly similar to those between physicians and patients. When a physician breaks the bad news to a patient with a new diagnosis, the stress reaction is often identical to an employee's reaction when he or she first hears about a new process, work reassignment, or, worse, a layoff. Most people, when confronted with change, are ambivalent. Even if they understand that change is required for organizational or personal success or survival, they equivocate, stagnate, and often resist change. Even clearly beneficial changes elicit overt or subtle resistance from patients, colleagues, and direct reports. Motivational interviewing techniques, for example, help both in clinical practice and organizational change management. Table 7.1 lists examples of change models for each change category. For a more extensive look at various change models and references, see Appendix 2.

As a leader, you are more prepared for change because you have been planning for it. You live it. You breathe it. Your mind is engaged in it. On the contrary, your team has not been as experientially immersed in the change as you have; therefore, you cannot use your own readiness as an indicator of others' readiness for change. Understanding where your

Table 7.1   Examples of Select Change Management Models

Enterprise Transformation	Individual Adjustment	Effective Change Manager
Beer Critical Path Method	Kubler-Ross 5-Stages of Grief	Stephen Covey's *7 Habits*
Kotter Leading Change Model	Bridges' Transition Model	William R. Miller and Stephen Rollnick Motivational Interviewing
The Prosci ADKAR Model	Kurt Lewin's Unfreeze-Change-Refreeze	Egan's Skilled Helper Model

team is at is critical to success. Provide a venue for people to voice their concerns and take the time to listen attentively to people closest to the change operation as they will assist you with understanding the current state, the amount of change effort that will be required to achieve the future state, and what adjustments may be needed for the implementation to succeed.

Thus, a significant portion of the leader's role is assessing and understanding where people are starting from and the potential impact of the change on them:

- What is their experience with similar changes?
- What was the success or failure of prior initiatives?
- Are they anxious to solve the problem?
- Are they curious or even excited about the possible improvements associated with the change?
- Are they worried about changing the status quo?
- What is people's capacity to handle new changes?

Asking these questions will help determine how to leverage various change management models to design the most effective approach.

Mindset of the Change Manager

The importance of the change manager's mindset should not be underestimated. Change is very personal, and even positive change can be challenging. It is often a give-and-take process. First, the leader envisions the end result of the change and imagines the process of getting there.

Then the leader evaluates the change process through the eyes of those affected and considers the change disruption from their perspectives. Lastly, the leader engages openly, directly, and transparently with those affected, willing to be challenged, pressing through resistance when appropriate, and role modeling desired behaviors along the way.

COACH'S CORNER: EVEN GOOD CHANGE IS STRESSFUL

Let's consider a personal example. Imagine that you and your partner have lived in an apartment for the last few years, but now with a growing family, you are looking for the right opportunity to move into a house. You find the perfect house, and the entire family is excited about the move, but it requires a couple of significant changes: your partner's commute will be about 30 minutes longer, and your kids will attend a new school. How will you help support your family in this exciting time? How can you assess how they are experiencing and perceiving the change so that you can better support them? You can establish ways to check in with them. You can listen. You can adjust to show your support. You can be a positive change agent at home, supporting your family through challenging transitions.

Maybe this includes driving the kids to school for the first few weeks. Maybe it is getting dinner started since your partner will get home later. It would be reasonable to expect your partner to be more tired and frustrated with the longer commute, and kids might be anxious about a new school and forming new friendships. Their feelings could easily lead to tense conversations, disagreements, and resentfulness. The same is true for organizational changes. People impacted by the change could feel tense, pressured, stressed, and resentful that their work processes are changing. Focus on how the change affects others and less on how it affects you. Ask curious questions to clarify your understanding of how others see the change. See the change through their eyes, validate their fears, listen without defensiveness, and empathetically demonstrate that you recognize and understand their feelings.

Having the right mindset is important but not always easy to achieve. Some think that being a good change manager is about being positive. This is important, but too much positivity, especially when delivered superficially or insincerely, diminishes trust and respect. A good change manager listens and adjusts their style and approach based on the needs of the team and the individuals involved.

Years ago I attended a course on accelerating the pace of change. I learned to begin with the end in mind – you create the vision of what is the end state you want to get to. You look at the capacity for change: Did your group just go through five changes, and this is the sixth in a month, so they're going to be dead tired from it? You look at the prior change success rate: Were the last three projects your department went through successful? Were they on time or did they fail? All of that impacts a person's opinion of the change project you are leading. So, get your history. Find out what those changes were so you can speak to them, and share how this change will be the same or different. You also define your measures of success and you write them down – now, before you start. What are the objectives? What are your financial targets? What are your strategic targets? What are your human targets? You develop tools to measure those successes objectively and make sure all the sponsors agree with it. I can't tell you how many times people started a project and later said "Well, this isn't the outcome I wanted!" Guess what? The targets and goals were never written down, never objectified for others to look at and agree to. After you develop the measures of success, you can follow these measures to see if you are achieving what you expected/had planned. When you face resistance, know that it's not bad; don't try to cover it up; don't try to run away from it. Change is difficult, just like putting your watch on your left wrist every day instead of your right. That is change and something as simple as that is difficult. The amount of resistance is equal to the amount of change. Also, if people feel like they can't go back, they're going to resist even more! Even if it's as simple as changing their exam room or moving where the fax machine is placed. You have to understand that impact and negotiate that the future state will be better than the current state. And, if it isn't, you agree to go back. You've got to create the path and buy in for this change to happen so that people are supportive rather than resistant to it.

Scott Smith, *MD, SVP & Medical Director Value-Based Care, Millennium Physician Group*

Leadership Strategies for the Change Manager

Deploying new systems and processes is like swimming through murky waters: you do not know if – or when – you may encounter dangerous whirlpools. As a leader of change, the often-unpredictable human reactions to altering the status quo will undoubtedly challenge you emotionally and psychologically. It takes work and a lot of energy.

> *If you don't spend time strengthening your emotional intelligence, you will struggle to handle yourself well in the heat of public outcries aimed directly at you as the change leader.*
> **Janelle Banat**, *Founder and CEO, Footlamp Consulting, LLC*

Below are three Leadership Strategies to assist you in navigating challenging change journeys:

1. Build up an emotional bank account by building trust before change.
2. Demonstrate respect for people by involving those affected by the change.
3. Sustain changes by implementing visual management and standard work.

Building these strategies into both Big Changes and Little Changes makes the difference in the success and sustainability of a change initiative. The difference between change initiatives that "stick" and those that do not lie with the intentional work done by leaders and those implementing the change.

Build Up an Emotional Bank Account by Building Trust Before Change (Covey, 2013)

Leaders are change agents, the human catalyst for improvement, action, and organizational progress. As a change agent, your frame of mind and the behaviors you exemplify significantly influence not only others involved in the change but also the success of the change itself.

> *In a new leadership position, nothing is going to happen unless you can build that relationship of trust. People don't know who you are, you're*

not a proven entity, and for you to come in and if you start making changes, people will ask, "Who do they think they are?" It's really about gaining support and empowering people to say what they think.

Debbie Zuege, *Chief Nursing Officer*
Kaiser Permanente Colorado (Retired)

Stephen Covey, the author of *The 7 Habits of Highly Effective People*, emphasized the need to understand others before expecting others to understand us. The focus on others is key to any change management effort. Building an "emotional bank account" is a personal investment in others that can be tapped into during transformations. Covey highlighted five behaviors necessary for maintaining an emotional bank account in good standing (2013).

1. First, one must attend to the little things because "In relationships, the little things are the big things." Small deposits of kindness, such as providing a listening ear or helping during times of personal challenges, build a reservoir of goodwill and trust that can be tapped into later.

2. The second behavior is keeping commitments and always following through with your promises. It is important not to make promises you know you cannot keep. Say "no" if you can't deliver on a commitment, and take the time to demonstrate respect to the individual by talking openly about why you are unable to deliver on a commitment.

3. The third behavior identified by Covey is to clarify expectations. Setting clear, unambiguous, and reasonable expectations will ensure that you, as a leader, and your team are on the same page. This is even more consequential when you implement new workflows or systems or ask others to adopt new behaviors or skills.

4. The fourth behavior identified by Covey is showing personal integrity. Honesty is by far the most admired characteristic in leaders, as found in studies in numerous countries over the last several decades (2013).

5. Covey's final behavior is to apologize sincerely when you make a withdrawal from the emotional bank account. We are only human. Errors of judgment, execution, and communication will occur sooner or later. As a leader, learning to be transparent about your disappointments and mistakes will not compromise your standing with people. Quite the opposite: it will gain respect and signal

to others that failure is okay; it is acceptable. Studies in medicine show that admitting and sincerely apologizing for errors surprisingly decreases litigation costs. Physicians now recognize that mistakes are an opportunity to improve the safety and quality of healthcare (Kachalia et al., 2010).

COACH'S CORNER: THE EMOTIONAL BANK ACCOUNT

Stephen Covey's concept of the emotional bank account has stuck with me for years since I first learned about it. It helped me manage my relationships at work, both as a physician and as a leader, and my home life as a parent, wife, and daughter. When we have a bank account, we deposit small amounts of money in it to build substantial savings for future withdrawals when we plan to buy a car or a house. In relationships, positive actions are the same as making a deposit in an emotional bank account. Making a mistake or hurting someone's feelings is a withdrawal. When we undertake a big transformation or change effort, we can inadvertently hurt people's feelings, disturb the equilibrium, or bring negative energy to our relationships. This is a huge emotional bank account withdrawal, and to compensate for it, we need to prepare with a lot of small and big deposits of positive acts beforehand.

Building up an emotional bank account is a slow process that happens over time, over the course of multiple effective exchanges and encounters. Building a great rapport and a deeply trusting relationship takes time on the front end – and will pay off later in times of stress and change. Cutting corners or moving too quickly to introduce change before the preparatory leg work is completed will surely backfire and impede or slow down the change process, not to mention the potential of damaged relationships, decreased trust, and lack of respect.

Building an emotional bank account is important in clinical practice, too. Research has demonstrated that a physician who sees a patient several times and develops a good rapport with them is less likely to make medical errors. When patients see a new clinician for a serious medical condition, they are more likely to end up in the hospital than if their long-term primary care physician had seen them (Rose et al., 2019). In the authors' experience, studying patient satisfaction rating data over the years, new

Table 7.2 Best Practices for Building Trust Before Introducing Change

Trap	Implementing change before building relationships will backfire even if the change is positive.
Best Practices	■ Get to know people on a deeply personal level before initiating a project or change effort. This often requires one-on-one meetings focused not on business but on getting to know people as fellow humans. ■ Build trust, listen without prejudice, project openness, and demonstrate integrity. ■ Go out of your way to help and support others without expecting anything in return.
Questions to Ponder	■ How will I lay the groundwork for building trust before initiating change? ■ What approach will I use to build deep personal relationships?

doctors, independent of their work experience or style, were consistently rated lower in their first years with the organization. Ratings improved as the number of repetitive interactions with patients increased. There are parallels between a physician advising lifestyle changes, such as a healthy diet and a regular exercise routine, to a leader advising work-style changes, such as timely and efficient referral processing or patient message management. Table 7.2 presents best practices for building trust before introducing change.

COACH'S CORNER: COACHING WITHOUT TRUST

My first few patient complaints were eerily similar. One patient remarked, "The doctor called me obese and advised diet and exercise." On the surface, I could pat myself on the back, satisfied that I was doing the right thing and giving sound medical advice. I did not realize I provided advice before my patient developed trust in me and felt a personal connection. In my early years as a physician leader, I had a similar experience while trying to help doctors be more efficient with their patient management. I'd had a lot of experience implementing efficiencies: having five kids at home, I developed many shortcuts and efficiency hacks to help me complete my work without repetitive or unnecessary tasks. In attempting to help my colleagues, I figured if I could just show them – or cajole them or push them "for their own good" – they would love it, accept it, and celebrate me as a leader who truly cared about them. I meant well, thinking any doctor would want help to get them out of work on time. The reaction was quite the opposite. No one welcomed my unsolicited advice. It did not take me long to realize that I had to build relationships before I could make any change, no matter how beneficial it might be for patients or my colleagues. I had to make some deposits in the "emotional bank account."

Demonstrate Respect for People by Involving Those Affected by the Change

A capable executive leader understands their job is to create and communicate the organization's vision and to help others see the distant horizons that need to be reached. They create maps to show how to get their team, department, or organization from point A (current state) to point B (future state). Effective executives focus on the vision and strategy and leave the tactics to middle managers, who in turn work with their frontline teams to navigate and keep the ship afloat. In contrast, a less effective executive gives out static directives, deploys change in a rigid top-down fashion, and leaves no space for others to add ideas. The first executive is demonstrating respect for their people; the second executive is not. The first executive is leveraging the expertise and talents of its workforce to succeed; the second executive is silently signaling that "I have all the answers. I am not interested in your input."

> *My style is to deliberate and to discuss the change in advance to get a sense from the people I work with, what they think about it. By the time the change happens, I already know that the lion's share of the people are behind it. If you approach change this way, you don't even need to call it a change. It's more of an evolutionary step, something you take to the next level.*

> **Eli Y. Adashi**, *MD, MS, MA (ad eundem), CPE, Former Dean of Medicine and Biological Sciences at Brown University*

Jeff Liker, Professor of Industrial and Operations Engineering at the University of Michigan, has spent a lifetime studying Toyota's method for developing exceptional people (leaders and frontline employees), teams, and, consequently, products. In his books (*The Toyota Way* and others), Liker delves into Toyota's focus on its people: setting very high but clear expectations, developing individuals through "learning by doing," and expecting frontline teamwork, continuous improvement, and innovation. Frontline employees are not only allowed to contribute to the change efforts but are expected and encouraged to do so.

> *Nobody likes following someone's detailed rules and procedures when they are imposed on them. Imposed rules that are strictly policed become coercive and a source of friction and resistance between management and workers. However, people, happily focused on doing a good job, appreciate getting tips and best practices particularly if they have some flexibility in adding their own ideas.*

(Liker, 2004)

Research conducted at the Massachusetts Institute of Technology (MIT) by James Womack and his colleagues Daniel Jones and Daniel Roos gave birth to the lean management movement that permeated not only the automotive industry but also the service and healthcare industries worldwide. Womack named "Respect for People" as one of the two pillars of *The Toyota Way*. He identified the involvement of workers in problem-solving hand in hand with their managers as the highest level of respect (2007).

Respect for people as a change management strategy means investing time to help people understand the "why" behind a change and see the benefits for them, their team, and the entire organization. Typically, three groups of people are involved in a transformational effort: executives, middle managers, and frontline managers. The success or failure of any change effort is therefore highly dependent on the executive and local leaders' ability to ensure each and every employee can see the vision for the future, understand the risks of maintaining the status quo, accept change even if painful, and master the new skills and behaviors needed for success. Communication is by far the most effective and least utilized instrument of change. Both executive and middle manager communications must happen concurrently. Communications about Big Change should include the big picture, the vision, and the destination. Communications about Little Changes should address the "why" behind the change as well as what will be important to the people impacted by the change, specifically "What's in it for me?" and "How will I be affected?"

In their book *Making Sense of Change Management: A Complete Guide to the Models, Tools, and Techniques of Organizational Change*, authors Esther Cameron and Mike Green noted that

> *One of the most striking conclusions to draw is that employees need to hear about change from two people – the most senior person involved in the change and their line manager. The senior manager is best suited to communicating business messages around the change, whereas an employee's line manager is best suited to communicating more personal messages. This ties in with the notion that the overarching vision and strategic direction once communicated needs to be translated into a local context.*

(Cameron and Green, 2015)

It is often said that "People do not mind change; they mind being changed." Change can be something you either do with people, or you do to people. The latter will inevitably create resistance and undermine your improvement effort. Larry Anderson and Ron Oslin stated in their eloquent article in *Target Magazine* that the use of clinical methods (e.g., motivational interviewing) in business helps avoid wasting time in "wrestling to achieve compliance," and instead focuses time on "dancing together to achieve real change" (2015).

Following a major redesign of primary care at the Palo Alto Medical Foundation (PAMF), Dorothy Hung, researcher and director of the Center for Lean Engagement and Research, studied the effects of the implementation and the change efforts on team members. Her research concluded that the pilot site team – the staff and physicians deeply entrenched for six months in the redesign of workflows, reconfiguration of teams, and the standardization of their shared physical spaces – highly rated their satisfaction and engagement with the change process and its results. Subsequent teams, who had minimal involvement with elements of the redesign and merely adopted the products developed by the pilot site, were much less satisfied with the change process, perceiving it as imposed upon them in a top-down fashion from management. As involvement in the redesign process decreased, so did engagement in the change process and satisfaction with the results. "When change is outsourced to consultants and 'experts,' it rarely works" (Ashkenas, 2013). Successful redesign is based on "encouraging frontline engagement with change efforts, allowing flexibility in tailoring the intervention to local environments, and keeping the lines of communication open for feedback across work functions" (Hung et al., 2016).

Eisenstat, Spector, and Beer recognized this same phenomenon decades earlier, specifically that letting departments "reinvent the wheel" leads to the more organic and successful spread of change initiatives.

> *The temptation to force newfound insights on the rest of the organization can be great, particularly when rapid change is needed, but it would be the same mistake that senior managers make when they try to push programmatic change throughout a company. It short-circuits the change process.*

(1990)

Table 7.3 presents best practices for involving those affected by the change.

Table 7.3   Best Practices for Involving Those Affected by the Change

Trap	"Copying and pasting" change or adopting it as-is without improvement and adaptation to meet the needs and realities on the ground.
Best Practices	■ Make change a participatory and immersive experience. Engage people who are going to be affected the most in the change process. Do not do it *to* people, rather do it *with* people. ■ Let your proposed changes be improved or adjusted, even to a small degree, by the team. You will gain understanding, support, and buy-in, which in turn will accelerate acceptance and ownership.
Questions to Ponder	■ How will I allow people affected by the change to put their fingerprints on the new process?

Sustain Changes by Implementing Visual Management and Standard Work

You have applied rigorous change and communication strategies and successfully led your team to the future state. Now that the new process, technology, or workflow is implemented, the hard work of sustaining change begins. It is not enough to expect that a single communication or presentation will be sufficient to establish and sustain new routines and behaviors. In nature, as in the workplace, everything experiences entropy, the tendency to go back to disarray unless systems are in place to prevent it. Consider the effort required to keep your tidy and organized garage from becoming a cluttered mess. It matches the effort Sisyphus exerted to push a boulder up a mountain. Relaxing for even a moment results in a crushing backslide. To anchor the change you worked so hard to implement requires that a system is in place to prevent backsliding. What elements might be important to include in this system? How will it be managed? This section describes visual management and leadership routines (sometimes described as Leader Standard Work) as key elements in your system for sustaining and managing change.

Like a storm warning issued by the National Weather Service, a visual management system signals when problems are observed, and with enough lead time, adjustments to prevent or mitigate potential mishaps can be made. Similarly, in medicine, physicians receive an early warning signal via the electronic medical record when prescribing a medication that may be contraindicated for the patient. To mitigate a poor medical outcome for the patient, the physician has the opportunity to prescribe a safer alternative therapy. When implementing a new process or workflow, identify the most critical steps or time in the process and "attach" a visual early warning system to them to alert you when a standard or threshold is about to be breached. Pay attention to the warning system; be alert for its signals and have a response plan ready to execute.

For example, imagine your department has just implemented a new process for handling electronic patient messages, and the standard is that all messages are responded to within 24 hours of receipt. Because your department is staffed during regular business hours (and not evenings or weekends), two visual alerts may be needed to manage the process on a daily basis: first, a count at 7:00 a.m. of the patient messages needing attention that day. With this information, staffing assignments can be adjusted to ensure the volume of messages is managed. A second alert may be needed at 1:00 p.m. to indicate whether the number of messages yet to be handled exceeds the day's staff capacity. When notified at 1:00 p.m. that the standard may not be met, the manager still has time to take action to avert failure.

The most reliable method for monitoring your warning systems is to fold them into your leadership routines. Leader Standard Work (LSW) includes the activities you do on a regular basis (hourly, daily, weekly, monthly, quarterly, annually), such as formal and informal meetings, coaching, data review, reflection, problem-solving sessions, and others. These routines are a reflection of what you deem important; you allocate time to each of these routines because they are critical to the success of your department, division, or organization. They are important leadership activities.

Depending on the cadence of the critical steps in a new process, you may set up your LSW such that you "round" on the new process every day at 3:00 p.m. If problems are observed at 3:00 p.m., there is still time before the clinic closes at 6:00 p.m. to resolve them.

COACH'S CORNER: SUSTAINING CHANGE

Train everyone in the new way of working or behaving. Remove anything that makes it easy to revert to the old process. Make sustaining change easy. For my patients who start a new exercise routine, I often advise them to have exercise clothing and sneakers right by the bedside. As soon as they wake up, it is there to remind them and to help them avoid distractions that get in the way of the new routine. If patients need to take medications and have a hard time remembering, I advise them to place medication bottles or pillboxes right next to the toothbrush and toothpaste, assuming that they have a daily oral hygiene routine. Committing to change is only the first step; making it easy to adopt the new behavior is what sustains change.

Sustaining change is hard work, requiring your undivided attention as a leader. Change starts with you. Create a system that will ensure you and your team's work performance and behaviors are consistent with a new process. Make it easy to do the right thing. New processes should be visible, supported by unambiguous metrics, and integrated into daily routines (not on top of old routines). Think about your own LSW and how to incorporate a new process into it. There are different approaches to LSW.

Though we do not deeply explore the concept of LSW, we believe it is an important leadership practice worth introducing here. LSW is a method that helps move you from unproductive firefighting to stable leadership routines. LSW helps you stay focused on activities that Stephen Covey describes as "Important and Non-urgent." Think about all the various activities you do as a leader: formal and informal meetings, coaching, data review, reflection, problem-solving, and others. Review what you do daily, weekly, monthly, quarterly, and yearly. Think about how you can incorporate into your LSW a new system or process change that you are determined to sustain.

LSW should be easily accessible, perhaps displayed on a whiteboard or flipchart, printed and attached to a clipboard, or documented in a software program. Begin by listing your standard work to include your regular leadership activities, the cadence (daily, weekly, monthly) that they are completed, and measurable deliverables for each one. The example below demonstrates how a specific change can be successfully cascaded through an organization using visual management and standard work.

COACH'S CORNER: STANDARD WORK AND VISUAL MANAGEMENT TO SUSTAIN CHANGES

A healthcare organization had to quickly improve its rate of patients' preventative screenings and procedures, with the ambitious goal of addressing 100% of preventative care needs, such as ordering and fulfilling lab, imaging, and vaccination orders. Luckily over the years, the organization had built and continuously improved a robust IT solution that displayed in real time which preventative care needs patients had completed and which remained unfulfilled. Although available for a decade, this robust tool was not used consistently across the enterprise. Multiple presentations and communications had failed to inspire teams and individuals to act in the past. The immense potential to save lives and reduce the cost of unnecessary clinic, emergency room, and hospital visits was just one click away.

Once the call to action had been effectively communicated, clinical teams rallied to design an elegant and simple process to improve their rates of preventative health screenings. Everyone on the team with any contact with the patient was instructed to open the system, access the list of unfulfilled care needs, and share the list with the patient, even offering to assist with scheduling a test or procedure if needed. First, a clear metric was developed and communicated as a strategic quality goal. The metric, target, and current value were displayed on the executive dashboard and reviewed quarterly. As part of LSW for every level of the organization, a cadence of check-ins on this metric was established that allowed quick review of progress as well as coaching and problem-solving to get to the goal. In clinical areas, the process for rooming patients before the physician visit included a review of all the preventative measures due, with clinic staff reminding patients about tests, scheduling what was needed, and administering all the vaccinations. Similarly, physicians doing virtual visits would perform the same process. Standard work for non-clinical areas, including local call centers, also incorporated processes to schedule preventative visits and tests.

Various departments had metrics posted visually on physical and virtual huddle boards. Physicians and staff could see how their performance on the metric compared to one another. This created healthy competition. Building this change into LSW and teams' standard work on various levels guaranteed intentional and persistent focus on the change. Though the cadence of review varied, with executives checking the metric quarterly, directors checking monthly, and frontline clinical teams monitoring it weekly, everyone could easily see if they were winning or losing and how far they were from the goal. Visualizing and standardizing the process of deploying this prevention initiative will undoubtedly result in saved lives by detecting early breast and colon cancers, preventing hip fractures and exploding aortic aneurysms, ensuring compliance with life-saving medications, and vaccinating against serious diseases.

Think of everything you can do that will help you and your teams sustain a new normal. Much has been published about developing standards, training staff to meet the standards, and ensuring mastery of the new process. Invest time in learning more about this as a part of your learning journey.

Creating standard work (documenting the sequence of the critical steps in a process) prevents getting bogged down in unending conversations about the change. It normalizes change through an immersive and personally engaging experience. Standard work visualizes and embeds the change in new work routines and behaviors. Facilitate the development and coaching of standard work with your teams, peers, and direct reports.

Make change visible. One of the most effective ways to keep change energy up is to have a regular cadence of huddles (short, in-person stand-up or virtual meetings) that are data-driven, where goals and progress are reviewed, opportunities for improvement are identified, problems are solved, and successes are celebrated. Data helps the team see if they are winning or losing. Research shows that small wins are encouraging and "Even ordinary, incremental progress can increase people's engagement in the work and their happiness during the workday" (Amabile and Kramer, 2011).

People often accept and adopt change faster when they live it versus simply thinking about it. The adage, "It's easier to act your way into a new way of thinking, than think your way into a new way of acting," is attributed to various authors. (Pascale, Sternin, and Sternin mention it in their book *The Power of Positive Deviance: How Unlikely Innovators Solve the World's Toughest Problems* (2010)). Creating a system that supports the right behaviors will ensure you and your teams live the change. Visualizing change and embedding the new work processes in leader, team, and individual standard work will help everyone "act their way into a new way of thinking." Table 7.4 presents best practices for sustaining change with visual management and standard work.

Table 7.4   Best Practices for Sustaining Change with Visual Management and Standard Work

Trap	Change is not codified in the standard work.
Best Practices	■ If you agree with your team on a new process, co-design the step-by-step standard work that the team agrees to. Print it out and make it visible. ■ Review progress and identify further process improvements in every meeting or huddle. Add discussion of the change and associated metrics to your Leader Standard Work.
Questions to Ponder	■ Have I made the change or process visible to others in the organization? ■ Do I regularly discuss new processes and metrics? ■ Am I coaching people to perform the new process? Am I auditing the process? Have I included coaching and auditing in my Leader Standard Work?

Leadership Strategies: Bringing It All Together

Seemingly Little Changes can inadvertently and unexpectedly become Big Changes. Change management is considered by many to be the most stressful and demanding part of leadership.

Volumes are published on various change management approaches, but in the end, good change managers focus on:

- Building deeply emotional connections with those affected by changes.
- Involving people in co-designing change or providing valuable input.
- Implementing systems and processes to sustain the new normal and prevent backsliding.

The following example shows what the three change manager Leadership Strategies can look like in action.

COACH'S CORNER: STANDARDIZING CLINIC SUPPLIES AND EXAM ROOMS

One of the authors was working closely with a clinic's leadership team to decrease unwarranted variation by standardizing the layout and contents of all the exam rooms and its inventory of in-clinic medications. Before attempting this consequential change, the leaders invested time in building close relationships with clinicians and staff through a series of personal engagements and team-building activities.

The "why" for this change was clinicians' reluctance to move around the clinic since the rooms were not set up to their liking (i.e., they were not standardized). Leadership also hypothesized, "If all the exam rooms contained agreed-upon supplies and handouts, stocking would be simplified with less chance of running out of needed items." Since an exam room was often perceived as a sacred physician space, setting them up in a standardized way without physicians' input was fraught with danger. One leader went around the clinic collecting all the handouts and supplies. She brought everything to the physician meeting and placed all the items on the table in front of them. Her first goal was to standardize handouts, then move to standardizing the supplies if time allowed. There were 105 different handouts but only eight slots in the document holder to house them. A lively discussion ensued when physicians were asked to select only the handouts they actually used and which they absolutely could not do away with. To everyone's surprise, most handouts were not used by anyone; they were relics from years ago and not relevant to current practice. After some negotiations back and forth, the doctors selected eight handouts that were helpful to everyone and decided to put them in all 28 exam rooms. For several doctors who needed a few additional handouts, folders with these documents were placed on their exam room tables. A similar process was used to review supplies and clinic-administered medications. In the process of standardization, physicians found numerous supplies and medications that were ordered month after month, later discarded, and reordered again without anyone using them. Clinicians narrowed the list of injectables they used and, based on the scientific evidence, coalesced around only a few that were essential. After standardizing handouts, supplies, and medications, a regular review process was implemented.

When the leadership team shared their experience of standardizing and drastically reducing clinic-administered medications, senior leaders were eager to spread this change enterprise-wide to save costs. They copied the medication list from the pilot clinic and asked all other clinics across the company to standardize their in-clinic medications based on it. On the surface, it made sense that if this "change" worked in one clinic it should work in all. But other clinics resisted this change. After a few weeks, this effort to standardize in-office medications was dropped without much fanfare.

In the first clinic, since clinicians were part of the change process, they not only did not resist it but they learned the value of working together and simplifying their practice environment while simultaneously saving money for the organization. However, when the standardized in-clinic medication list was spread enterprise-wide, the change failed to take place, as physicians in other departments were not allowed to "reinvent the wheel" and develop their own standardized clinic-specific medication lists.

Establishing a personal connection before attempting change and allowing people affected to participate and put their fingerprints on the change will decrease resistance and increase buy-in. If you are trying to motivate a team to embrace a new way of doing things, let them have a say in the change, give them several choices to select from, and allow further innovation within the established boundaries.

The GUIDES Framework and the Change Manager

Let's return to the fictional Dr. Jenny Chang mentioned at the beginning of the chapter. She called her executive coach in panic, disappointed and taken aback by physician resistance to what she had perceived as a positive change for them. Her coach suggested she return to those practices in the Midwest to get to know their leaders better and understand the pain points and concerns before attempting any change initiative.

Jenny met with her coach the following week to work through the three Leadership Strategies and the GUIDES Framework to devise a personal Change Manager developmental plan. The coach asked her questions to understand better her mindset and approach to Little and Big Changes:

- How do you approach building relationships and emotional connections with new colleagues and reports?
- How do you prepare to introduce new initiatives and decrease resistance?
- In your opinion, what are the top three reasons why change initiatives stick? What are the top three reasons why they fail?
- Can you share an example of a successful change you implemented and why you think it succeeded?
- Why do you think you encountered resistance in your current job with integration and the pay-for-performance model?

This concludes the exploration of the three Leadership Strategies: (1) build up an emotional bank account by building trust before change, (2) demonstrate respect for people by involving those affected by the change, and (3) sustain changes by implementing visual management and standard work.

In Chapter 2, we asked you to think of someone you consider a great change manager. As you consider them now, to what extent do you think they embody and demonstrate the three Leadership Strategies we have discussed? What other change management skills or characteristics do they exhibit that make them effective?

Next, access and print the GUIDES Development Plan template in Appendix 1 and create a development plan to assess and improve your change manager skills. See Figure 7.2 as an example of a plan to improve the strategy "Sustain changes by implementing visual management and standard work."

GUIDES Development Plan – Change Manager

Step 1: GATHER inputs to evaluate your skills gaps and opportunities for development.

1. **Record your own assessment of your degree of confidence in these skills.**

To what extent are you confident in your ability to:	Not at all	Somewhat	Great deal
Build up an emotional bank account		x	
Demonstrate respect for people		x	
Sustain change by implementing standard work and visual management	x		

2. **Reflect on your answers to the questions above. Record your additional thoughts.** *I have a lot to learn about visual management and standard work. I'm worried about being able to explain it and sustain it. How do I ensure others find value in visual management and standard work?*

3. **Ask for feedback from others (e.g., trusted colleagues, your coach, or direct reports) on the skills, and take notes.** *I was advised to start with LSW and activities focused around sustaining newly implemented changes. I know this is important but clearly will need help.*

4. **What does your additional research tell you about this attribute?** *It is easier for people to change their behaviors through specific actions (by "doing" vs. "thinking"). And, individuals have to grow and change as well.*

Figure 7.2 Example of GUIDES Development Plan for Change Manager.

Step 2: UNDERSTAND and interpret the data you collected.

The following questions help you understand and interpret the data you collected in the GATHER step. Spend a few minutes thinking about these questions. Record your thoughts and responses.

1. **What did you learn from your self-assessment?** *Many of the prior change efforts I was involved in quickly disintegrated as my attention moved on to the next new initiative.*

2. **How did you interpret feedback from others (e.g., trusted colleagues, your coach, or reports)? Were you surprised? Did their feedback match your self-assessment?** *I tend to initiate many new changes but don't take adequate time to ground the change, to ensure it sticks long term.*

3. **What were your key takeaways from the research? Were you surprised by anything you learned?** *I was surprised at how often change efforts fail and how critical it is to adopt new behaviors and standardize new processes. The research shows that I'm not unique in this but I will need to figure out how to ensure long-term sustainability of change initiatives.*

Step 3: IDENTIFY your strengths and opportunities.

Spend a few minutes thinking about each of these questions. Record your thoughts and responses.

1. **Which skills do you want to develop further?** *Developing standard work for processes and leaders, starting with myself.*

2. **Which skills are foundational?** *Building visual management systems for activities and processes, as often "out of sight" means "out of mind" for me and my teammates.*

Figure 7.2 (Continued)

3. Which skills are your highest priority? *LSW is my highest priority, as it will allow me to focus on critical activities and avoid unnecessary firefighting. On an individual level, firefighting has always been important to me so this will be especially challenging.*

Step 4: DESIGN your leadership development plan.

What are your development priorities? Record two or three high-priority opportunities and actions.

Area for Development	Developmental Opportunity	Actions to Take	Resources Needed	Target Date	Success Metrics
Change Manager	*Implement visual management*	*Create visual board*	*Board, magnets, tags*	*4/1/24*	*# huddles/ week conducted at the board (over time this should evolve into the effectiveness of the visual board)*
Change Manager	*Create and implement standard work*	*Develop LSW*	*Board or software for a digital version*	*4/15/24*	*% of LSW completed/ week*

Look over your development plan, then consider these questions. Record your thoughts below.

1. Does this plan address the foundational opportunities identified in your self-assessment, research, and input from others? *Yes, I get a chance to develop both a visual management board and my LSW.*

2. Does your plan take into consideration the personal triggers that could help or hinder your development? *Maybe. I've never been comfortable starting something that I'm also learning. I'm not sure if I have any triggers at this point, but I'm open to assessing this question in the future.*

Figure 7.2   (Continued)

3. **Is the plan incremental and doable?** *This may be a more monumental than incremental personal change, but it is critical for my success in sustaining change.*

4. **Are you excited about your plan? Why or why not?** *For someone like me who is more visual and needs to see change through, this builds accountability for me personally as well as my team.*

Step 5: EXECUTE your development plan.

Put your development plan into action! As you proceed with the execution of your plan, spend a few minutes thinking about each of these questions. Record your thoughts and responses.

1. **What circumstances or triggers will signal that "now" is the time to act and practice new behaviors?** *My LSW will be reflected in my scheduling software as well as visualized on the board. It will also be incorporated into my 1:1 meetings.*

2. **What specific behavior(s) or action(s) will you try? How far are you willing to push your comfort zone?** *I will have reflection time scheduled both daily and weekly to review how much of my standard work I completed and what may have prevented me from completing it.*

3. **How do you know if you are improving and becoming more successful with this attribute and as a leader?** *Number of completed items/activities (green magnets) vs. number of activities skipped (red magnets). Feedback from my team on my effectiveness but more importantly, how it helps or hinders their success.*

4. **How will you gauge the impact of your actions or behavior changes? What responses will you be watching for??** *Overall team performance on metrics associated with the changes implemented. Feedback from team members.*

Figure 7.2 (Continued)

Step 6: SELF-REFLECT on your execution of the development plan.

Spend a few minutes at the end of the day and/or week thinking about each of these questions. Record your thoughts and responses.

1. **Was I mindful of my development today/this week? What did I do well? What could I have done better?** *I was able to complete 70% of the LSW activities I planned this week. I could have improved by asking my team for feedback, then reflecting on it and incorporating it for next week.*

2. **How did others respond when I intentionally led in a new way? Were people more (or less) engaged with me as a leader?** *My direct reports developed their own LSW and they shared how it helps them prevent unnecessary firefighting and allows them to focus on what is important.*

3. **Was I mindful of my triggers? How did I respond to those?** *Yes, I was paying attention to the distractors, and purposely bringing myself back to what was planned for the week.*

4. **What will I do differently tomorrow/next week? What should I be watching for?** *I will move rounding with my teams earlier in the day (assuming that works for their schedules and responsibilities) and will not check my email more than twice per day.*

5. **What else do I need to do or learn to further my development of this attribute?** *I should check in with my team on what activities they think I should focus on, using my LSW as a guide to support them.*

Figure 7.2 (Continued)

Bibliography

Amabile, Teresa, and Steven J. Kramer. "The Power of Small Wins." *Harvard Business Review* (May 1, 2011). https://hbr.org/2011/05/the-power-of-small-wins

Anderson, Larry, Tony Chamberlin, and Ron Oslin. "Lean Coaching." *Target Magazine* (Summer 2015). www.onesystemonevoice.com/resources/TargetSummer15_LeanCoaching_Reprint.pdf

Ashkenas, Ron. "Change Management Needs to Change." *Harvard Business Review* (April 16, 2013). https://hbr.org/2013/04/change-management-needs-to-cha

Cameron, Esther, and Mike Green. *Making Sense of Change Management: A Complete Guide to the Models, Tools and Techniques of Organizational Change*, 4th ed. London; Philadelphia, PA: Kogan Page, 2015.

Covey, Stephen R. *The 7 Habits of Highly Effective People: Powerful Lessons in Personal Change*. 25th anniversary edition. New York: Simon & Schuster, 2013.

"Developing People Improving Care | NHS Improvement." Accessed August 15, 2019. https://improvement.nhs.uk/resources/developing-people-improving-care/

Eisenstat, Russell, Bert Spector, and Michael Beer. "Why Change Programs Don't Produce Change." *Harvard Business Review* (November 1, 1990). https://hbr.org/1990/11/why-change-programs-dont-produce-change

Hung, Dorothy, Caroline Gray, Meghan Martinez, Julie Schmittdiel, and Michael Harrison. "Acceptance of Lean Redesigns in Primary Care: A Contextual Analysis." *Health Care Management Review* 42 (March 2, 2016): 203–212. https://doi.org/10.1097/HMR.0000000000000106

Kachalia, Allen, Samuel R. Kaufman, Richard Boothman, Susan Anderson, Kathleen Welch, Sanjay Saint, and Mary A.M. Rogers. "Does Admitting Mistakes to Patients Lead to More Lawsuits?" *Annals of Internal Medicine* 153, no. 4 (August 17, 2010): 1–28. https://doi.org/10.7326/0003-4819-153-4-201008170-00001

Liker, Jeffrey K. *The Toyota Way: 14 Management Principles from the World's Greatest Manufacturer*. New York: McGraw-Hill, 2004.

Pascale, Richard T., Jerry Sternin, and Monique Sternin. *The Power of Positive Deviance: How Unlikely Innovators Solve the World's Toughest Problems*. Leadership for the Common Good. Boston, MA: Harvard Business Press, 2010.

Rose, Adam J., Justin W. Timbie, Claude Setodji, Mark W. Friedberg, Rosalie Malsberger, and Katherine L. Kahn. "Primary Care Visit Regularity and Patient Outcomes: An Observational Study." *Journal of General Internal Medicine* 34, no. 1 (January 2019): 82–89. https://doi.org/10.1007/s11606-018-4718-x

Wiltsey Stirman, Shannon, John Kimberly, Natasha Cook, Amber Calloway, Frank Castro, and Martin Charns. "The Sustainability of New Programs and

Innovations: A Review of the Empirical Literature and Recommendations for Future Research." *Implementation Science: IS* 7 (March 14, 2012): 17. https://doi.org/10.1186/1748-5908-7-17

Womack, James P., Daniel T. Jones, and Daniel Roos. *The Machine That Changed the World: The Story of Lean Production–Toyota's Secret Weapon in the Global Car Wars That Is Revolutionizing World Industry*. London: Free Press, 2007.

Chapter 8

Learner-in-Chief

Leadership and learning are indispensable to each other.

John F. Kennedy

Becoming an effective leader takes time and the learning process never ends. It's okay to make mistakes but it's not okay to not learn from your mistakes. You can always learn something from others and should always try to do so.

M. Sean Rogers, *MD, MBA, Regional Medical Director, Optum CA*

Leadership Case Study: Building a Learning Culture

Dr. Rudolph Cobb had hoped to leave work early that Thursday afternoon. Instead, he found himself in the midst of the monthly Operating Room (OR) team meeting. The team grappled with an OR scheduling problem they had been trying to solve for over a month. Block time was a hot topic among surgeons. Several physicians wanted to adopt a 12-hour block time, while others wanted to stay with the current eight-hour blocks. In addition, surgeons couldn't agree on how many ORs they should keep open to allow for emergent add-on cases. Nurse managers expressed concern that all the proposed solutions were not addressing the real "elephant in the room," the issue of variable OR utilization among surgeons. As Dr. Cobb listened to the team's discussion, he believed he might be able to offer a solution, but he also realized he did not fully grasp the problem and the interpretation

DOI: 10.4324/9780429352355-8

of the supporting data. He wanted to help the team solve this problem but needed to learn more about block time and OR utilization best practices. Leaving the meeting, Dr. Cobb wondered how to go about learning more. How could he close his knowledge gaps? Who should he approach? What questions should he ask? How could he learn more about the problem without displaying his ignorance?

Dr. Cobb quickly realized that the organizational culture in the Ambulatory Surgical Centers did not support learning on the job. Rather than valuing knowledge sharing, exploring ideas, and relying on previous lessons learned, the organization valued high levels of expertise in its clinicians and administrators. As a new Executive Director overseeing three Ambulatory Surgery Centers, he didn't want his lack of knowledge on display for all to see! Instead, he searched PubMed and Google Scholar for articles that would help him out. He contacted his former colleagues in other surgical centers. Finally, he decided that looking into his own organization's history on this topic would also come in handy, so he met with several of the surgeons.

Introduction

Most leaders are in the positions they are in now because of previous successes in their careers. It is natural to want to continue doing what has worked in the past and avoid discovering new paths and perspectives. Drawing on our past experiences is how we develop as leaders. However, relying primarily on experiential leadership can lead to skewed and distorted learning. A Learner-in-Chief is someone who continuously learns and leads with curiosity. They are always students, open to new information, ideas, and perspectives that are different from their own. With more than the end goal in mind, a curious leader explores the path to the end goal and engages others by asking questions that lead to unbiased and diverse answers. Learners-in-Chief ask curiosity-based questions that begin with words or phrases such as "I wonder …", "Tell me more about …", "How should I think about …", and "Help me understand … ." They suspend their preconceived notions and expect to be surprised; they are willing to hear a contrasting point of view and learn from diverse experiences. This level of curiosity and continuous personal growth facilitates experimentation, creates a learning atmosphere, and ultimately leads to innovation.

This chapter defines the role and mindset of the Learner-in-Chief and focuses on the key Leadership Strategies that facilitate maturing your abilities in this area and creating your personal Learner-in-Chief development plan.

Physician Leader as Learner-in-Chief

What does it mean to be a Learner-in-Chief? A Learner-in-Chief is comfortable saying, "I do not know," a concept that physicians may find challenging to accept at times. Years of clinical training, filled with rote theoretical and practical experiential learning, is what prepares highly trained clinicians. A practicing physician who does not know the solution to a medical or surgical problem may not be highly regarded. Physicians are trained to be experts, and society looks to them with an expectation of unfaltering expertise. In contrast, it is far more important for a leader – whether physician or administrative – to continuously learn and experiment rather than to have all the answers. A leader is just one of many experts on a team willing to display humility and risk exposing personal knowledge gaps to others. Some physician leaders are dedicated learners within their clinical specialties but do not pursue other learning avenues.

COACH'S CORNER: LEADERS GO FIRST

Early in my consulting career, I was retained by a combined hospital and ambulatory clinic system to guide their organization through the annual strategic planning process. Immediately following a meeting with the executive team to finalize the consulting plan for the next six months, the chief medical officer (CMO) pulled me aside. Noting that the consulting plan included training and coaching of the executives, the CMO felt that this part of the plan was unnecessary. The CMO respectfully said, "I don't need training or coaching, I've been doing this a long time. Tell me what you need from me and I'm happy to do it." My response was,

I appreciate your experience, but it's important that the leaders "go first" each step of the way in this new process. I want to be sure you are prepared to go first because your organization and team need you to lead by example.

The CMO was taken aback. However, that early tension dissipated quickly, and our working relationship progressed to one of mutual respect and trust. It's not that the CMO didn't want to learn and grow as a leader; rather, this person genuinely didn't think it was necessary to take these steps, having been very successful in the role for many years. In our many discussions, I drew parallels for this leader between continuous clinical learning as a physician and business learning as a leader. Not surprisingly, throughout my career, I met many physician leaders who didn't apply rigorous clinical learning habits to their business roles. Fortunately, this CMO embraced coaching and learning and, as a result, has become an exceptional healthcare leader.

All leaders must role model personal learning, stimulate team learning, and, ultimately, catalyze organizational learning. The payoff for fostering a culture of continuous learning and the systems and practices that reinforce it is realized in improved performance and achieving strategic goals. It makes sense to invest in continuous learning and inspire others to do so as well.

Mindset of the Learner-in-Chief

The Learner-in-Chief's mindset relies on being open-minded to learning in various settings and situations:

- Learners find nuggets of knowledge from expected and unexpected encounters and interactions.
- Learners set up experiments to solve problems and pursue innovative solutions.
- Learners rely heavily on the experience of others, not just their own.
- Learners avoid firefighting and jumping to preconceived solutions that do not leverage the knowledge and expertise of those around them, including their teams.

Physician leaders should be accountable for producing new ideas and contributing to the vision in a new way. They should be going out to conferences and other learning opportunities and bringing

back information and ideas to the organization. You can drive an
organization crazy if you have a new idea every day, but it's better to
have more input rather than less input, and to keep the ideas flowing.

Larry Gray, *MSBA, Managing Director, Gray Dynamics LLC*

COACH'S CORNER: A LESSON IN SINCERITY

I worked with a physician who was an incredible clinician. He had excellent patient outcomes, high satisfaction scores, and seemingly great engagement with his clinical team. He was asked to take on an interim leadership role primarily for being such an outstanding and highly respected clinician in the organization. Over a few months, it became apparent that his stellar clinical skills didn't translate as effectively into leadership skills. I was surprised because he actively engaged with other members of leadership; he seemed to listen, and he usually started questions with "How should I think about this?" or "Teach me more about that," and he often shared his reflective thoughts. Through extensive dialogue and coaching, his leadership blind spots came to the surface. As a physician, he developed a talent for ensuring his clinical advice was followed to a tee. He knew how to engage his patients, so they were more apt to adhere to what he prescribed. Similarly, he expected his team to follow his guidance and his preferred standards. He thought he had a method to engage his team to basically execute what he decided without consultation with them. This sounds great, right? In a clinical practice setting, this approach may have worked. And at first, this approach seemed to be quite effective in the new leadership role. However, everyone soon realized that he already had the answers in his mind even before he engaged his team. He cajoled the team into giving him the answers and outcomes he was looking for. He was not interested in learning from – or with – his team, and thus, he unintentionally caused people to disengage from him. I reflected with this leader on the "why" behind his team's disengagement. He understood that his team cooled off to his inquiries for input as they sensed his lack of sincerity. He agreed not to ask for opinions if he did not intend to follow through or incorporate ideas from others. He committed himself to remaining curious and open to changing his thinking, opinions, and decisions.

Fortunately, as trained scientists, physician leaders usually possess a natural curiosity and intellectual humility to pursue even greater discoveries in the realm of leadership and organizational effectiveness. Being open-minded and curious sounds simple, but living this mindset can be challenging, especially during times of stress or when the prevailing organizational culture encourages firefighting and not learning – and reflection-based problem-solving. Traditional management that focuses on symptom management and not system management creates perpetual firefighting cycles that discourage learning. As new challenges arise, leaders simply jump to solutions. They do not take time to learn from the history of their organization. They do not deeply understand the problems they need to solve. And worst of all, they reinvent failed solutions when best practices exist inside and outside of the organization.

George Koenigsaecker dives into the topic of organizational firefighting in his book, *Leading the Lean Enterprise Transformation*, saying,

> *Getting an organization out of the firefighting mode – that is, to resolve problems at the true root-cause level instead of putting out the fires that spring up throughout the day – turns out to be very hard to do, because it involves changing adult behaviors.*

(Koenigsaecker, 2009)

He further explains that a lack of organizational learning creates barriers to transformation.

As a leader, a Learner-in-Chief mindset of open-mindedness, intentional learning, and pursuit of innovation helps you, your team, and your organization overcome tendencies of firefighting and prematurely implementing solutions ahead of understanding the problem at hand.

Leadership Strategies for the Learner-in-Chief

What advice might Dr. Rudolph Cobb (introduced at the beginning of this chapter) receive from his leadership coach? Rudolph instinctively understood that he must first role model learner behaviors to change the culture in the Ambulatory Surgical Centers. In addition to practicing a Learner-in-Chief mindset, his coach suggested engaging in the following five Leadership Strategies, the practices that demonstrate a commitment to continuous learning and building a workplace that values diverse learning opportunities and encourages personal growth:

1. Sharpen observational skills.
2. Go to Gemba (the "actual place," where value is created for the patient or customer).
3. Use each encounter as a learning opportunity.
4. Seek out new learning opportunities.
5. Spend time in reflection.

"Look for opportunities to learn in all your daily activities and within each and every human interaction," Dr. Cobb's coach advised.

> *Hone keen listening and observation skills and use them as you personally observe the care of patients and walk in the shoes of our customers. This practice of going to Gemba (the actual place) is, without a doubt, a learning experience that will inspire your teams to design patient and customer-centric workflows and processes. Encourage your leaders to visit other departments in your organization as well as external institutions, to learn best practices. Use this newly acquired knowledge as a springboard for accelerated improvement.*

Conversations like the one between Dr. Rudolph Cobb and his coach are opportunities to open oneself to genuinely seeking feedback and being receptive to receiving it. Learning takes place in multiple venues: leadership courses at work, online publications, books, podcasts, structured courses, and conferences. Personal reflection time is another opportunity to learn as you think over interactions you have had throughout the day and the week, and consider what could have been done better or differently. In each of these experiences and venues, you are learning and maturing, building your power to skillfully adjust your approach and way of thinking in the future.

Sharpen Observational Skills

> *There are three classes of people: those who see, those who see when they are shown, and those who do not see.*

> **Leonardo da Vinci**

Years are spent perfecting a physician's observation skills to ensure timely diagnosis and treatment. With experience, a physician can quickly determine, even before their patient utters a word, whether the patient is sick enough to go to the hospital or healthy enough to be safely treated as an outpatient. Collecting a medical history and performing a physical exam serves to support or dispel the physician's observation. Honing observation skills as a leader is just as important. The healthcare setting provides numerous opportunities for leaders to observe many types of interactions between physicians, staff, and patients.

Observation skills are equally important when evaluating a process or workflow. Taichi Ohno, the father of the Toyota Production System, often asked leaders to stand inside a chalk circle drawn on the floor near the production line. They were instructed to observe production processes and note any process inefficiencies (Nakane and Hall, 2002). This technique was intended to teach leaders to focus on a process without assumptions and preconceived notions and to look for opportunities for improvement and redesign. Though busy physician leaders do not have time to strictly follow this technique (and staff and patients may find it strange to see physicians standing in a circle and not interacting with anyone for long periods of time), it is encouraged that leaders "walk in their patients' shoes," perhaps by shadowing Call Center employees or observing clinical, surgical, and virtual workflows. The challenge is to observe without judgment and not jump to conclusions or provide unsolicited solutions to frontline teams. Observation skills go hand-in-hand with listening skills. Open yourself up to the information flow around you. Create time and space for learning and acquiring new and often unexpected information. To stop, observe, and listen without judgment is a meditative experience requiring intentionality and practice.

COACH'S CORNER: IMPROVING PREVENTATIVE HEALTH MEASURES

I recently coached a director-level physician leader on methods for increasing the rate of preventative testing by physicians. The metric was clear and part of a strategic quality improvement initiative. I asked the leader to observe as I demonstrated the workflow in the electronic medical record and described the process physicians would be required to follow. She watched the step-by-step process reserving questions to the end. Sitting back and observing the process was eye-opening to the leader. Until then, she had not understood the process required to achieve the metric. To inspire physicians to embrace and follow the necessary steps, she needed to understand the process herself; only then could she help physicians fold the new workflow into their daily routines. When she later presented the new metric and process steps to physicians, she did so with confidence, coaching the team on ways to incorporate the process into their patient interactions. Observing, learning, and sharing the new process gave her credibility as a leader and helped physicians adopt this new initiative without significant resistance.

Other opportunities to practice observation skills are in one-on-one interactions and group meetings. In these settings, observe your audience, study their mood, and reflect on their state of being. Leaders who "see" beyond the words and pay attention to non-verbal cues quickly ascertain:

- How their presence affects the team. Are people relaxed and comfortable in the presence of their leader?
- The level of attentiveness of the group. Are people making eye contact with the leader, or does their gaze wander?
- The mood in the room. Are people tense? Engaged? Open and authentic? Or are their words guarded and filtered?

For some leaders, learning to "see" may require the help of a trusted colleague or coach. For example, consider scheduling a debrief session with a trusted colleague who attended the same meeting. Compare notes. Are your observations about the team's level of engagement the same as your colleague's? How did you assess openness, body language, and eye contact? Talk about the specific observations that led to your assumptions. The value of this exercise becomes evident in subsequent interactions as cues are picked up, acted upon, and more authentic and productive conversations emerge.

COACH'S CORNER: THE SHY PHYSICIAN LEADER

One of the authors had an opportunity to observe a physician leader with years of leadership experience. His business acumen was impeccable, and he understood better than most the intricacies of strategic thinking versus tactical execution. However, it was observed that he wasn't connecting with the physicians he led. When facilitating meetings, he spoke with his head lowered and his gaze focused on his notebook, not once raising his head to see the reaction from the audience. He wasn't consulting any notes; it was simply his natural style not to make eye contact with others when he was speaking. As he wasn't looking at anyone, he couldn't observe and internalize how his comments were received or processed. His unintended monologue made dialogue impractical leading to boring and unengaging meetings.

After coaching and reflection, he realized that this habit of looking down was due to shyness. With practice and feedback, he improved his facilitation skills, determined to establish eye contact with participants throughout the meeting. He made it a point to look up, though it wasn't easy and did not feel natural to him as he spoke. When he noticed a curious or questioning look on someone's face, he would stop and ask probing questions that would lead to a lively and engaging discussion. Over time, looking up and observing his audience became habitual and required no effort, resulting in closer relationships with his colleagues and more productive conversations.

As discussed in Chapter 4, reading the audience helps leaders adjust their style, tailor their approach, and create an environment of openness and trust, ultimately leading to numerous learning opportunities for the leader and team. Observation skills are especially critical in Gemba (the actual place) when leaders "go see" what is actually happening in places where organizational value is created, such as patient care areas, call centers, and prescription refill teams (www.lean.org/lexicon-terms/gemba/).
Here, leaders uncover challenges experienced by frontline employees and customers and learn about opportunities for improvement. As a true Learner-in-Chief, this can be a very exciting and game-changing leadership development experience. Table 8.1 presents best practices for sharpening observational skills.

Table 8.1 Best Practices for Sharpening Observational Skills

Trap	Presenting or "selling" change without personally observing and understanding new processes or workflows.
Best Practices	■ Observe processes or workflows in real time and in the actual place where they take place to understand what is happening and not simply what you think is happening.
Questions to Ponder	■ Do I understand the new process or change well enough to effectively present it to my team? ■ Based on my process observation, what questions should I anticipate from physicians and staff, and what answers facilitate their buy-in? ■ What non-verbal cues should I pay attention to so I better understand how well my team will embrace the change?

Go to Gemba

Gemba is a Japanese word that roughly translates to the actual place where work is performed. In manufacturing, it is a production or assembly line. In medicine, it is a hospital unit or a clinical department. In a virtual environment, it is a sales meeting or a patient video visit. By regularly going to Gemba, leaders can make better decisions. They learn directly from the people who are creating value for patients and customers. Being in tune with the operational realities of the business, such as observing the direct delivery of care to patients or listening to incoming telephone calls at the Call Center, makes leaders better strategic thinkers, better change agents, and trusted partners in solving problems throughout the organization. Leaders who "manage from the ivory tower," spending most of their time orchestrating changes from the office and focusing on data-filled reports, tend to make decisions that are often disconnected from the realities of the business. Leaders who regularly go to Gemba learn about the work and its challenges and are much more capable of assessing the organization's overall capabilities. Similar to the challenges a physician faces when trying to assess or solve a patient's medical problem without speaking to them or seeing them, it is equally challenging trying to lead a department or organization without actively engaging with its people and processes.

COACH'S CORNER: GO SEE THE PATIENT

"Remote management" is not unique to business; it also occurs in the practice of medicine. As a physician educator who has coached many medical students and residents in Internal Medicine, I saw a similar tendency among physicians in training. During rounds, a medical student and a resident gave me a perfect patient presentation, with all the right data elements and everything fitting nicely into the clinical picture. When I took the team to the patient's bedside and sat down next to the patient to observe them and ask how they were actually doing, the nicely painted picture evaporated. The real clinical picture that appeared was quite different from the one previously presented. When asked about the discrepancy in clinical presentations, the resident often referenced the prior shift notes and a few well-researched studies from respectable journals as their sources of information. "But did you speak with the patient yourself? Did you examine them?" I inquired, hiding my frustration. The answer, usually, was "No." Without fail, my response got their attention: "Listen to your patients! Patients are generous and will lead you to the diagnosis. Save yourself time digging through the notes of others, and, instead, get your facts directly from the source." Going to Gemba is important in delivering high-quality patient care, too!

Why would we allow problem-solving to occur if the problem owners haven't gone to see the problem themselves?

Dr. John E. Billi

For many leaders, spending time in Gemba is a seismic shift in their management style and behavior. The benefits of Gemba management are truly transformational. Go to Gemba to:

- Check your assumptions about the work and test/confirm the data.
- Solve organizational challenges.
- Learn from the people who create value and are closest to customers and patients.
- Engage in problem-solving activities.
- Build a more dynamic and effective team.

Leaders often have lofty plans of what they want the organization to do, while the organization actually has fundamental problems with its basic capabilities. This is what the workers are most concerned about. They can't get a pillow for the patient in the ER. Or they have the wrong instruments when they open the OR trays. There is a disconnect between the leaders' and the workers' views of the organization's capabilities. Going to Gemba bridges this disconnect. When leaders go to Gemba, they see the real work in the real workplace and interact with the workers. The problem, though, is most of the time, when they go, leaders are shown stuff, or they go to be seen instead of going to learn. Going to Gemba is an opportunity to learn more about how the work is done; how complicated it is; how difficult it is; how far people have to walk; how they don't have the supplies they need; how buzzers and phones are going off every 10 to 15 seconds. So Gemba, or the place where work is happening, is, I think, the best educator for leaders.

John E. Billi, *MD, Professor Emeritus and Former Chief Engineer, Michigan Quality System, University of Michigan*

Leaders must be fully present while in Gemba, ensuring their body language projects openness, curiosity, and neutrality. Observing the cues that people project tells leaders how they are being received: Is the team responding with energy? Are they engaged in the conversation? Or do they seem distracted, uninterested, or reserved? In response to these observations, leaders can adjust their style and approach to be seen as accessible and eager to learn. As a byproduct of these actions, leaders grow team trust and engagement.

Gemba is a time of discovery, and the more open-ended questions leaders ask, the likelier it is that teams will open up and share their ideas for improvement. This is no different than physician interactions with patients. Opening up a conversation with curiosity will uncover what is really happening with the patient without introducing bias or risking premature closure. Going to Gemba with a learner's mindset is humbling. Though typically accustomed to solving every problem, this is not the leader's job. Instead, their role is to assess how well the team identifies and understands the problem before attempting to solve it. It is also important to understand what lens the team is looking through. Coach the team to see problems from multiple perspectives: the patient's, physician's, and staff member's. What do you see when you go to Gemba?

COACH'S CORNER: PRIORITIZING GEMBA TIME

At one organization, the management team took seriously the importance of spending time in Gemba. They protected the hours between 10:30 a.m. to 1:00 p.m. every Wednesday for Gemba. This allowed focused time for observing and participating in frontline team huddles and problem-solving session and coaching their leaders. This time was also used for personal development and reflection. It is challenging to have the discipline to do this each week without the interruption of meetings that couldn't get scheduled for any other time or managing the problems of the day. If the leaders prioritize Gemba, the organization will follow.

General Questions to Consider in Gemba

- What is really happening?
- How and why is this process/system/area different from what you expected?
- What disrupts the work? How do the disruptions impact other areas/departments?
- How do staff know what work they should be doing? How is their work prioritized?
- Is doing the "right thing" in the "right way" crystal clear to even the casual observer?
- What happens when problems are encountered? Is there a system to get issues resolved, or does the individual have to figure it out?

The Overall Appearance of the Area, Department, and Clinic

- Are needed work items (tools, equipment, supplies) physically located where they are used?
- Is there anything in the work area that does not belong there?
- Is the work area comfortable and orderly?

Work Quality

- What waste do you observe in the work area or in processes? Are resources (such as time, talent, and materials) being consumed unnecessarily?

- Where might mistakes be made in the process? What keeps these mistakes from happening?
- How are issues of poor quality, mistakes, defects, and rework handled? Does the team engage in root cause analysis to understand the contributors to poor quality?
- What are the quality and safety implications for patients and teams in this environment?

The Flow of People, Processes, and Information

- Does the overall flow of work (people, materials, information) appear smooth, organized, and calm?
- If the processes were flowing perfectly, how would they look? How do they actually look?
- Are communications seamless between staff, physicians, and patients?

Table 8.3 presents best practices for going to Gemba.

Use Each Encounter as a Learning Opportunity

Every interaction is an opportunity to learn, only if we are interested in improving rather than proving.

Abhishek Shukla

Table 8.2   Best Practices for Going to Gemba

Trap	A leader who manages remotely (away from where value-adding work is happening) is at risk of making decisions based on assumptions and not facts on the ground.
Best Practices	Make going to Gemba part of your Leader Standard Work. That is, build time into your leadership routines to go to Gemba on a regular and reliable schedule.
Questions to Ponder	■ How often do I get out of my office to observe value-creating work and to recognize the great work of my frontline staff? ■ What open-minded questions should I ask so I can learn about the work and its challenges? ■ How will I ensure I am coaching while I am in Gemba (and not problem-solving or directing frontline teams)?

Whether in a meeting, a one-on-one conversation, or spending time in Gemba, each encounter is a learning opportunity. This is the third Leadership Strategy for the Learner-in-Chief. Learning opportunities present themselves in many ways, venues, and settings, and exceptional leaders are alert to them. To lead and influence, leaders must first get to know their people: their past experiences, current circumstances, and future desires. Leaders must learn to see work struggles from the point of view of the people performing the work.

> *The biggest challenge I see is hubris, the presumption of excellence. Leaders are very reluctant to acknowledge that they have a lot of problems in their organization. And they're reluctant to acknowledge that they don't have all the skills and knowledge that they need in order to make it good. We need the opposite of hubris. We need humility. We must adopt a learner's mindset: "I'm a learner. I'm curious. I don't know everything. I come to hear others' opinions. I'm going to try and ask good questions rather than giving answers."*
>
> **John E. Billi**, *MD, Professor Emeritus and Former Chief Engineer, Michigan Quality System, University of Michigan*

COACH'S CORNER: ADOPTING ENGAGEMENT CONVERSATIONS

At one organization, the management team used standardized "engagement conversations" to help leaders stay connected and learn from frontline teams and leaders. The intentionality and structure of the interactions with suggested questions helped leaders focus on the needs of frontline teams, discover communication gaps, and unearth improvement opportunities. Leaders practiced how to ask questions and how to avoid pitfalls that might occur during structured one-on-one interactions. They learned to make engagement conversations meaningful and productive while ensuring staff felt a sense of psychological safety. Leaders were coached to remain open, and not defensive, about what they heard, especially if they received feedback about their leadership practices. A learner values the gift of feedback and the people willing to share it. Engagement conversations were an opportunity to learn, reflect, and improve leadership effectiveness and strengthen teams.

ENGAGEMENT CONVERSATION QUESTIONS

- What does a successful day at work look like? (The purpose of this question is to hear what matters to the employee.)
- What have you done well recently? (The purpose of this question is to discover achievements and recognition preferences.)
- Are there any barriers getting in the way of your work today? (This is important for understanding improvement opportunities.)
- What can I do better to inform you about changes affecting your job? (It is critical to understand communication gaps with staff.)
- On a scale of 1–5 (5 = excellent), how would you rate your morale at work? (It is helpful to gain an overall sense of satisfaction with each employee.)
- Is there anyone you would like to recognize and why? (This is possibly the most powerful question because it creates positive team cohesion.)

ENGAGEMENT CONVERSATION PITFALLS TO AVOID

- Do not over-commit. Be transparent about what actions you are going to take, then follow up accordingly, and update the employee as needed.
- Do not use this conversation for any other agenda; genuinely focus on engaging with your team members.
- Do not discuss what you heard during other engagement conversations.

You can change culture … one conversation at a time.

Jack Cochran, *MD*

In addition to engaging in work-related conversations, every one-on-one interaction is an opportunity to get to know people on a personal level. People want to feel cared for, attended to, and have a personal connection with their leaders. When they see their leaders as caring and human, employees are likely to share their concerns and engage in improvements, just as patients engage more enthusiastically to better their health if they have a deep and personal connection with their caregivers.

AUTHOR'S REFLECTION: FROM "ME, ME, ME" TO "THEM, THEM, THEM"

As a physician, what I treasure most is getting to know my patients on the deepest level. Each human life is a book. It is a web of stories made up of triumphs and defeats, highs and lows, and twists and turns. Early in my career, I was hyper-focused on "helping patients" and ensuring I had a "fix" for each complaint. As soon as they started talking, I hypothesized potential diagnoses, formulated treatment plans, and prepared answers to questions. I was confident in what my patients needed since I had trained for years and years to be right, not make mistakes, and practice evidence-based medicine. As efficiently as a robot, I could swiftly analyze data, inputting it all in my brain along with all the millions of other facts and factoids I had accumulated and integrated over time. It was hard and often tiresome intellectual work that left little space or time for patients' non-clinically relevant personal experiences, emotions, and reflections. My patient interactions were about me: my clinical judgment, my ability to ascertain the right diagnosis, and my power to convince patients to execute my treatment plans flawlessly. Me, me, me … It wasn't fun. It felt very transactional. But worst of all, it wasn't delivering patient outcomes that I "expected" and had trained for.

Social and outgoing by nature, I was craving relational physician–patient interactions. I learned with practice that patients also longed for a personal connection with me, an emotional bond, and often my friendship. I evolved from transactional to relational interactions. Now I learn from each patient and each interaction to discover their unique personal journey and to see how my medical diagnosis and treatment plan fits into their life, environment, culture, and experience. Prior to this personally immersive experience with each interaction, I often unconsciously prejudged patients based on their appearance, education level, the language they used, and cultural upbringing. As I got to know all my patients on a deeply personal level, I learned that, in some ways, we are all the same, and in some ways, we are very much different. What made us different was not age, social status, ethnic background, or sexual orientation but our uniquely beautiful personal stories. Their stories taught me much about living and doctoring and inspired me to relate better, understand more deeply, and advocate intensely for the care my patients deserved. Now, I focus on them, them, them … Sitting back and listening without judgment opens my mind to uncover new facts and let patients drive our co-discovery of relevant medical and personal facts that penetrate the deepest part of my brain, heart, and soul, changing me forever, not only as a physician but also as a leader.

The concept of transactional versus relational interactions is not unique to medicine. It is very much applicable to management and leadership. To intentionally make every interaction relational and not transactional transforms them from cold to warm, mechanistic to organic, and robotic to human. In this learning process, we discover the unique attributes and experiences of the other person that helps us relate differently, understand deeply, and engage openly. Learning and getting to know others as fellow human beings with their unique life stories is the antidote to prejudice and bias. It fosters diversity and inclusion. Learning to see business dilemmas from diverse points of view and perspectives will open horizons to unconventional solutions and help answer challenging questions with unexpected answers.

In addition, every interaction is an opportunity to find new leaders. Both authors discovered many talented individual contributors during rounding (or Gemba walks) who had a passion and eye for improvement, an unquenchable thirst for learning, and, most of all, the burning desire to help patients and their teams – traits that define leadership excellence. Many informal leaders who, with the right coaching, will excel in leadership often don't know how to create opportunities to join the ranks of formal leaders. The following Leadership Case Study continues the Learner-in-Chief journey of Dr. Rudolph Cobb (introduced at the beginning of the chapter) as he recognizes the leadership potential of a colleague while in Gemba.

Leadership Case Study Continued

Dr. Rudolph Cobb, now two years into his tenure, is rounding with the hospital's CEO, Dr. Dan Berger, who hired him to lead the Ambulatory Surgical Centers. Both leaders are on a mission to change their culture to that of a learning organization. They step into the perioperative area. It is early in the Covid-19 pandemic when personal protective equipment (PPE) is in short supply. People are on edge, not knowing how, when, or if they might become infected with the virus. Yesterday, the hospital made a hard decision not to test patients before surgeries because tests are in short supply, and the current evidence for preoperative testing is not convincing. The two leaders run into Shira, an outspoken, opinionated general surgeon, and an informal leader that other surgeons look up to.

Shira: Dan, you guys in the executive suite must be out of your mind! No pre-op Covid testing? Why? What are you thinking? I know there's no evidence for testing, but what evidence can we expect to have so early in the pandemic? Covid is a nightmare that gets worse every day. Our nurses are freaking out. None of us can be sure that our masks protect us in the OR. We feel like we're walking into a trap every time we operate.

Dan: Shira, the executive team wants to support you as best as we can. We're rounding here now to learn and understand how this situation affects all of you. I know everyone is on edge, and I need your help to figure out why everyone is so set on testing. We'd also like to hear what alternatives you are thinking about.

Shira: I called around to a few hospitals in the area. I trained with their surgeons. I have no clue where they are getting their supplies, but they are testing each and every patient before surgery. I honestly do not worry so much about myself. I am young and healthy, but many of our nurses are older, and we are hearing so many reports of older patients dying of Covid. Two things keep me up at night: first, what if the local press learns that we are not testing patients when everyone else is? And second, what if our nurses refuse to come to work, fearing for their own safety?

Rudolph: I'm worried about those things, too, Shira. What do you propose?

Shira: I've met informally with most of our surgeons, and we brainstormed some possible solutions with our nurses. They suggested we hold off on elective surgeries for now. I know that would be a huge financial hit, but if we reduce surgeries in half, we will have enough PPE and Covid swabs to test everyone pre-op. Many of us can take our vacations now, and once we get back to our normal operations, we will work overtime, including weekends, to work down the backlog of elective surgeries.

Shira paused, as she wanted to give Dan and Rudolph time to consider her proposal and assess its merits. Dan and Rudolph realized Shira had handed them a solution to the problem on a silver platter. She was a smart surgeon with no formal leadership role. She was tough and fair. And she was clearly collaborative and resourceful, engaging other surgeons, nurses, and staff in understanding the problem, learning what other hospitals were doing, and solving the problem with out-of-the-box solutions. She had even considered the risk to the hospital's reputation.

Dan said, "Thank you, Shira. I appreciate everything you've done to find workable and safe solutions to this problem. Please go ahead and explain your proposal to the Chief Operating Officer. And I will touch base with her later today," Dan nodded to Rudolph and they left the area.

As the leaders left the perioperative department, Rudolph turned to Dan and reflected in excitement, "With a few more leaders like Shira who unabashedly drive problem-solving and change, we could change the culture so much faster." He continued, "Dan, what do you think about coaching and preparing Shira for a role to lead one of the Ambulatory Surgical Centers?"

Rudolph was proud as he thought about this moment. He had struggled the last two years to change the organizational culture from one that was top-down to building a more collaborative learning environment, with frontline teams driving improvement and innovation. Managing the Covid-19 response had forced him to concentrate all the power in the command center, leaving little space or appetite for the opinions of frontline physicians and staff. But at this moment, he recognized in Shira the behaviors and skills he had been advocating for: the drive to understand and solve problems and learn from others without hubris, politics, or double-speak. Table 8.3 presents best practices for using encounters as learning opportunities.

Table 8.3 Best Practices for Using Encounters as Learning Opportunities

Trap	Formal interactions with leaders and teams feel distant and cold, which stifle initiative and ingenuity.
Best Practices	Make every interaction feel relational and not transactional. Build trust and personal connections before jumping to action.
Questions to Ponder	■ What actions can I take to make an interaction feel more relational?
	■ What leadership behaviors may be perceived as transactional?
	■ What situations may appropriately require a transactional leadership approach?

Seek Out New Learning Opportunities

Leadership, like any other discipline, requires a keen focus on acquiring new expertise, honing skills, and modifying unproductive behaviors. Seeking new learning opportunities is the fourth Leadership Strategy for the Learner-in-Chief. In his book *Outliers*, Malcolm Gladwell popularized the idea that achieving greatness in any field requires 10,000 hours of practice (2008). Though leadership cannot be compared to playing chess or the violin, a curious mindset with intentional learning and deliberate practice will undoubtedly bring one closer to mastery. Peter Senge, in his book, *The Fifth Discipline*, popularized the term "learning organization" (2006). As a fan of W. Edwards Deming, who developed the "System of Profound Knowledge," Senge championed individual, team, and organizational learning as an antidote to the "prevailing system of management" where focus on short-term outcomes trumps learning and systems thinking and leads to short-sighted decision-making and endless cycles of hiring and laying off workers. "Learning organizations are possible because not only is it our nature to learn, but we love to learn," (2006). Senge explains that these five disciplines of a learning organization are the centerpiece of individual change that builds learning organizations:

1. Systems Thinking.
2. Personal Mastery.
3. Mental Models.
4. Building Shared Vision.
5. Team Learning.

Continuous learners envision a better version of themselves, starting with honestly assessing where they are now and determining what to achieve next. Learners can overcome feelings of powerlessness to change their mental mode or behaviors by focusing intentionally on continuous personal improvement and reimagining themselves.

Being open to learning from others – not to copy them, but to build off their knowledge – opens a world of opportunities for experimentation and iteration. Through books, articles, conferences, or consultations with other leaders or organizations, we learn what is possible, broaden our horizons, and deepen the knowledge base that can be tapped into immediately or in the future. It is often said that "Everything that can be invented has been invented," which underscores the recognition that most new ideas, innovations, or discoveries are built on the shoulders of others. Make it a habit to learn from various sources to aid with modeling new processes, solving complex problems, or developing new lines of business. Learning from others is an integral step in the GUIDES Framework, and is underscored in the following case study, "Redesigning Primary Care Flow," where learning from others informs innovative and transformative thinking.

COACH'S CORNER: REDESIGNING PRIMARY CARE FLOW

A patient called to request an appointment with his primary care physician for a health concern. He experienced one delay after another and became increasingly frustrated as he told his story over and over when he was transferred to several staff members. His electronic chart bounced between them, and he was eventually scheduled for an appointment with a random physician. His primary care doctor could have solved his medical problem immediately, had he been connected directly to her.

Instead, the patient's physician was busy managing the overwhelming volume of paperwork and electronic virtual patient care, which often kept her working through lunch breaks and several hours after her regular clinic day ended. To cope, she was in the process of interviewing for an internal transfer to a hospitalist job that would not require so much time spent on electronic messages. Her response to this problem was not unusual in primary care or medicine in general in the United States: high physician burnout and turnover, resulting in inefficient and often poor patient care and health outcomes (as studied and published in numerous medical and business articles).

Recognizing this all-too-familiar burnout scenario within the clinical team, the physician leader of the practice worked closely with the administrative dyad partner to learn about various successful primary care models in healthcare: the National Health Service of the United Kingdom, Mayo Clinic, Cleveland Clinic, ThedaCare Health System, Intermountain Healthcare, and many others. Research conducted by author and professor Thomas Bodenheimer, MD, at the University of California San Francisco, defined successful Primary Care models as ones that create "joy in practice" for healthcare professionals while providing first-rate patient care. Additional research led the dyad leaders to Virginia Mason Medical Center (VMMC) to study "flow" in Primary Care. VMMC was at the forefront of continuous improvement and innovation in healthcare, and clinic leaders spent three days at their Seattle, Washington, campus learning the basics of primary care redesign. Their instructors challenged the team to imagine future models of care and prototype them right there and then. To redesign the delivery model, the dyad partners consulted with other healthcare organizations, learning various elements of successful models and critically assessing what could be adapted to their organization. Ultimately, they assembled a pilot team, developed a business case, and drafted a step-by-step implementation plan. The model was then presented to executive leaders and approved. As one of its guiding principles, leaders were committed to iterating and adjusting the model quickly, based on lessons learned as the redesign project was underway. The model itself was simple and elegant and included elements that are now common in many primary care settings: physicians and staff were co-located and worked in flow, ensuring patient concerns were addressed without delay. Unnecessary hand-offs and care touches between team members were avoided. Physician and staff workflows were standardized, driving out redundancy and any activities that added no value to patients. Everyone was trained in practices to achieve the standard, and care teams huddled several times a day, sometimes to review patients on the schedule and other times to reflect on how their day was going and what small improvements could be made to ensure the next day's flow was better. When implemented, the redesigned primary care model improved patient satisfaction, access to care, and message response rate, and most of all brought back "joy in practice" to physicians.

Table 8.4 presents best practices for seeking new learning opportunities.

Spend Time in Reflection

To pay attention, this is our endless and proper work.

Mary Oliver

Spending time in reflection is the fifth Learner-in-Chief Leadership Strategy. The GUIDES Framework is rooted in self-reflection ("S" stands for

Table 8.4 Best Practices for Seeking New Learning Opportunities

Trap	Relying on your own experience or that of your siloed area in the design of new systems and processes.
Best Practices	■ Benchmark your process redesign to best-in-class organizations. ■ Adopt and adapt best practices from outside your department, organization, and country.
Questions to Ponder	■ In designing this new process, which organizations can I learn from? ■ Are there publications that can help benchmark our organization's processes and results with other organizations? ■ In solving this problem, which areas or departments in my organization have solved a similar problem and have a best practice that we can adopt and improve upon?

SELF-REFLECT). As previously mentioned, the unproductive yet common culture of firefighting and rapid solutioning leaves no space for reflection, the deliberate practice of slowing down, looking back, and critically assessing your actions, behaviors, interactions, wins, and failures. It can be difficult to engage in reflection; the brain is constantly busy, planning, analyzing, brainstorming, and judging. Therefore, if not scheduled, reflection will not happen because precedence is given to the "tyranny of the urgent."

No sustainable learning happens without reflection, which results in the repeat of errors and the reinvention of ineffective solutions, locking into place a reactive cycle of "problem-solution-problem-solution." Reflection teaches us how to be proactive. It prepares practitioners to anticipate challenges and avoid missteps. Paying attention and slowing down enables reflection on what is being observed. Reflection can be done in many ways and applied to innumerable situations. It could be prospective (future-oriented), contemporaneous (here and now), retrospective (past-oriented), or blended. Let's examine an example of "blended" reflection.

COACH'S CORNER: APPROACHES TO REFLECTION

Imagine you are preparing for an upcoming difficult conversation or meeting. First, take time to reflect on your emotional and physical state, your readiness to effectively manage conflict, and your capacity for empathy today, now. Reflect on your home and work stress, sleep patterns, and state of well-being. Then, reflect on your prior experience in similar situations. And, if you are experiencing a situation now that is similar to circumstances you encountered in the past (with a similar process or problem or people with similar styles), analyze what worked well in the past and what you could have done differently. Think about your personal triggers that may have derailed the conversation. Now, think or envision the future interaction. What steps can you take to be more effective (e.g., listen more, ask questions, sit back, look relaxed, pay attention to non-verbal cues, empathize, or "seek to understand")? In what ways can you affect your state of being if you are feeling overwhelmed, fearful, or not otherwise prepared for the challenge at hand? Can you meditate or do a visioning exercise to get yourself emotionally ready?

This blended approach to reflection (past, present, and future) will help you identify preparatory steps, including any needed support from others. Different challenges require different support systems. At times you may need your mentor, boss, or coach. Other times, you may need guidance from your partner, friend, or colleague. Occasionally, all you need is to get enough sleep to be your best emotional self. Reflection may drive you to avoid the interaction altogether or change the timing if you do not feel ready now. As with any skill, reflection requires intentionality and practice to make it a habit. Mastery requires time and repetition. Include reflection in your Leader Standard Work (the leadership routines and activities you follow on a regular basis), discussed in greater detail in Chapter 7. Practice reflection daily. Apply it to both professional and personal situations.

AUTHOR'S REFLECTION: LESSONS ON THE PRACTICE OF PERSONAL, TEAM, AND ORGANIZATIONAL REFLECTION

LESSON 1: FOCUS REFLECTION ON "YOU" AND NOT "OTHERS"

Early in my career, I would mentally prepare for the day while getting dressed for work, then during the commute home, I would reflect on the day's events. Typical, right? I still do this, by the way. However, most of my reflection would occur when a colleague and I would debrief from a meeting or conversation. We would typically talk about the things that didn't go well and how we wish the others involved had done something differently. We would then strategize about how to change "the others" involved. Not surprisingly, we had little impact since this reflection was ad hoc, not intentional, and wasn't focused on my personal growth and development. Instead of focusing on "changing others," I needed to focus on my lessons learned and specific steps to change, learn, and improve myself first and foremost. My approach to personal reflection is continuously evolving as I learn with each reflection opportunity. Generally, I divide my reflection into three stages:

1. Pre-performance reflection (one-on-one interaction, meeting, or large event facilitation):
   ■ What are the desired outcomes?
   ■ What is my mindset, mood, and mental capacity readiness?
   ■ Which people do I have to work with beforehand to get them to the right mindset?
2. In-the-moment reflection:
   ■ Are we achieving the intended outcomes?
   ■ Is the team or the group going in a different direction from the desired direction?
   ■ What is my mindset, mood, and mental capacity at the moment?
3. Post-mortem (after the fact) reflection:
   ■ What went well?
   ■ What could have been done better?
   ■ What follow-up work do I need to do to achieve what was planned?

If I am grumpy, sleep deprived, or emotionally exhausted, I will have a different meeting since people unquestionably take cues from me. Since most communication happens non-verbally, it is not what I am saying but how I am saying it and what non-verbal signals I am sending to the audience that affect the meeting. I have this intentional awareness that depending on my mindset, mood, and mental capacity, my facilitation can go spectacularly well or be a complete dud. So, I think of steps to improve my emotional state and place visual triggers that help me stay in the productive mental space throughout an interaction or a meeting. I always ask myself: "Do I know and realize the leadership shadow I cast?"

LESSON 2: REFLECTION IS A HIGHLY PERSONAL ENDEAVOR

I coached one healthcare Chief Executive Officer (CEO) for almost five years. He had been a CEO for over 20 years and had been quite successful. His style was more traditional, and personal reflection was not something he did with intention. It took some time, but we finally found an approach that worked for him. At the end of each day, he scheduled 30 minutes for reflection. He would do this outside of his office to avoid interruptions. He reviewed his calendar and thought about each meeting and each interaction. As he reflected on his day, he would answer four questions:

1. What went well today, and why did it go well?
2. What didn't go well today?
3. What did I do to contribute to that situation, and what could I have done differently?
4. What behaviors did I model today?

At the beginning of the next day, he would review his notes and commit to how he would lead differently. This was not easy for him. This took a couple of years to become part of his work and leadership style. Once this became routine for him, the organization started performing at a much higher level.

LESSON 3: TEAM REFLECTION MATTERS

I coached a medical director in a pediatric hospital for a couple of years. It was hard for him to make time for personal reflection. He was very committed to improving his leadership and initiated a reflection exercise with his team. In their bi-weekly anesthesiology meeting, they covered the agenda, which ended with team reflection. I must admit that I was a bit skeptical at first because the meeting usually had 15–18 people in it, and I worried about it turning into a gripe session. However, this physician leader structured the team reflection to positively impact the group. He asked the following questions and allowed a response from one to two people.

- What are you most proud of clinically since our last meeting?
- What are you doing to improve your own processes?

This leader would end the meeting by giving his own answers after he listened with curiosity to his team's reflection. After a few months, he told me that the hardest part was openly talking with his peers about something that was not going well and that he was trying to improve. The personal exposure left him feeling vulnerable. Ultimately, it proved to be the best leadership behavior he could have exhibited. The department became more cohesive and could openly and safely talk about opportunities for improvement.

LESSON 4: LEARNING ORGANIZATIONS REFLECT TO IMPROVE

As a hospital administrator, I spent much time working with my team to maintain regulatory readiness. The Joint Commission, established in 1951, is the largest hospital accreditation agency. As you can imagine, preparations for the next Joint Commission visit required an inordinate number of ongoing compliance activities. To accelerate our efforts, we allocated scheduled meeting times to regularly assess our readiness and the gaps between our targets and our current performance. We identified the next actions to help us be better prepared for assessment. This is an example of enterprise-wide, cross-functional reflection: assess the current state and make plans to adjust (iterate) to get to the future state (vision, strategy, goals) based on what is learned. This cadence of learning and improvement guaranteed we would pass all the regulatory requirements with flying colors. The importance of this intentional cross-functional reflection approach cannot be understated.

Table 8.5 presents best practices for spending time in reflection.

Leadership Strategies: Bringing It All Together

A leader who considers themself a Learner-in-Chief will make great strides in creating a learning organization. A learning organization is one that not only continuously improves but also creates a culture of innovation, growth, and exceptional performance. Consider the challenges that Covid-19 brought to the healthcare field. Leaders and teams were Learners-in-Chief out of necessity. They learned to operate differently with rapid iterations in an ambiguous and unpredictable environment and were forced to turn expedited learning into innovative processes and practices to care for patients. Think about what has been learned through that process and how those learnings can revolutionize our leadership (and healthcare).

As a Learner-in-Chief, reflect on how you really feel about learning and learning with others. As leaders, the learner role exposes vulnerabilities; this can feel uncomfortable and cause a level of anxiety or even fear.

Table 8.5 Best Practices for Spending Time in Reflection

Trap	A culture of firefighting that leaves no time for individual or organizational reflection.
Best Practices	■ Block time on your calendar for reflection. Include daily and weekly reflection sessions. ■ Journal your lessons learned and improvement opportunities.
Questions to Ponder	■ Did I lead with an open mind and curiosity? How do I know? How was I perceived? ■ What did others learn from me today (focus on your positive and negative behaviors and traits, and less on technical content)? ■ What will I do differently tomorrow?

Leaders may acknowledge their vulnerabilities with questions such as, "Will I lose credibility if I don't know something? Will the team think I'm not able to perform as a leader? Will I be able to learn new skills and behaviors at this stage in my career? What will others think if I have to ask multiple questions to learn something new?" These are all normal questions that come up as you truly understand the magnitude of becoming a Learner-in-Chief.

COACH'S CORNER: LEARNER-IN-CHIEF STRATEGIES IN ACTION

What do the five Leadership Strategies for the Learner-in-Chief look like in action? Several years ago, a nursing leader with whom I worked closely and mentored in operational excellence asked, "Why can't we reimagine the role of a registered nurse in primary care?" Though this was not my area of expertise, I was excited to learn more about a new patient care model and coach an enthusiastic learner. First, we needed to find a willing physician and a nurse to partner with us to design a new model. Then we could develop and implement a pilot followed by several iterations before spreading the model more broadly across the department. After spending some time thinking through possible candidates, we agreed to work on the model with "Dr. Brown" and "Melanie," the registered nurse. This wasn't a random choice. Though neither of them was in a formal leadership position, we noticed a spark of enthusiasm emanating from both during clinic rounds. They were full of ideas on how to make care delivery more efficient and patient-centered. Before the design session, which included our executive sponsor, a nursing education specialist, and a union representative, every participant was asked to do extensive research on any published models and unpublished best practices inside and outside of our organization. We searched PubMed, reviewed abstracts from nursing conferences, and called our contacts in other institutions. We didn't limit our research to the United States. Armed with the newly acquired knowledge, we met to brainstorm and design our pilot. From our research, we gathered insights to weave together transformative new processes for a pilot. Our goal was to analyze part of the current physician load that could be safely transferred to the registered nurse. We postulated that if a physician and a nurse are co-located (sitting in visual proximity to each other), the nurse could handle a much higher volume of patient phone calls and emails, freeing up the physician to see more patients and manage complex clinical issues in real time.

When the pilot started, "Dr. Brown" led reflection huddles at least twice a day, to determine what was going well and what could be improved the next day. We also held the first biweekly and later weekly design team huddles to check in with the pilot team and see what barriers or challenges they encountered, lending our support and guidance. Daily reflections and iterations of the pilot, bi-directional real-time feedback, and "Dr. Brown's" clinical teaching quickly expanded "Melanie's" knowledge base and confidence to take on more complex patient tasks. The pilot results were closely tracked, with patient satisfaction, message turn-around time to resolution, and available appointments improving greatly. But most importantly, "Dr. Brown" and registered nurse "Melanie" were loving their clinical work more and more every day. They talked about "joy in practice" (Sinsky et al., 2013), and sharing their excitement energized all of us. Throughout the process of this redesign, implementation, and iteration of the role of the registered nurse in primary care was the unexpected professional development of two excellent leaders, "Dr. Brown" and "Melanie," who transitioned soon after into formal leadership roles.

The GUIDES Framework and the Learner-in-Chief

Let's return to the fictional Dr. Rudolph Cobb mentioned in the beginning of this chapter. Puzzled, he turned to his executive coach: "If learning is not taking place openly in the workplace, then it must be happening in the shadows." His coach asked:

- What role do you have in changing the culture?
- What can you do to make it safe for everyone to explore new ideas?
- How can you influence others to ask questions to understand problems more deeply?

The more Dr. Cobb thought about it, the more excited he became about leading physicians and teams that were curious, willing to experiment, and anxious to learn. He decided he was responsible for leading that cultural change and modeling the traits of a "Learner-in-Chief."

This concludes the exploration of the five Leadership Strategies: (1) sharpen observational skills, (2) go to Gemba, (3) use each encounter as a learning opportunity, (4) seek out new learning opportunities, and (5) spend time in reflection. In Chapter 2, you were asked to think of someone you consider to be a great Learner-in-Chief. To what extent do they embody and demonstrate the five Leadership Strategies we discussed? What other skills or characteristics do they exhibit that make them effective? Now, access and print the GUIDES Development Plan template in Appendix 1 and create a development plan to assess and improve the Learner-in-Chief attribute. See Figure 8.1 as an example of a plan to improve the strategy "Spend time in reflection."

GUIDES Development Plan – Learner-In-Chief

Step 1: GATHER inputs to evaluate your skills gaps and opportunities for development.

1. **Record your own assessment of your degree of confidence in these skills.**

To what extent are you confident in your ability to:	Not at all	Somewhat	Great deal
Sharpen observational skills		X	
Go to Gemba		X	
Use each encounter as a learning opportunity			X
Seek out new learning opportunities		X	
Spend time in reflection	X		

2. **Reflect on your answers to the questions above. Record your additional thoughts.** *After reading this chapter, I know I must focus on "Spending time in reflection" while also working on the other four strategies. I'm not sure how to make time for reflection due to all my responsibilities and ever-changing demands.*

Figure 8.1   Example of GUIDES Development Plan for Learner-in-Chief.

3. **Ask for feedback from others (e.g., trusted colleagues, your coach, or direct reports) on the skills, and take notes.** *My coach helped me understand that I should schedule regular reflection time in order for it to become a habit.*

4. **What does your additional research tell you about this attribute?** *Reflection needs to be part of my Leader Standard Work every day and every week. I can adopt a set of reflection questions to guide me.*

Step 2: UNDERSTAND and interpret the data you collected.

The following questions help you understand and interpret the data you collected in the GATHER step. Spend a few minutes thinking about these questions. Record your thoughts and responses.

1. **What did you learn from your self-assessment?** *I spend too much time firefighting, leaving me with no time to process what has happened during the day or the week. It's hard to learn from my mistakes in this mode. Honestly, it's hard to accept mistakes because I work so hard and don't mean to make leadership mistakes.*

2. **How did you interpret feedback from others (e.g., trusted colleagues, your coach, or reports)? Were you surprised? Did their feedback match your self-assessment?** *My coach values reflection time above all other leadership tasks. She finds me rarely to be introspective, as I am often drowning in the tyranny of the urgent. I know I need to prioritize developing in this area.*

3. **What were your key takeaways from the research? Were you surprised by anything you learned?** *The simple act of scheduling reflection time as an appointment on my calendar ensures I have dedicated time every day to focus on reflection. However, the largest takeaway is to think of this time as non-negotiable.*

Figure 8.1 (Continued)

Step 3: IDENTIFY your strengths and opportunities.

Spend a few minutes thinking about each of these questions. Record your thoughts and responses.

1. **Which skills do you want to develop further?** *Asking insightful reflection questions of myself, my direct reports, and even other leaders.*

2. **Which skills are foundational?** *Slowing down and processing what went well and what could have gone better during a specific timeframe. Then, adjusting my approach for next time.*

3. **Which skills are your highest priority?** *Reviewing my actions and activities to better understand what was valuable to me personally (my development as a leader), my team (their growth and learning), and my organization (actions contributing to the mission and strategy).*

Step 4: DESIGN your leadership development plan.

What are your development priorities? Record two or three high-priority opportunities and actions.

Area for Development	Developmental Opportunity	Actions to Take	Resources Needed	Target Date	Success Metrics
Learner-in-Chief	*Spend time in reflection*	*Schedule reflection time*	*Outlook calendar*	*10/1/23*	*% completed without changes to the schedule*

Look over your development plan, then consider these questions. Record your thoughts below.

1. **Does this plan address the foundational opportunities identified in your self-assessment, research, and input from others?** *Yes, this plan will help my learning through intentional reflection on my leadership abilities, plans, activities, actions, and results.*

Figure 8.1   (Continued)

2. **Does your plan take into consideration the personal triggers that could help or hinder your development?** *Yes, I tend to swirl in urgent, short-term activities and often not getting to the not-urgent, long-term critical matters.*

3. **Is the plan incremental and doable?** *Yes, I am going to start with weekly reflections, scheduling time every Monday morning at 8 a.m. so I can reflect on the prior week and plan the current week. I know I'll need to increase this to every day, but I have to start somewhere.*

4. **Are you excited about your plan? Why or why not?** *Very much so, I hope to gradually reduce the amount of time I spend in urgent activities, from 80% to 40% over the next two months.*

Step 5: EXECUTE your development plan.

Put your development plan into action! As you proceed with the execution of your plan, spend a few minutes thinking about each of these questions. Record your thoughts and responses.

1. **What circumstances or triggers will signal that "now" is the time to act and practice new behaviors?** *Missing a reflection session will trigger me to schedule another one the same day or next day. I don't want to fall back into firefighting mode.*

2. **What specific behavior(s) or action(s) will you try? How far are you willing to push your comfort zone?** *I will schedule check-in reflection meetings with my team so they can help me reflect on my actions and behaviors with the goal of moving away from firefighting and swirling unproductively.*

3. **How do you know if you are improving and becoming more successful with this attribute and as a leader?** *I will judge my success by how many reflection sessions I complete vs. the number planned, and I will be checking in with my team and my boss.*

Figure 8.1 (Continued)

4. **How will you gauge the impact of your actions or behavior changes? What responses will you be watching for?** *I will monitor my state of mind: Do I feel anxious and overwhelmed? Do I feel deliberate and in control? I will be watching how my team reacts to the change in my behavior: Do they seem stressed or calm?*

Step 6: SELF-REFLECT on your execution of the development plan.

Spend a few minutes at the end of the day and/or week thinking about each of these questions. Record your thoughts and responses.

1. **Was I mindful of my development today/this week? What did I do well? What could I have done better?** *I did well this week. I spent 30 minutes reflecting on my prior week, lessons learned, and opportunities for improvement, plus another 30 minutes to prepare for my meetings this week.*

2. **How did others respond when I intentionally led in a new way? Were people more (or less) engaged with me as a leader?** *Too early to say. After three months of sustained improvement, I will send an informal survey to see if the team noticed any changes in my leadership behaviors. In the meantime, I will inquire informally and adjust based on their feedback.*

3. **Was I mindful of my triggers? How did I respond to those?** *Yes, I stopped myself every time I started swirling, bringing myself to the planned activities.*

4. **What will I do differently tomorrow/next week? What should I be watching for?** *I may begin journaling my lessons learned or ideas that surfaced during the week. Maybe this can help future leaders.*

5. **What else do I need to do or learn to further my development of this attribute?** *I think I am ready for short daily reflections.*

Figure 8.1 (Continued)

Bibliography

Gladwell, Malcolm. *Outliers: The Story of Success*, 1st ed. New York: Little, Brown, 2008.

Koenigsaecker, George. *Leading the Lean Enterprise Transformation*. Boca Raton: CRC Press, 2009.

Lean Enterprise Institute. "Gemba." www.lean.org/lexicon-terms/gemba/

Nakane, Jinichiro and Robert W. Hall. "Ohno's Method: Creating a Survival Work Culture," *Target* 18, no. 1 (First Quarter 2002): 6–15. www.ame.org/sites/defa ult/files/target_articles/02-18-1-Ohnos_Method.pdf.

Senge, Peter M. *The Fifth Discipline: The Art and Practice of the Learning Organization*. Rev. and Updated. New York: Doubleday, Currency, 2006.

Sinsky, Christine A., Rachel Willard-Grace, Andrew M. Schutzbank, Thomas A. Sinsky, David Margolius, and Thomas Bodenheimer. "In Search of Joy in Practice: A Report of 23 High-Functioning Primary Care Practices." *The Annals of Family Medicine* 11, no. 3 (May 1, 2013): 272. https://doi.org/10.1370/afm.1531

The Deming Institute, "The Deming System of Profound Knowledge." https://dem ing.org/explore/sopk/

Chapter 9

Problem-Solver

Don't start with the problem, start with the people, start with empathy.

Bill Burnett and Dave Evans, authors *Designing Your Life*

Having no problems is the biggest problem of all.

Taiichi Ohno

Leadership Case Study: Bringing Problems Out of the Shadows

Dr. Alicia Zervoudakis sat in her new spacious office, slightly distracted. This promotion to Chief Medical Officer (CMO) had been her highest professional goal, and at times, it had seemed unattainable. But here she was, three weeks after starting her "dream" job, second-guessing the decision to move her family across the country. Why did she have this gnawing sensation in her stomach? She had known this job wasn't going to be a cakewalk. In her opinion, the Chief Executive Officer (CEO) needed to make some drastic changes in the executive suite to solve the hospital's many presenting problems: financially, they were bleeding money; talented doctors were leaving en masse; and regulators were concerned with the recent spike in the facility's nosocomial infections. Dr. Z. didn't dread these challenges. If anything, challenges energized her. What worried her was the hospital's current culture, specifically its leadership culture. Everywhere she went, everyone she spoke to and everything she observed exuded no sense of urgency. This artificial normality in the face of a looming disaster frightened her. Just as she had done in all of her prior leadership positions, Dr. Z. dove into learning all she could about her new organization's executive leadership style and culture, team dynamics and learning, systems to escalate safety concerns, and, most importantly, its attitude toward problem-solving. It was the latter one that gave her pause: problems were never mentioned. Doctors and nurses were either tight-lipped or indifferent to raising concerns or bringing up challenges to delivering patient care. As she built closer relationships with some of the surgeons, it became painfully obvious that surfacing problems was dangerous. The practice was not encouraged or celebrated. Quite the opposite, identifying problems was seen as a negative reflection on leaders, and this attitude was coming from the highest levels. Dr. Z. observed that her immediate boss, the hospital's CEO, propagated this culture; she knew without a doubt that unless she could influence the CEO to see problems as gems or gifts to be uncovered and solved across the enterprise, the hospital and her new job were doomed. "Am I ready to manage up?" Dr. Z. asked herself.

Introduction

Workplace problems present themselves at both strategic and tactical levels in any organization. In your role as a leader, you may be involved in responding to changing market conditions, a raging pandemic, medical supply procurement issues, or staff turnover. You may lead a problem-solving team, brought together to improve a clinical or administrative process that isn't producing the necessary outcomes. In all these situations, and others where problem-solving is needed, leaders engage in – and model – a thinking process that strives to understand the root cause of the problem using facts and data. Leaders engage those who do the work in solving the problem, take a systems view of the potential solutions, plan experiments to test the hypotheses, and iterate solutions (sometimes called countermeasures) based on an analysis of the outcome data. This approach to problem-solving may seem familiar to physicians as it closely resembles their approach to solving clinical problems, including the intentional participation of others in the process. Physicians and patients solve clinical problems through shared decision-making, while physicians and staff solve their practice problems together as a team. Likewise, in leadership, most problems are solved more effectively in a consultative and collaborative fashion with others. In this role, leaders model a methodical problem-solving approach, facilitate small and large groups in the problem-solving process, and set the pace along the way.

> *I promote decentralized scientific problem-solving, which is every worker taking initiative every day to find and fix the root cause of their most important problem. And what is the leader's role in that? The leader's job is to help, to create the environment in which the workers are empowered to do that. They're not punished for criticizing or complaining, or taking time to improve the work. Leaders create the environment in which all work is turned into an experiment. It's just like when we watch the results every time we give a patient a new blood pressure medicine. That's an experiment.*
>
> **John E. Billi**, *MD, Professor Emeritus and Former Chief Engineer, Michigan Quality System, University of Michigan*

This chapter discusses the mindset and Leadership Strategies that will position physician leaders to be effective problem-solvers.

Physician Leader as Problem-Solver

Leadership is all about solving problems, the big and small ones, and everything in between. It is akin to finding an appropriate clinical treatment or remedy. Learning to approach each problem in a structured and methodical manner will help get leaders and teams out of firefighting mode and ensure they are solving the right problems. Figuring out the problem to solve is by far the biggest challenge for any leader. Leaders may have a tendency to find solutions for the wrong problems. Just like clinical decision-making is iterative, so is problem-solving in business. The **GUIDES** Framework used to improve leadership skills also can be employed for problem-solving business challenges: **G**ather background data, **U**nderstand the problem to solve, **I**dentify the root causes of the problem, **D**esign experiments, **E**xecute the planned experiments, and **S**ustain results while continuing to iterate further. GUIDES is very similar to the SOAP (Subjective-Objective-Assessment-Plan) clinical framework, the PDCA (Plan-Do-Check-Act/Adjust) improvement cycle created by Walter A. Shewhart and socialized by W. Edwards Deming, and the Scientific Method developed in the 17th century, as shown in Table 9.1.

Table 9.1   Comparison of Problem-Solving Frameworks

GUIDES	SOAP	PDCA	Scientific Method[a]
Gather current state information	**Subjective** (history)		Make an observation
Understand the problem to solve	**Objective** (physical exam, diagnostic tests)		Ask a question
Identify root cause and gap	**Assessment** (differential diagnoses)	**Plan**	Form a hypothesis
Design the future state	**Plan**		Make a prediction
Execute the action plan	Treat	**Do**	Test a prediction
Study and Sustain results; iterate further; document standard work	Reassess treatment success (follow-up)	**Check** Act/Adjust	Iterate: create a new hypothesis or prediction based on the results

Note: [a]www.khanacademy.org/science/high-school-biology/hs-biology-foundations/hs-biology-and-the-sci entific-method/a/the-science-of-biology.

Physicians repeat the SOAP process countless times with their patients and pride themselves on painstakingly developing a differential diagnosis before initiating treatment. Why is it, then, that often, as physician leaders, we jump to "treatment" before completing a thorough diagnostic assessment of a non-clinical problem? Why is it still rare to see leaders approach business problems with the same level of intention as physicians: dissect the problem, find root causes, and develop differential diagnoses?

When a patient case does not go well in the clinical setting, doctors usually get together to understand the underlying cause, specifically focusing on diagnostic errors. A common cognitive bias of "premature closure" results in many undesirable outcomes. Not taking time to understand the problem, jumping to the final diagnosis too fast, and not brainstorming differential diagnoses can harm and, at worst, kill patients. In a clinical setting, most of the time should be spent listening to the patient, eliciting the history, and backing up the history with the physical exam and diagnostic test data. Only then would one formulate a potential differential diagnosis. In the business setting, leaders should spend a disproportionate amount of time understanding and formulating the problem and backing it up with data. To not do so risks the realization of Stephen Covey's maxim: "If the ladder is not leaning against the right wall, every step we take just gets us to the wrong place faster."

> *In clinical practice, clinicians solve many problems every day. They see a patient, they document the encounter, they order necessary tests, make needed referrals and they are "done." At least they are done until test referrals and consult notes come back. Their mindset is to finish all of today's work today. People in management may get the satisfaction of checking things off a to-do list, but rarely is a project started and solved the same day. There are more steps in the process of getting something done, and often the manager "owns" the project (or problem) day after day, without being able to refer it out and wait for test or consult results. So I would tell clinician leaders to let go of the expectation that things should get "done" quickly. Which is not to say that things should drag on or decisions shouldn't be made timely, but know that most administrative work is of a longer duration. Clinician leaders should also be aware that much of management and leadership work is about influencing. It is more like motivating a patient to make lifestyle changes than it is like excising a skin lesion.*
>
> **Lloyd David**, *MBA, CEO of The Polyclinic and Western Washington Group President for Optum Care (Retired)*

Mindset of a Problem-Solver

The Problem-Solver leader is committed to developing the capabilities of others to solve problems. It can be challenging to suddenly transition from single-handedly owning every problem and solution to being a problem-solving leader, problem-solving facilitator, and, more importantly, a problem-solving coach. The first step is a mindset shift: acknowledging that leaders are not expected to have every answer and that eliciting ideas from others is not a sign of personal or professional weakness. A leader's mindset should be one of openness to learning from others and a belief that others can solve problems, too. In a sense, it should be a relief that no one person has to have all the answers; instead, rely on people close to the problem to experiment and find solutions to simple and complex problems. By coaching others to problem-solve, leaders acknowledge the expertise of the talented and highly trained people in the organization, develop their capabilities to find answers to work dilemmas, and model strong leadership.

Your job is not to create solutions to problems – your job is to communicate the "why" to your team and then remove barriers so that they can create the solutions.

M. Sean Rogers, *MD, MBA,*
Regional Medical Director, Optum CA

It isn't easy to ask others what they think and then wait patiently while they formulate an answer. It can be just as difficult for them. Being asked to contribute their opinion may be a new experience for staff, especially if the organization has (or had) a traditional hierarchical culture. They may be wary of volunteering an idea or answer. Be patient. Facilitate problem-solving in a psychologically safe manner; suspend your bias for quick action and allow space for building a trusting relationship.

Now, what makes a good physician leader or physician coach? My definition of a leader is someone who solves problems but, more importantly, coaches and mentors others to solve problems. They create an environment in which problem-solving can occur. The physician, as a leader, makes sure it's safe for people to raise problems. They handle the issue in a blame-free environment. Humility helps with this. People don't get into medical school because of being humble, and often the residencies have pummeled humility out of them. Sometimes humility might be seen as a sign of weakness. So, we often favor the decisive physician or surgeon, who's able to jump to conclusions quickly and grasp the situation rapidly and move forward. As opposed to the qualities of a good leader: being humble and curious. Asking good questions helps with solving the problem with a learner's mind – with a curious mind. Instead of the usual "take charge" surgeon, I need the medical director of a surgery clinic to come in and say, "I'm not sure what's going on; help me understand. I want to learn about what your roles are. And, I want to learn about what problems you have. And, I want to learn about which of those you're working on now. And what you think are causing them and what experiments you're going to try? And what happened when you ran your last experiment?" When in medical school did you learn that?

John E. Billi, *MD, Professor Emeritus and Former Chief Engineer, Michigan Quality System, University of Michigan*

By following a structured problem-solving approach, being respectful and others-focused, the culture will begin to shift. Just as the physician leader's mindset shifts from "I have all the answers" to "I coach and develop others to get to the answers," the team will embrace a new way of thinking and acting: solving problems independently, collaboratively, and innovatively. Recall these two adages as you support yourself and your team in reshaping the mindset: "Go slow to go fast" and "Strive for progress, not perfection." That is, proceed in a measured fashion and focus on making daily incremental improvements. Mindset change is just the beginning of the problem-solving transformation journey. The next section presents three strategies that will demonstrate the "how" of credibly leading teams in problem-solving.

Leadership Strategies for the Problem-Solver

Before diving into leadership strategies, let's review the six Leadership Attributes presented in previous chapters that are fundamental to the Problem-Solver attribute: Strategic Thinker, Coach, Learner, Effective Communicator, Team Builder, and Change Manager:

- As a strategic thinker, a leader helps teams align problems with organizational vision, strategy, and department goals.
- As a coach, a leader guides and facilitates the identification of problems, root causes, and solutions.
- As a learner-in-chief, a leader learns about best practices and benchmarks and encourages teams to learn from others within and outside of their department or organization. Great leaders know that not recreating previously failed solutions, but iterating them instead will speed up the process of improvement and innovation.
- As an effective communicator, a leader facilitates interactions, discussions, and brainstorming meetings that contribute to a psychologically safe environment and stimulate innovative thinking.
- As a team builder, a leader encourages and stimulates teams to experiment and not be incapacitated by analysis paralysis or fear of failure.
- As a change manager, a leader ensures that the solutions developed are adopted and successfully sustained over time by engaging the team and meeting them where they are from a mindset perspective.

Mastery of these six Leadership Attributes benefits the problem-solving process, as demonstrated in the three Leadership Strategies for the Problem-Solver:

- Engage and prepare the team.
- Master problem-solving methods.
- Facilitate the problem-solving process.

Engage and Prepare the Team

To engage and prepare your team for problem-solving, spend time with the team in Gemba – the place where value-creating work takes place. The value of going to Gemba is described in several chapters throughout the book, as it is such a powerful experience and key to being a successful leader. In some organizations, the word "rounding" is used instead of Gemba as it is a familiar concept for physicians, similar to daily rounding with clinical teams in the hospital and problem-solving patient care cases. Traditionally this activity takes place in person: in clinical and non-clinical areas. Covid-19 uprooted business as usual, and now both clinical and non-clinical work often happens virtually. Rounding virtually can challenge leaders and often requires creativity to match the same experience as in-person Gemba. Fortunately, many patient flows happen within the electronic medical record or other electronic systems. Going to Gemba (or rounding) in person or virtually will deliver huge benefits throughout the problem-solving process:

- Observing patient flows and workflows in-depth and in real time.
- Connecting with teams in their usual work environment (physical or virtual) versus a more formal setting of a conference room.
- Validating assumptions about the problem that is being solved.
- Understanding how to realistically implement changes and sustain improvements.

In the context of problem-solving, understanding realities on the ground is critical in uncovering pain points, testing hypotheses, and validating assumptions. Seeing the work being done, talking to the people doing the work, and asking questions to check your understanding of current performance and potential gaps helps prepare the team for problem-solving. It also demonstrates that leaders are genuinely open and curious.

Teams will be excited to see leaders learning from them and with them. This is critical in creating a psychologically safe environment for problem-solving.

> *I tell people that when you are in management, you are in sales. You have to sell a problem before you can sell a solution. Which is to say that you need to get people to recognize that there is a problem before you can get them engaged in exploring possible solutions. Sometimes that is a matter of shining a light on something, e.g., when I do Gemba rounds, I often ask if we are able to give patients everything they want. It's a bit of an awkward question because people hate to tell me, "No, we can't." But it's one way to get people to acknowledge reality in a non-analytical way. Sometimes you can do this by presenting data, but often people want to explain away the data. But if you sell them on the goal first, they are more likely to buy into the data and acknowledge what the data is telling them. Selling the problem doesn't necessarily mean that I can sell my solution. When we engage people in designing solutions, they seem to own it without having purchased it. I guess what I'm selling then is the chance to make a difference, to make things better.*
>
> **Lloyd David**, *MBA, CEO of The Polyclinic and Western Washington Group President for Optum Care (Retired)*

It is difficult to tackle problems and find solutions while cocooned within the walls of an office and not going to the places where the actual work is happening. Leaders risk relitigating old problems, rehashing retired plans, and reusing outdated solutions. Instead, humble and curious leaders reject the hubris of self-importance and an "I have the answer" attitude. They spend time with frontline teams, rounding and learning what is actually happening. They recognize that people who care for patients or work directly with customers have a wealth of expertise. Learning from these value-creators and problem-solving with them, leaders tackle real and relevant problems that support organizational strategy, success, and advancement. Problem-solving without learning from frontline care teams is like fishing without a fishing rod.

Problem-solving can occur on the fly during huddles or on Gemba walks, as demonstrated in the Case Study Message Management. Later in the chapter, the focus is on more formal structured problem-solving used to redesign small- and large-scale processes that span across several functions or departments. As discussed in Chapter 8, any one-on-one interaction or meeting is an opportunity for learning. And this learning often happens through problem-solving at the frontlines of medical care.

CASE STUDY: MESSAGE MANAGEMENT

Dr. Eric Johnson, the chief of primary care, noticed that electronic messages from patients seeking medical advice were not being responded to in a timely manner. Some messages had been sitting in a physician's electronic queue for days, creating delays in care and irritating patients. In response, patients phoned the clinic repeatedly, leading to increased call volumes and long wait times. Other patients, not knowing what else to do, went to urgent care clinics and emergency rooms, driving the total cost of care unnecessarily high.

Eric approached Irene, the newly promoted nurse manager, with his concerns about patient care delays and dissatisfaction. She pointed out that there was nothing to be done to speed up message management, saying, "I think patients should just make an appointment with their doctor if they don't get a response." It happened that Brian, a college intern studying healthcare management, was shadowing Irene that day. At that moment, Eric saw an opportunity to model and introduce problem-solving concepts to Brian and Irene. Given the current stressful work environment, Eric specifically wanted to use this as an opportunity to build team cohesion. Eric engaged Brian and Irene, "I'd like to talk to our frontline staff to learn more about this problem. Before we go to the clinic, though, could we think about what questions we might want to ask when we get there?"

After a few minutes, they came up with a short list of questions:

- Do we know our current message management process?
- When and how was the staff trained in the process?
- Is the process documented? Is it visually displayed for staff to see?
- When was this process last reviewed and updated?
- How do we know whether our current process meets our patients' needs?
- Is there a better process?

Irene said, "Eric, that's a lot of questions, but I think some of the staff members who have been here for a while can give us answers." The three of them went upstairs and opened the door to the department, where they were greeted by Diane, a medical assistant who just finished the patient rooming process and had a few minutes to chat. Irene introduced Diane to Brian and explained their purpose for coming to see her.

"Diane, would you show us your current process for managing the avalanche of patient messages that come in?" Irene asked. After observing the process for a few minutes, Irene asked more questions. "Diane, are all of the medical assistants trained in this process? Do you know if they are all comfortable with the process? Are they all following it?"

Diane, warming up to the problem-solving process, said, "Oh, sure! Let me show you!" They walked across the hall and stood before a visual display of graphs on the wall near the nursing station. There was a colorful chart of team assignments, including responsibility for managing patient messages. Diane proceeded to explain the other documents they were looking at, including a map of the message management process, a skills competency checklist documenting that all of the medical assistants had been well-trained in completing the process, and recent audit results showing that the medical assistants were clearly performing the process reliably. Next, Diane brought their attention to the fishbone diagram (sometimes called an Ishikawa diagram) dated three months ago, when the staff had identified the root causes of the delayed response time and proposed improvements to the process, which had been implemented successfully. They then spent some time looking at the patient message turnaround-time data. They could see that the process was not meeting the turnaround-time standard at least once or twice a week.

Finally, Eric said, "Before we jump to conclusions, let's dive into the data and see which messages are sitting the longest without responses to the patient. Diane, are you seeing any patterns? Why do you think this process breaks down?"

Diane thought for a moment, then said,

Well, it looks like most of the unanswered messages are from the patients of just two doctors. Dr. Gomez's nurse is out on a three-month medical leave, and Dr. Bell's medical assistant is out on vacation. Sometimes, we have just one medical assistant responding to patient messages for four doctors. Ordinarily, we would have three or four medical assistants covering this workload, but with the shortage of medical assistants and all the restructuring going on around here, we sometimes don't have the right number of medical assistants on the floor.

"Wow, I did not realize how challenging things were," Irene replied. "Do you have any ideas on how we can make it better?"

"I can't speak for everyone on the team," Diane mused,

but I think we need to assign coverage on a daily basis for message management the same as we do for rooming patients. Maybe we could talk about this problem with the whole team in the huddle tomorrow morning. I think other folks may have some ideas, too.

Eric thanked Diane for her analysis of the problem. He then asked Irene for her impressions of the situation and what she thought should be done next. Irene said,

My understanding of the problem has really changed by coming here and speaking with the people who actually do the work. I'm glad I didn't try to come up with a solution while we were downstairs in the office. I'd like Diane to help lead this discussion in our huddle tomorrow with the medical assistants and the rest of the clinical team so they can come up with any changes to the process and a plan for trying it out. We'll be able to test it fairly quickly and see if the changes improve our message turn-around time. Hopefully, we can help our patients get the information they need as quickly as possible and avoid expensive after-hours care in the emergency department.

Before leaving the clinic, Eric took a moment to summarize their problem-solving experience.

Brian, we call the rounding experience "Going to Gemba." That's a Japanese term that means going to the actual place where work is happening. It is always better to make decisions based on the facts on the ground and not from our assumptions or preconceived notions formed behind closed doors. And, sometimes, the facts aren't in the reports we get, which makes going to Gemba a critical step in problem-solving.

In the case study above, Dr. Eric Johnson focused on facilitating the problem-solving session using questions designed to encourage frontline engagement in understanding and solving the problem. He coached the team on verifying data with facts, determining the likely root causes, and deciding what remedy (treatment) should be tried. Diane, the medical assistant, had access to all the data to assess the situation and responded positively throughout the discussion. By the end of Eric's impromptu problem-solving session, Diane was eager to bring the problem to her teammates the following day. Eric's open approach to facilitating problem-solving with questions – and not answers – role models the leadership strategies discussed in this chapter.

The team must be ready to engage effectively in the problem-solving process. Spending time with the team allows leaders to assess the readiness of individual team members and build relationships with them. From this informal assessment, leaders can create a more thoughtful plan for facilitating the team through the problem-solving process. Leaders must be cognizant of their "presence" when they are with frontline teams, as body language, facial expressions, and tone of voice may need to be adjusted based on the subtle non-verbal messages received from the team. In general, asking questions while engaging with a genuine interest to listen and learn creates a milieu for brainstorming, experimentation, and discovery. Edward Schein recommends an approach called humble inquiry, describing it in his book *Helping*, as "The fine art of drawing someone out, of asking questions to which you do not already know the answer, of building a relationship based on curiosity and interest in the other person" (2009). There are a few ground rules to make the team engagement experience valuable and less intimidating for everyone involved:

■ Introduce yourself to the staff in the area and explain why you are there. You should do so without impeding patient flow or interrupting staff that are working. Be as quiet as you can.

■ Demonstrate respect for people. Know who is working in the area and know something about them. Give praise!

■ Avoid prologues. Don't spend too much time explaining who you are. If they are surprised to see you, that's a problem. Build trust first.

■ Avoid starting questions with "why," especially in the beginning. Use "what" or "how" to start the conversation. Use "why" to carry the dialogue forward.

■ Observe the process through the eyes of your patients or customers.

Table 9.2 Best Practices for Engaging the Team in Problem-Solving

Trap	Depriving your team of the opportunity to figure out answers to their problems by providing unsolicited ideas and solutions.
Best Practices	■ Use open-ended questions to understand realities on the ground and the challenges that your team is experiencing. ■ Coach your team to problem-solve using facts and data.
Questions to Ponder	■ How will I assess team readiness to solve a specific problem? ■ How will I approach a team that has been conditioned to have problems solved for them by their supervisors?

- Engage people in thinking about why we need to improve and encourage them to find creative solutions.
- Never use the word "not" to modify "why." It is tempting to provide your opinion or an answer. People expect leaders to solve problems. Your "why not" robs them of the opportunity to develop solutions themselves. Let them learn how to problem-solve, even if it takes longer.
- Never use the words "maybe" or "I guess." Using these words typically means that you are trying to problem-solve. Stop speculating about how to address an issue. Allow the team the opportunity to do this.
- Speak the language of the area. Listen with an open mind to whatever lessons it will yield.

Table 9.2 presents best practices for engaging the team in problem-solving.

Master Problem-Solving Methods

Employing a structured problem-solving approach prevents fixing the wrong problem. Under stress, while firefighting, it is easy to focus on quick fixes that improve things temporarily but, ultimately, make overall system performance worse, not better. It is also easy to lose sight of who is the ultimate customer and tackle only issues that are plainly visible. However, some critical problems are hidden, uncovered only in a deep dive problem-solving session involving the right subject matter experts and validating the data and information by going to Gemba. To tackle these challenges, keep a line of sight to the organization's overall strategy and the department's goals. Ultimately, any healthcare problem should focus on improving several areas within the Quadruple Aim (patient experience, clinician experience, cost, and quality of care), an iteration of the Triple Aim advocated by Dr. Donald Berwick and the Institute for Healthcare Improvement (Berwick et al., 2008).

The iterative problem-solving approach encourages solving problems at the point of care based on data, facts, and observations in Gemba. Iterative problem-solving works hand-in-hand with frontline physicians and staff who ultimately know the finer details of complex patient care. It organically incorporates change management principles as change is made *with* people and not *to* people. This is even more critical for any change affecting physicians who are independent scientists at heart. They are data and evidence-driven and may resist a "just do it because I told you so" directive. They spend their days (and nights) in the patient care setting, ultimately positioned better than anyone else to make change happen or, conversely, to resist any efforts to improve. Coach teams to:

- Problem-solve iteratively.
- Ask open-ended questions.
- Experiment without fear of failure.
- Continuously learn.
- Pay attention to problems, processes, and results.

This approach develops the team's collective expertise while addressing real day-to-day challenges. A focus on progress – and not perfection – encourages teams to test a series of hypotheses and not wait for flawless solutions. It may seem counter-intuitive, but significant progress is made when failures are treated as learning opportunities. Many physicians and physician leaders have a hard time with this concept of "failing fast." Iterative problem-solving is learning from experiments. Table 9.3, based on *Gemba Walks* by James Womack, compares iterative and traditional problem-solving (2013).

The GUIDES Framework can be used for iterative problem-solving just as it is used for personal leadership development throughout this book. This is a versatile tool that can help solve small and large problems at the team or enterprise-wide levels. This framework makes the scientific method of experimentation and the PDCA cycle more accessible and applicable to you as a healthcare leader. It parallels the SOAP framework of clinical evaluation but adds more detail to refining healthcare systems and processes.

The GUIDES Framework is based on the A3 problem-solving method,

Table 9.3   Characteristics of Iterative and Traditional Problem-Solving (based on *Gemba Walks* **by James Womack)**

Iterative Problem-Solving	Traditional Problem-Solving
Problems are solved in Gemba with frontline clinicians and teams using facts and data.	Problems are solved remotely by managers relying on assumptions.
Problem and process focused.	Solutions focused.
Facilitators or coaches ask questions.	Leaders give answers.
Uses iterative experiments as its implementation plan.	Uses carefully planned solutions as its implementation plan.
Failures are valued as learning opportunities.	Failures are seen as embarrassments.

popularized by Toyota. On a single page, a description of the problem, the hypothesis, and the improvement to be tested are presented on an 11" × 17" piece of paper. Figure 9.1 blends the GUIDES Framework and A3 problem-solving and includes six familiar steps:

Step 1: **G**ATHER current state information (voice of stakeholders and process, best practices).

Step 2: **U**NDERSTAND the problem to solve (the gap between current performance and future goals).

Step 3: **I**DENTIFY root causes and drivers of the gap (fishbone, 5 whys, driver diagram).

Step 4: **D**ESIGN the future state (process map, standard work).

Step 5: **E**XECUTE (action plan, deliverables).

Step 6: **S**USTAIN (reflect, iterate next steps).

Gather information about the current state:

■ Get the "voice" of stakeholders and process.

■ Collect data to characterize current process performance.

■ Identify best practice information within and outside of the area and organization.

Soliciting the "voice" of stakeholders (patients, providers, staff, management, and executives) is not difficult to do but it can be time-consuming. This is not something to be rushed. There are a few rules of thumb to take

GUIDES A3 Title:
Date:

Improvement Sponsor:
Improvement Team:

1. **GATHER** current state information (process data, voice of stakeholders and process, best practices)

2. **UNDERSTAND** the problem to solve (the measurable gap between the current state and the goal)

3. **IDENTIFY** root causes of the performance gap, using tools such as fishbone diagram (Ishikawa diagram) or 5 Whys

4. **DESIGN** the future state (create a process map; document the standard work for the team and the leader)

5. **EXECUTE** the action plan (identify the action steps and deliverables)

WHAT	WHO	WHEN	OUTCOME

6. **SUSTAIN** the results (stabilize, reflect, and iterate)

Figure 9.1   GUIDES A3 Framework for Iterative Problem-Solving.

into account as problems are explored from the perspective of patients, colleagues, and other stakeholders:

■ Be intentional. Prepare for conversations; actively listen without distractions; follow up as appropriate.

■ Seek out diversity. Involve people of different ages, races, genders, and tenures within the organization. Seek out a spectrum of opinions from people who are both quiet and more vocal; those who are both engaged and disengaged; those who want change, and those who are content.

■ Be curious. Lead with open-ended questions (What problem we are trying to solve? What are your pain points? How would you describe an ideal state or customer experience?), not preconceived ideas of the problem. Expect to be surprised and nurture an environment of respect and trust.

■ Go where they are. Engage people during usual one-on-one conversations, huddles, and team meetings. Talk with patients in the waiting room (with permission) and use interviews and surveys as applicable.

How many stakeholders are appropriate to include in the "voice of" exercise? There is no magic answer to determining the number of people to include, but a better understanding of the problem will emerge with more, but not too many, people involved (ideally, between eight and 12 people). Hearing the "voice of the process" is equally vital. Observe and document the process and collect data. Encourage teams to observe and create a map of the current flow of patients and information, including the amount of time it takes to move through the various process steps, the number of people involved in the process, and the number of times the process is handed off to another person or department. Determine how well the process meets patient and customer requirements. Identify the steps in the process where value is created and, equally important, the steps that can make or break the process outcome. How well do those steps perform? Are those steps reliable? Capable? Process mapping and value stream analysis are tools used to visualize the process as it exists now and are well-described in other books and on the internet. In the *Understand* and *Identify* steps of the GUIDES Framework, the team may see that some process steps are not valuable to patients or teams and could be omitted or redesigned.

A deep *Understanding* of the problem being solved is based on all the information gathered from diverse "voices" of stakeholders and the process. Leaders may assume they know what others think about the problem. But, getting the "voice" of key stakeholders helps build engagement. Observing the process directly is critical for a better understanding of the problem. Learn, listen, and be curious. Go to Gemba, verify assumptions with data and facts, and map the current state of the process or procedure. Take some time to assimilate the data you've gathered.

- Is the data consistent with what patients and team members said?
- Does the data support what was observed in Gemba?
- Is additional assessment warranted?

Aligning sponsors and teams around the problem is by far the most challenging step in any problem-solving process. It is worth repeating: solving the wrong problem is the biggest waste of all. The problem is the *measurable gap* between the current state and the goal. Local problem-solving goals should be connected to strategic goals and initiatives. Local teams should have a clear line of sight to the organization's overall performance. Avoid non-specific and wordy problem statements that can't be measured. Ensure problem statements include specific metrics, goals, and a timeline:

- Instead of *GI Call Center doesn't respond timely to phone calls and electronic messages* try *GI Call Center's response time to telephone and electronic messages is currently five minutes. Our goal is to achieve a response time of three minutes within two months.*
- Instead of *Primary care patients have long delays getting appointments for annual exams* try *Average number of days wait for an annual exam in primary care is currently six days. Our goal is to achieve an average of three days within six months.*

In the *Identify* step, coach teams to explore the causes of the performance gap. Use any of the brainstorming techniques to identify the root causes of the problem, such as a fishbone diagram (sometimes called an Ishikawa diagram), the "5 Whys" method, or other root cause analysis and driver diagrams. Experiment with other methods to help the team think out of the box and identify underlying reasons for the gap in performance. If the chosen tool or approach does not work, try another one. Regardless of the tool and approach used, your team's and organization's success, alignment, and engagement start with brainstorming and problem-solving together in a psychologically safe environment.

After creating a physical or virtual current state process map, ask the team to identify wasteful steps that bring no value to the customer, team, or process. Use this knowledge in the *Design* step to create a new or future state process map that incorporates the "voices" of stakeholders and process, removes redundant steps, and implements solutions or countermeasures to the identified root causes of the problems.

Designing the future state should not focus on perfection but on improvement. Remember, this is an ongoing experiment consisting of multiple iterations and observations of the results while striving for continuously improved processes and performance. Some leaders get bogged down trying to anticipate all the possible pitfalls in a new system or process and proactively trying to fix them. Expect that some things meticulously designed and planned will not perform as intended. Eric Ries popularized the term "minimally viable product" in his book *The Lean Startup*. Ensure the design of the new process has all the needed steps to satisfy patients or customers (a minimally viable product), then depend on iterations to improve the process even further (2011).

Now it is time to roll up your sleeves and integrate all the information you and your team gathered and processed in the Gather, Understand, and Identify steps of the GUIDES Framework. You mapped out the current state, found broken or redundant process steps, and identified the root causes of the issues at hand. You learned from various process stakeholders and other areas in the organization the best practices to use in the design process. You are ready to create your first prototype of the improved or new process. Map it out together with your team.

In the *Design* phase, pay attention to standard work. Any new process must be clearly documented to be easily explained and taught. Documented standard work and an accountability system are essential to maintaining the new process and preventing backsliding to doing things the old way. Explore the concept of standard work with your team.

In the *Execute* phase, create an action plan. Based on the new process created, prepare an action plan with the steps needed to achieve it. Many great plans fail if not executed properly. Ensure each of the next steps is clearly defined and roles to implement changes are assigned with specific due dates. It is a good habit to come out of any meeting, whether problem-solving or otherwise, with the following questions answered:

- **What** are the next steps and action items?
- **Who** is responsible for completing each step and action item?
- **When** is the step or action item to be completed?

Ensure team members are aware of and commit to the action items and due dates. Peter Drucker reminds us that "Many brilliant people believe that ideas move mountains. But bulldozers move mountains; ideas show where the bulldozers should go to work" (www.goodreads.com/quotes/6539474-many-brilliant-people-believe-that-ideas-move-mountains-but-bulldozers). Focus on action, and don't let your team get stuck in analysis paralysis or the never-ending pursuit of perfection. Use what you learned in Chapters 5 and 7. Be intentional and focus on progress, process, and results.

The final step in the Iterative Problem-Solving GUIDES Framework is *Sustain*, where the focus is on both stabilizing the new process and looking for new opportunities to further improve it. Sustain is reinforced during the team's reflection time, reviewing the data and determining what works and what needs further development or improvement. Once the problem-solving activity is complete, the real work begins to ensure you are able to sustain the solutions you are experimenting with and then continue to improve them over time. As a leader, you should keep and use project plans and standard work to:

- Stay connected to the team.
- Monitor and measure results.
- Evolve the improvement work and take it to the next level.

Table 9.4   Best Practices for Understanding the Problem to Solve

Trap	Jumping to solutions before understanding the problem to solve and, as a result, solving the wrong problem.
Best Practices	▪ Ensure sufficient time is dedicated to defining the problem before attempting to solve it. Bring facts and data to the conversation. ▪ Once the problem is clearly defined and agreed upon, engage in root cause thinking to understand the underlying sources of the problem.
Questions to Ponder	▪ Is everyone on the team aligned around the problem to be solved? ▪ What organizational metrics will improve by solving the problem? Quantify the expected improvement.

This is your team's chance to iterate. What is their next hypothesis? What is their next experiment? Table 9.4 presents best practices for understanding the problem to solve.

Facilitating the Problem-Solving Process

Facilitating the problem-solving process can seem like a daunting task and an overwhelming responsibility. It doesn't have to be. Focus foremost on creating a collaborative, trusting, and psychologically safe environment for all problem-solving discussions.

> *One of the most important aspects of effective collaboration is the willingness of each person to acknowledge their own limitations and to have respect for the viewpoints of others. Setting aside personal ego and keeping the ultimate goal in mind is key to success. It is also important to develop a deep trust with the people you work closely with by regularly demonstrating an assumption of positive intent. If you don't understand what points they are trying to make or if it seems like they are headed in a direction that is uncomfortable, don't make assumptions. Use humble inquiry to gain a better understanding of their positions.*

> **M. Sean Rogers**, *MD, MBA, Regional Medical Director, Optum CA*

The following soft skills and strategies help facilitators establish a collaborative brainstorming environment:

- Start with a *personal* ice-breaker.
- *Listen* without judgment.
- Ask *non-leading* questions.
- Understand various viewpoints while *being neutral.*
- Champion the *no bad ideas* rule.
- Make space for *emotions* to be expressed.
- Draw out opinions with a *round robin* discussion.
- Make the discussion *visual and factual.*
- Leave problem-solving to the team.

In addition to the soft skills and strategies above, following a defined facilitation process or framework helps the team develop solutions efficiently without excessive swirl, while remaining focused on patients (or customers) and the organization's goals. The scope (goals and boundaries) and span (departments and functions involved) of the problem at hand will often define the problem-solving setting and facilitation method.

In organizations with a culture of continuous process or performance improvement, problem-solving may be built into routine business functions. Tackle small problems in daily or weekly improvement huddles. For example, in the Message Management case study presented previously, Dr. Eric Johnson engaged in impromptu problem-solving during his Gemba rounding.

To tackle large organizational problems that span several departments across the enterprise or the whole enterprise, facilitating multi-day design sessions is often needed. For example, as discussed in Chapter 3, many organizations develop a 12-month master plan of all the change activities across the enterprise. Once the performance gaps are identified, temporarily matrixed cross-functional teams can dive in and explore root causes of the problem, map patient or process flows, discover waste and redundancies in the process (steps that add no value to customers), and design process and system improvements that advance satisfaction, quality, and financial goals. As discussed previously, GUIDES offers a framework, the GUIDES Cross-Functional Redesign Model, to solve complex problems within and across departments. This model is explained below and is also accessible in Appendix 4. There are other problem-solving frameworks available as well. We encourage you to choose a framework that works for you and your team. Use it consistently to streamline your facilitation process and to prevent developing premature solutions based on wrong assumptions.

Large organizational problems spanning multiple departments or cross-functional redesigns require a few additional key steps (see Figure 9.2) before adopting the GUIDES-based facilitation model:

Step 1: Define the problem you are trying to solve.
Step 2: Secure sponsorship at the right level of leadership.
Step 3: Assess change readiness and timing.
Step 4: Align sponsors and stakeholders around the problem.
Step 5: Assemble a diverse team.
Step 6: Facilitate with GUIDES Framework.
Step 7: Spread best practice(s).

Step 1: Define Problem to Solve	Step 2: Secure Sponsorship at the Right Level of Leadership	Step 3: Assess Change Readiness and Timing Through Personal Conversations	Step 4: Align Sponsors and Stakeholders Around the Problem	Step 5: Assemble Diverse Team of Experts and Informal Leaders	Step 6: Facilitate with GUIDES	Step 7: Spread Best Practice
Collect current process metrics	Develop relationship and trust	Sponsors: How does this change align with the strategy and timing of other initiatives?	Goals	Conduct one-on-one conversations to build trust	Gather current state	Tell "Why Change?" compelling story
Define desired goals and metrics	Elicit sponsor needs	Formal Leaders: How do they feel about the change urgency and timing?	Metrics	Develop group norms	Understand problem to solve	Discuss WIIFM "What's in it for me?"
Quantify the gap (current vs. ideal or desired metric)	Develop compelling customer story	Informal Leaders: What kind of resistance to expect and why?	Scope	Align around common language and definitions	Identify root causes	Share pilot or new process results
Determine process boundaries and scope	Prepare "Why Change?" elevator pitch	Company Historians: How do past changes affect the future change or initiative?	Span	Cultivate "Go-getter" mindset	Design future state	Review GUIDES A3
Identify span (functions and departments) touched by the process or change	Identify risks if no change	Team Members: What is the team's preparedness and capacity for the change?	Definitions	Foster psychological safety	Execute action plan	Review new workflows and standard work
	Define sponsor role and responsibilities			Create role clarity and expectations	Sustain and iterate next steps	Iterate the process with local influence (adopt and adapt)

Figure 9.2 GUIDES Cross-Functional Redesign Model.

The following questions will guide you through the alignment and facilitation process. Not all problem-solving and process redesign requires this degree of detail. The larger the scope and span of the project, the less familiar sponsors and team members will be with each other, and the more helpful these steps and questions will be:

Step 1: Define the Problem You Are Trying to Solve (Consult with Company Historians and Colleagues)

- How does the process currently perform?
- What is the measurable target for this process?
- What is the gap between current and future (ideal) performance?
- What are the boundaries (scope) of the process to be fixed or redesigned?
- Which departments/functions (span) are touched by the process?

Step 2: Secure Sponsorship at the Right Level of Leadership

- Have I developed a trusting relationship with our sponsors?
- Do I understand sponsors' needs?
- Do I have a compelling story and a "Why change" elevator pitch?
- Can I articulate the risks of not changing (i.e., the risk of not doing anything)?
- Does the sponsor understand their role and responsibilities?

Step 3: Assess Change Readiness and Timing via Personal Conversations with Sponsors, Teams, and Formal and Informal Leaders

- How does this change align with the strategy and timing of other initiatives?
- How do formal leaders feel about the change, its urgency, and timing?
- What kind of resistance can I expect from informal leaders and why?
- How will similar changes in the past affect future change?
- What is the team's level of preparedness and capacity for change?

Step 4: Align Sponsors and Stakeholders Around the Problem Scope and Span

- Does everyone agree on goals and metrics?
- Does everyone agree on the scope and span of the process?
- Do we have a common language and definitions?

Step 5: Assemble a Diverse Team of Experts and Informal Leaders

- Who are the leaders touched by the current process?
- Who are the leaders that will be affected by the new process?
- Who might undermine the change if not engaged in its redesign?
- Does this team have a trusting relationship?
- Are roles clear?
- Does the team have a common language, group norms, and guiding principles?
- Does the team have the right mindset? Is it ready to solve problems?

Step 6: Follow the GUIDES Framework for Effective Facilitation

- **G**ather: What does the current state process map and performance data tell us? What does the voice of the process and the voice of stakeholders (patients, team, sponsors) tell us?
- **U**nderstand: What problem is being solved? What is the gap between current performance and our targets?
- **I**dentify: What root causes (or drivers) explain the performance gap? What steps in the current process provide no value to our patients or to the organization?
- **D**esign: What does the future state look like, with the patient (or customer) in the center and fewer process steps and hands-offs?
- **E**xecute: What are the action steps and deliverables? Who is responsible? When are the action items to be completed?
- **S**ustain: What is working well, and what needs to improve? What standard work will prevent the process or system from backsliding?

Step 7: Spread Best Practice

■ How does the current "Why change?" story apply to the next department or team?

■ How do we adjust the WIIFM (What's In It For Me?) to be relevant to the next function?

■ What results should be shared to influence the next group affected by this change?

■ Who are the appropriate formal and informal leaders to review the GUIDES A3, new workflows, and standard work?

■ How can the next team be supported to best iterate the process being spread (adopt and adapt)?

Once you step into a facilitator role, leverage the expertise of the group and be cognizant of not injecting your opinions excessively; ideally, only share your knowledge after everyone else has had a chance to speak up. Effective facilitation comes with practice. Experiment with your approach and reflect on what is most effective for you. Ask for feedback after each meeting to hear what went well and what could be improved. Table 9.5 presents best practices for effective team facilitation.

Table 9.5 Best Practices for Effective Team Facilitation

Trap	Facilitator gives ideas and solutions instead of facilitating and eliciting ideas from others.
Best Practices	■ Be clear which "hat" you are wearing. Ensure the team understands which perspective you are representing: facilitator, leader, team member. ■ Be agnostic to various points of view, leaving problem-solving to the team.
Questions to Ponder	■ What is the team's current dynamic? How will I ensure everyone feels psychologically safe? ■ How will I surface any resistance? How will I encourage everyone to participate and share ideas? ■ What non-leading questions can I ask to understand various points of view?

Leadership Strategies: Bringing It All Together

The Problem-Solver attribute relies heavily on many of the strategies presented in earlier chapters. For example:

- Coach the team to understand the problem in depth before they offer solutions. Coaching allows others to solve problems, making leadership easier, more effective, and more enjoyable.
- Go to Gemba (where the work is happening) to verify assumptions with facts to help the team solve relevant problems. Be intentional about identifying the gap between what exists now and what is desirable to your patients (or customers) in the future.
- Create an environment of psychological safety and trust that encourages surfacing problems and not hiding them.
- Engage teams in learning about the problem that needs to be solved. Tap into the ingenuity of others to come up with innovative solutions.

You have to develop trust before you can have a relationship that is going to work in terms of joint problem-solving.

Nancy Wollen, *Senior Vice President and Chief Operating Officer Kaiser Permanente of Colorado (Retired)*

As you practice going to Gemba and using the GUIDES Iterative Problem-Solving Framework (not to be confused with the GUIDES Framework for leadership development), consider working with a trusted colleague or coach. Learning structured problem-solving and facilitation requires intentional practice.

Teaching problem-solving methods to your team and coaching others how to facilitate process improvement and redesigns will greatly accelerate your team's capacity to fix what bugs them. Don't let great get in the way of good during quick problem-solving. Aim for progress, not perfection. Come up with a minimally viable product (Ries, 2011) to trial and experiment while keeping patient safety at the forefront. Make incremental and breakthrough changes based on the feedback and data. This iterative approach to tackling challenges and experimenting with new business ideas will undoubtedly drive deliberate organizational transformation for the better while creating a continuous learning environment.

The GUIDES Framework and the Problem-Solver

Let's go back to the fictional Dr. Z introduced at the beginning of this chapter. She reached out to her executive coach, who asked her think through the following questions:

- What system can you implement to make surfacing problems routine?
- What can you personally do to create psychological safety for your direct reports?
- How would you approach your leaders to create psychological safety for their team(s)?
- How would you coach teams to learn from others and come up with innovative solutions as they are problem-solving?
- How would you coach the CEO to show up in Gemba as an open-minded and respectful leader who asks questions and listens with curiosity?

As she reflected out loud on her coach's questions, Dr. Z. committed herself to role model a culture of learning and problem-solving without fear of retaliation and encouraging her CEO to do the same.

This concludes the exploration of the three Leadership Strategies: (1) engage and prepare the team, (2) master problem-solving methods, and (3) facilitate the problem-solving process. In Chapter 2, you were asked to think of someone you consider to be an effective problem-solver. To what extent do you think they embody and demonstrate the three Leadership Strategies? What other skills or characteristics do they exhibit that make them effective? Now, access and print the GUIDES Development Plan template in Appendix 1 and create a development plan to assess and improve the Problem-Solver attribute. See Figure 9.3 as an example of a plan to improve the strategy "Facilitate the problem-solving process." The GUIDES A3 Framework for Iterative Problem-Solving is also accessible in Appendix 3.

GUIDES Development Plan – Problem-Solver

Step 1: GATHER inputs to evaluate your skills gaps and opportunities for development.

1. **Record your own assessment of your degree of confidence in these skills.**

To what extent are you confident in your ability to:	Not at all	Somewhat	Great deal
Engage and prepare the team			x
Master problem-solving		x	
Facilitate the problem-solving process		x	

2. **Reflect on your answers to the questions above. Record your additional thoughts.** *After reading this chapter, I know I must focus on "Facilitate the problem-solving process" strategy while also working on the other two strategies.*

3. **Ask for feedback from others (e.g., trusted colleagues, your coach, or direct reports) on the skills, and take notes.** *My direct reports and colleagues who observed me facilitating shared that I often interject my opinions before others have an opportunity to share theirs. At times I appear impatient when the team has a hard time coming up with the problem to solve or root causes driving a problem.*

4. **What does your additional research tell you about this attribute?** *Using a structured brainstorming method allows for spontaneous and innovative ideas. This allows the team to flourish and decreases time wasted in circular discussions.*

Step 2: UNDERSTAND and interpret the data you collected.

The following questions help you understand and interpret the data you collected in the GATHER step. Spend a few minutes thinking about these questions. Record your thoughts and responses.

Figure 9.3 Example of GUIDES Development Plan for Problem-Solver.

1. **What did you learn from your self-assessment?** *I tend to be so passionate about the problem that I have a hard time remaining neutral. I fear that the team will not come to the right conclusion and next steps in a timely manner. I have to accept that I don't always have the best answer. Honestly, I often don't have the best solution.*

2. **How did you interpret feedback from others (e.g., trusted colleagues, your coach, or reports)? Were you surprised? Did their feedback match your self-assessment?** *My impatience with the facilitation process disengages some team members who feel that their opinion may not contribute to the discussion.*

3. **What were your key takeaways from the research? Were you surprised by anything you learned?** *Stick to a structured brainstorming method no matter how tempted I am to jump into solutioning.*

Step 3: IDENTIFY your strengths and opportunities.

Spend a few minutes thinking about each of these questions. Record your thoughts and responses.

1. **Which skills do you want to develop further?** *I would like to work on my facilitation soft skills. I think I understand the problem-solving process well and practice it, but patiently facilitating the team though structured problem-solving is not my strength.*

2. **Which skills are foundational?** *Remaining neutral, listening without judgment, and asking non-leading questions, keeping my opinions at bay.*

3. **Which skills are your highest priority?** *When I facilitate, I need to allow space for the team to brainstorm to solve the problem or design a process.*

Figure 9.3   (Continued)

Step 4: DESIGN your leadership development plan.

What are your development priorities? Record two or three high-priority opportunities and actions.

Area for Development	Developmental Opportunity	Actions to Take	Resources Needed	Target Date	Success Metrics
Problem-Solving	*Facilitate the problem-solving process*	*Facilitate improvement session: Disability Redesign*	*Help from my coach and team leadership.*	*11/1/23*	*Facilitation Success survey*

Look over your development plan, then consider these questions. Record your thoughts below.

1. **Does this plan address the foundational opportunities identified in your self-assessment, research, and input from others?** *I will practice involving and leveraging cross-functional team engagement and input using the GUIDES Framework and soft skills learned in this book.*

2. **Does your plan take into consideration the personal triggers that could help or hinder your development?** *Yes, I will write out reminders to remain neutral, keep my facilitator hat on, and encourage a "round robin" discussion to make sure everyone can share their ideas.*

3. **Is the plan incremental and doable?** *Yes, I will begin to focus on my ability to create space for others to solve problems.*

4. **Are you excited about your plan? Why or why not?** *Very much so, getting others to design solutions will make it easier to implement and sustain. They will have their fingerprints all over the new process/system.*

Figure 9.3 (Continued)

Step 5: EXECUTE your development plan.

Put your development plan into action! As you proceed with the execution of your plan, spend a few minutes thinking about each of these questions. Record your thoughts and responses.

1. **What circumstances or triggers will signal that "now" is the time to act and practice new behaviors?** *I will ask one of my trusted colleagues to signal to me when I start brainstorming and not facilitating.*

2. **What specific behavior(s) or action(s) will you try? How far are you willing to push your comfort zone?** *I may let the team know before I start facilitating that I tend to jump in with my ideas when too excited. I will give them permission to push back if it hinders the team's flow. I recognize this could be a challenging balance.*

3. **How do you know if you are improving and becoming more successful with this attribute and as a leader?** *At the end of each day I will ask for feedback and I will do my personal reflection.*

4. **How will you gauge the impact of your actions or behavior changes? What responses will you be watching for??** *I will observe team dynamics and see if my facilitation creates a psychologically safe place for everyone to share their ideas. I will also ask for objective feedback from trusted colleagues and/or my leadership coach.*

Step 6: SELF-REFLECT on your execution of the development plan.

Spend a few minutes at the end of the day and/or week thinking about each of these questions. Record your thoughts and responses.

1. **Was I mindful of my development today/this week? What did I do well? What could I have done better?** *During our three-day process redesign session, I did really well in the mornings but when I got tired I tended to revert to my old behavior in the afternoons.*

Figure 9.3   (Continued)

2. **How did others respond when I intentionally led in a new way? Were people more (or less) engaged with me as a leader?** *I am not sure and will have to check in to find out.*

3. **Was I mindful of my triggers? How did I respond to those?** *Yes, I was paying attention. As I got tired in the second half of the day, I was less likely to remain neutral.*

4. **What will I do differently tomorrow/next week? What should I be watching for?** *I will write out a few reminder words (stay neutral, remember which hat you wear, do round robin) and look at them before the morning and noon sessions and even during breaks.*

5. **What else do I need to do or learn to further my development of this attribute?** *I need to have my coach with me in the next process redesign meeting so they can observe me in action and coach me. I recognize this is an important step.*

Figure 9.3   (Continued)

Bibliography

"A Quote by Peter F. Drucker." Accessed July 6, 2023. www.goodreads.com/quotes/6539474-many-brilliant-people-believe-that-ideas-move-mountains-but-buldozers

Berwick, Donald M., Thomas W. Nolan, and John Whittington. "The Triple Aim: Care, Health, And Cost." *Health Affairs* 27, no. 3 (May 1, 2008): 759–769. https://doi.org/10.1377/hlthaff.27.3.759

Covey, Stephen R. *The 7 Habits of Highly Effective People: Restoring the Character Ethic*. Rev. edition, New York: Free Press, 2004.

Kahneman, Daniel. *Thinking, Fast and Slow*. New York: Farrar, Straus and Giroux, 2011.

Khan Academy. "The Scientific Method." Accessed July 18, 2019. www.khanacademy.org/science/high-school-biology/hs-biology-foundations/hs-biology-and-the-scientific-method/a/the-science-of-biology

Ries, Eric. *The Lean Startup: How Today's Entrepreneurs Use Continuous Innovation to Create Radically Successful Businesses*, 1st ed. New York: Crown Business, 2011.

Schein, Edgar. *Helping: How to Offer, Give, and Receive Help*. San Francisco: Berrett-Koehler Publishers, 2009.

Schein, Edgar H. and Peter A. Schein. *Humble Inquiry: The Gentle Art of Asking Instead of Telling*. San Francisco: Berrett-Koehler Publishers, 2013.

Womack, Jim. *Gemba Walks*. Expanded 2nd edition. Cambridge, MA: Lean Enterprise Institute, 2013.

Chapter 10

Conclusion

No great manager or leader ever fell from heaven, it's learned not inherited.

Tom Northup

A leader takes people where they want to go. A great leader takes people where they don't necessarily want to go, but ought to be.

Rosalynn Carter

Long before Covid-19, this book came to life when our ideas, research, writing, and interviewing commenced. Once the pandemic started, the writing process stalled as we were fully enmeshed in our organizations' response teams. During this time, at top of mind in every clinical practice and leadership team was the fear of getting Covid-19, navigating life in quarantine, looming job insecurity, adapting to homeschooling, and economic instability. When the writing process re-commenced, we realized that the leadership themes we recognized pre-Covid-19 were virtually the same themes throughout and after the pandemic. Leadership is about relationships. Leadership is about commitment to others. Leadership is about driving change. Leadership is about teaching. Leadership is about learning. During the pandemic, when the healthcare system was stressed to the brink, physicians and other healthcare professionals showed up at their best, leading bravely through uncertainty and fear, integrating their clinical and leadership skills, solving problems, iterating new clinical pathways in real time, and adapting to unprecedented change. Our care teams,

DOI: 10.4324/9780429352355-10

patients, and customers still need strong leaders today, those who can help navigate the volatilities and complexities of healthcare while keeping them psychologically and physically safe.

In combining physician expertise with leadership abilities, drawing invaluable lessons from both, exceptional value is brought to any organization. Preparedness as a physician leader to lead transformative changes – in government, hospitals, insurance companies, integrated care organizations, pharmaceutical companies, or private equity firms – is critical to reinvigorating and reimagining our failing health system. As we explored how to leverage and capitalize on your physician experience to enrich your leadership skills, we presented the attributes, mindset, and strategies needed for success. In addition, we introduced the Iterative Leadership Model with the GUIDES Framework to sharpen strategic thinking, communication, coaching, team building, change management, learning, and problem-solving skills. Through personal reflections, case studies, and insights from other physicians and business leaders, we hope we provided you with new perspectives to make your leadership self-improvement journey fulfilling. The leadership development journey is long term and continuous.

It is ambitious to attempt to practice all the strategies and implement all the best practices at one time, but it will be overwhelming to try to do so. Instead, pace yourself. Be intentional about how you structure and sequence your development plans. Aim for a steady pace and keep the learning momentum going. Assemble your portfolio of development plans from each chapter and:

■ Review. Prioritize. Sequence. Build and iterate.
■ Get feedback. Be vulnerable. Be genuine.
■ Give yourself space and time to change.
■ Don't rush. Be patient.
■ It will take time for others to see you differently.
■ Focus on progress, one step at a time.

As you develop your leadership skills and apply them to business situations, continue to connect your business acumen with your clinical expertise. Continue learning and asking insightful questions.

The Strategic Thinker

- How will I broaden my perspective to think holistically, long term, and innovatively?
- How will I share and translate strategy so my teams can see how the work they do connects and contributes to the organization's mission and vision?
- How will I help my teams know where to focus? How will I help them prioritize the critical activities that contribute to organizational success?

The Effective Communicator

- How will I help myself and other physician leaders communicate with humility?
- How will I foster a culture of feedback by asking rather than telling?
- How will I apply my patient communication skills to leadership interactions? How might I need to adjust my communication style as a leader?

The Coach

- How will I leverage my exam room coaching style to the business environment?
- Do I have a consistent coaching process? How will I develop one?

The Team Builder

- What behaviors will I role model to engage and develop the team so they can perform at the highest level?
- How will I facilitate interactions, discussions, and meetings to ensure we have a psychologically safe environment that stimulates innovative thinking?

The Change Manager

- How will I leverage my clinical skills (used in dealing with difficult or frustrated patients) to lead and sustain organizational changes, even when presented with resistance or apathy?
- How will I meet people where they are and engage them in change, much as I do with patients in shared decision-making?

The Learner-in-Chief

- How will I go about learning from others when I don't have an obvious answer to a clinical or leadership challenge?
- How will my team and I learn to observe processes or workflows without jumping in to fix it? How will we stay focused on what is actually happening and not what we think is happening?

The Problem-Solver

- In the spirit of the SOAP clinical approach, how will I ensure I spend adequate time collecting **s**ubjective and **o**bjective data on a business problem before jumping to **a**ssessment and **p**lan?
- How will I encourage iterative problem-solving using cycles of "try-fail-learn-improve-try," and promoting a "progress, not perfection" mentality while discouraging analysis paralysis?

Finally, invest in the development process. Invest in yourself and invest in your teams. Invest in learning and adopting the GUIDES Framework for coaching, personal development, team learning, and problem-solving:

Step 1: Gather information, data, and facts.
Step 2: Understand and make sense of the gathered information, data, and facts.
Step 3: Identify improvement opportunities.

Step 4: Design improvement or experiment plan.
Step 5: Execute the plan.
Step 6: **S**elf-reflect (personal/professional development) or **S**ustain (problem-solving).

P.S. If you find this book helpful, please leave a review on Amazon or Goodreads so we can learn from you.

Appendix 1

GUIDES Development Plan Template

Step 1: GATHER inputs to evaluate your skills gaps and opportunities for development.

1. **Record your own assessment of your degree of confidence in these skills.**

To what extent are you confident in your ability to:	Not at all	Somewhat	Great deal

2. **Reflect on your answers to the questions above. Record your additional thoughts.**

3. **Ask for feedback from others (e.g., trusted colleagues, your coach, or direct reports) on the skills, and take notes.**

4. **What does your additional research tell you about this attribute?**

Step 2: UNDERSTAND and interpret the data you collected.

The following questions help you understand and interpret the data you collected in the GATHER step. Spend a few minutes thinking about these questions. Record your thoughts and responses.

1. **What did you learn from your self-assessment?**

2. **How did you interpret feedback from others (e.g., trusted colleagues, your coach, or reports)? Were you surprised? Did their feedback match your self-assessment?**

3. **What were your key takeaways from the research? Were you surprised by anything you learned?**

Step 3: IDENTIFY your strengths and opportunities.

Spend a few minutes thinking about each of these questions. Record your thoughts and responses.

1. **Which skills do you want to develop further?**

2. **Which skills are foundational?**

3. **Which skills are your highest priority?**

Step 4: DESIGN your leadership development plan.

What are your development priorities? Record two or three high-priority opportunities and actions.

Area for Development	Developmental Opportunity	Actions to Take	Resources Needed	Target Date	Success Metrics

Look over your development plan, then consider these questions. Record your thoughts below.

1. **Does this plan address the foundational opportunities identified in your self-assessment, research, and input from others?**

2. **Does your plan take into consideration the personal triggers that could help or hinder your development?**

3. **Is the plan incremental and doable?**

4. **Are you excited about your plan? Why or why not?**

Step 5: EXECUTE your development plan.

Put your development plan into action! As you proceed with the execution of your plan, spend a few minutes thinking about each of these questions. Record your thoughts and responses.

1. **What circumstances or triggers will signal that "now" is the time to act and practice new behaviors?**

2. **What specific behavior(s) or action(s) will you try? How far are you willing to push your comfort zone?**

3. **How do you know if you are improving and becoming more successful with this attribute and as a leader?**

4. **How will you gauge the impact of your actions or behavior changes? What responses will you be watching for?**

Step 6: SELF-REFLECT on your execution of the development plan.

Spend a few minutes at the end of the day and/or week thinking about each of these questions. Record your thoughts and responses.

1. Was I mindful of my development today/this week? What did I do well? What could I have done better?

2. How did others respond when I intentionally led in a new way? Were people more (or less) engaged with me as a leader?

3. Was I mindful of my triggers? How did I respond to those?

4. What will I do differently tomorrow/next week? What should I be watching for?

5. What else do I need to do or learn to further my development of this attribute?

Appendix 2

Personal and Organizational Change Models

Beer Critical Path Change Model (Eisenstat et al.,1990)

Based on extensive management research, Michael Beer demonstrated that successful transformations happen not through top-down company-wide training courses and culture programs but through a laser focus on the teams that perform value-creating work and are best positioned to spread change organically or, as he describes it, through "revitalization."

> *Successful change efforts focus on the work itself, not on abstractions like "participation" or "culture" … The most effective senior managers … recognized their limited power to mandate corporate renewal from the top … they defined their roles as creating a climate for change, then spreading the lessons of both successes and failures.*

Steps	Description	Beer's Pearls of Wisdom (Eisenstat et al., 1990)
Mobilize *commitment to change* through joint diagnosis of business problems.	A broad team of committed leaders who jointly diagnose a business problem and develop solutions.	"The starting point of any effective change effort is a clearly defined business problem."
Develop a *shared vision* of how to organize and manage competitiveness.	Develop and communicate a vision of gaining competitiveness with the new information flow, task alignments, roles, and responsibilities.	"Once a core group of people is committed to a particular analysis of the problem, the general manager can lead employees toward a task-aligned vision of the organization that defines new roles and responsibilities."
Foster consensus for the new vision, competence to enact it, and cohesion to move it along.	Develop and facilitate consensus around the vision and build new skills, capabilities, and competencies to make it come to reality.	"People's understanding of what kind of manager and worker the new organization demands grows slowly and only from the experience of seeing some individuals succeed and others fail."
Spread revitalization to all departments without pushing it from the top.	Individual departments and divisions organically spread change and "reinvent the wheel" of implementing the vision through new flows and competencies.	"The temptation to force newfound insights on the rest of the organization is great, but it only short-circuits change."
Institutionalize revitalization through formal policies, systems, and structures.	Establish new enterprise-wide systems, structures, and standardized procedures that align with the new vision to prevent backsliding to the "old ways."	"There comes a point where general managers have to consider how to institutionalize change so that the process continues even after they've moved on to other responsibilities."
Monitor and adjust strategies in response to problems in the revitalization process.	Continuously improve the systems and processes by solving new problems and sharing lessons across the organization.	"The purpose of the change is to create an asset that did not exist before – a learning organization capable of adapting to a changing competitive environment. The organization has to know how to continually monitor its behavior – in effect, to learn how to learn."

Kotter Model (1996)

Stages	Steps	Traps
Establish a Sense of Urgency	Identify crises, potential crises, and opportunities based on competitive market review analysis.	High complacency culture will result in failure.
Create the Guiding Coalition	Assemble a team (5–15) with key people who have adequate power to guide change.	People who do not buy into change will undercut it.
Develop Vision	Create an uplifting, clear, practical vision with simple strategies to achieve it.	Plans without vision or vague vision not relevant to internal and external realities.
Communicate Vision	Over-communicate change in person and through multiple vehicles/channels of communication.	Member of guiding coalition, not role-modeling change in behaviors and under-communicating vision.
Empower Employees to Act	Remove obstacles, encourage out-of-the-box thinking and risk-taking.	Bureaucratic barriers and management actions not aligned with transformation efforts.
Generate Short-Term Wins	Achieve visible early wins and recognize people for their accomplishments.	Failure to create achievable goals with accompanied clear metrics.
Keep Up Urgency	Build momentum after early wins, "do not let up," and work on the next improvement.	"Declare victory too soon."
Anchor Change in the Culture	Demonstrate how the new behaviors, systems, and processes boost organizational improvement.	Let traditional culture undermine change effort.

Kurt Lewin's Unfreeze-Change-Refreeze Model (Burnes, 2004)

Stages	Description	Preconditions
Unfreeze	Help people understand their present performance skills and capabilities that contribute to day-to-day inefficiencies and poor processes – resulting in poor customer experience or the company's bottom line.	Psychological safety to be able to accept disconcerting information and open up to change.
Change	Invest time and money to introduce and coach new skills, behaviors, and habits to improve work processes, flows, and systems. Encourage continuous learning and improvement.	The learner is open to new information.
Refreeze	Anchor new behaviors, skills, and habits in new systems and processes that are aligned with the change effort.	New behaviors are role modeled by leaders.

The Prosci ADKAR Model (Hiatt, 2006)

Elements	Description	Factors
Awareness	Understand the risk of not changing: internal and external threats.	- Nature of change - Alignment with a vision - Risks of not changing - Organizational impact - Personal impact
Desire	Have a personal drive and internal motivation to carry out change.	- What's in it for me (WIIFM)? - Perception of the organization - Personal situation - Intrinsic motivation
Knowledge	Learn new behaviors, jobs, processes, systems, and workflows.	- Knowledge base - Capacity to learn - Educational resources - Access to knowledge

Elements	Description	Factors
Ability	Execute change, translating knowledge into practical actions.	- Psychological readiness - Physical abilities - Intellectual skills - Time to learn and improve skills - Availability of coaching/mentoring
Reinforcement	Sustain change through internal and external drivers.	- Reward and recognition of new behavior - Absence of negative reinforcement - Accountability systems

Stephen Covey's Seven Habits Model (2013)

Stephen Covey, author of *The 7 Habits of Highly Effective People*, introduced a personal change model that can be both helpful to leaders managing change and frontline employees who are living through it. Change is a highly emotional and personal experience that is psychologically taxing for leaders and their reports. Learning how to be patient and not overreact when you face the unknown, trying to understand the other before expecting to be understood, and finding mutually acceptable paths forward are just a few of the many pearls of wisdom that Stephen Covey contributed to the change management discourse.

Habits	Description
Be proactive	Do not be reactive; you control your life and experiences – "between stimulus and response, you have the freedom to choose."
Begin with the end in mind	Envision your future and methodically march toward it – "If your ladder is not leaning against the right wall, every step you take just gets you to the wrong place faster."
Put first things first	Understand the difference between urgent and important – "not doing everything that comes along is okay."
Think win–win	Create mutually beneficial solutions, not "win-lose."

Habits	Description
Seek first to understand, then to be understood	Listen empathetically and build deep personal relationships – "diagnose before you prescribe."
Synergize	Focus on teamwork to combine talents and achieve more than individual efforts – "creative cooperation."
Sharpen the saw	Continuously learn and improve – "investment in ourselves."

The Kubler-Ross Grief Model (2018)

The Kubler-Ross Model was popularized in the 1960s when psychiatrist Elisabeth Kubler-Ross published her book *On Death and Dying*. Intended to present a model of psychological adjustment to dying, it became a timeless model for change management. It intensely focused on the process of adjustment to radical change and how a human psyche transitions through grief. The process of change that mostly focused on macro-level organizational change suddenly had a model to explain micro-level individual adjustment to restructuring, reorganization, layoffs, and other radical operational transformations.

Stages	Description	Change Management Parallels
Denial	A patient pretends that the given terminal diagnosis is not real: "No, not me, it cannot be true."	Employees believe it cannot be true or real when confronted with reorganization or layoffs. "This is not really happening – management will change their mind."
Anger	Realizing that the diagnosis is real, a patient experiences "feelings of anger, rage, envy, and resentment." "Why me?"	The realization that change is inevitable creates feelings of discontent, dissatisfaction, and at times anger. "I am refusing to do this. This is ill-advised and will harm customers."
Bargaining	A patient bargains, usually with God, by "entering into some sort of an agreement that will postpone the inevitable happening …"	Negotiations to either minimize, reshape, or avert change ensue. "If you seriously want me to do this, I will need tons of time, more money, and staff."

Stages	Description	Change Management Parallels
Depression	"When the terminally ill patient can no longer deny his illness … his anger and rage will soon be replaced with a sense of great loss."	Sadness and low morale set in due to losing the status quo and fearing the unknown. "I can't imagine working here once they move me to a different department. I may as well resign."
Acceptance	"If a patient has had enough time … and has been given some help in working through previously described stages, … he will contemplate his coming end with a certain degree of quiet expectation."	If management communicates effectively and provides an empathetic ear, this acceptance of a new normal takes place sooner than later. "I understand they had to do it to survive. There were not so many options but to combine the departments."

Bridges' Transition Model (Bridges and Mitchell, 2000)

William and Susan Bridges developed a model that deals with human response to change. Leaders must understand that each individual affected by changes is undergoing a psychological transition. The length of the transition varies between people. Learning to coach through the transition will ensure the success of the change effort.

> *Transition is the state that change puts people into. The change is external (the different policy, practice, or structure that the leader is trying to bring about), while transition is internal (a psychological reorientation that people have to go through before the change can work).*

Stages	Description	Role of Managers
Ending	Understanding losses and letting go: the prior comfortable state of being, sense of identity, perceived reality.	- Explain "why" of change succinctly. - Communicate change steps diligently. - Understand loss of "status quo" grieving. - Be an empathetic listener and help most affected employees psychologically and financially.

Stages	Description	Role of Managers
Neutral Zone	In-between state when people let go of their losses but do not yet adopt new behaviors or embrace the future	- Be patient, do not rush or push. - Describe the future vision again and again. - Review step-by-step plans on how to get there. - Explain what is required of people to get there.
New Beginnings	People embrace new reality, attitudes, behaviors, skills, and competencies.	- Restate new processes and expectations. - Coach and role model new behaviors and attitudes. - Train in new skills and provide many opportunities to practice.

Miller and Rollnick Motivational Interviewing (2013)

The practice of Motivational Interviewing took the world by storm resulting in the new field of research with 25,000 citations of the work and more than 200 randomized trials. Initially developed and studied for alcohol addiction in 1983, it spread across numerous fields, including leadership and change management. It is a collaborative and empathetic approach to change that is focused on eliciting personal motivation, reasons, and commitment to change goals. Each process in the model is built upon another.

Process	Descriptions	Role of Change Manager
Engaging	Initial engagement, developing relationships, building connection.	Ask open-ended questions and listen without judgment with reflection and affirmation.
Focusing	Focus on the agenda, change goals discovered.	Clarify direction, future change goals.
Evoking	Elicit person's motivation for change, capture their own ideas.	Help the person to voice arguments for change.
Planning	Strengthen change talk and negotiate goals and plan.	Help develop a specific action plan.

Egan's Skilled Helper Model (2010)

This model created by Gerard Egan, PhD, was intended for professional helpers, specifically human services professionals who are often counselors to their clients. This model focuses on the way people think, feel, and express emotions. Helping others to change should be grounded in the past but unapologetically focused on the future. This model is powered by goal setting, planning, and execution.

Stages	Description	Tasks
The Current Picture	Clarify key problems necessitating change.	- People tell their stories. - Develop stories and help reframe them constructively in a new perspective. - Focus and work on problems that make a difference and have value.
The Preferred Picture	Identify, select, and shape the problem; manage goals.	- Help people to imagine and identify possibilities for the better future. - Choose challenging and realistic goals that are real solutions to the key problems. - Find incentives that will help people commit to the change plans.
The Way Forward	Develop plans and strategies to get to goals.	- Review strategies to achieve goals. - Choose strategies that best-fit resources. - Assemble chosen strategies into a viable plan.

Bibliography

"Bridges' Transition Model: Guiding People Through Change by Managing Endings." Accessed September 2, 2019. www.mindtools.com/pages/article/bridges-transit ion-model.htm

Bridges, William, and Susan Mitchell. "Leading Transition: A New Model for Change." *Leader to Leader* 16, no. 3 (2000): 30–36.

Burnes, Bernard. "Kurt Lewin and the Planned Approach to Change: A Re-Appraisal." *Journal of Management Studies* 41, no. 6 (September 2004): 977–1002. https:// doi.org/10.1111/j.1467-6486.2004.00463.x

Chowdary, Nagendra V. "Executive Interviews: Interview with Michael Beer on Change Management." June 2007. http://ibscdc.org/executive-interviews/Q&A_with_Michael_Beer.htm

Connelly, Mark. "Kubler-Ross Five Stage Model." August 30, 2018. www.change-management-coach.com/kubler-ross.html

Connelly, Mark. "The Kurt Lewin Model of Change." November 15, 2016. www.change-management-coach.com/kurt_lewin.html

Covey, Stephen R. *The 7 Habits of Highly Effective People: Powerful Lessons in Personal Change.* 25th anniversary edition. New York: Simon & Schuster, 2013.

Covey, Stephen R. *The 7 Habits of Highly Effective People Personal Workbook.* New York: Simon & Schuster, 2003.

Egan, Gerard. *The Skilled Helper: A Problem-Management and Opportunity-Development Approach to Helping*, 9th ed. Belmont, CA: Brooks Cole, Cengage Learning, 2010.

Eisenstat, Russell, Bert Spector, and Michael Beer. "Why Change Programs Don't Produce Change." *Harvard Business Review* (November 1, 1990). https://hbr.org/1990/11/why-change-programs-dont-produce-change

Hiatt, Jeff. *ADKAR: A Model for Change in Business, Government, and Our Community*, 1st ed. Loveland, CO: Prosci Learning Center Publications, 2006.

Kotter, John P. *Leading Change.* Boston, MA: Harvard Business School Press, 1996.

Kotter, John P., and Dan S. Cohen. *The Heart of Change: Real-Life Stories of How People Change Their Organizations.* Boston, MA: Harvard Business School Press, 2002.

Kübler-Ross, Elisabeth. *On Death and Dying.* 1st Scribner Classics ed. New York: Scribner Classics, 1997.

Miller, William R., and Stephen Rollnick. *Motivational Interviewing: Helping People Change*, 3rd ed. New York: Guilford Press, 2013.

Nohria, Nitin, and Michael Beer. "Cracking the Code of Change." *Harvard Business Review* (May 1, 2000). https://hbr.org/2000/05/cracking-the-code-of-change

Schein, Edgar H. "Kurt Lewin's Change Theory in the Field and in the Classroom: Notes Toward a Model of Managed Learning." *Systems Practice* 9, no. 1 (February 1, 1996): 27–47. https://doi.org/10.1007/BF02173417

GUIDES A3 Framework for Iterative Problem-Solving Template

GUIDES A3 Title:
Date:

Improvement Sponsor:
Improvement Team:

1. **GATHER** current state information (process data, voice of stakeholders and process, best practices)

2. **UNDERSTAND** the problem to solve (the measurable gap between the current state and the goal)

3. **IDENTIFY** root causes of the performance gap, using tools such as fishbone diagram (Ishikawa diagram) or 5 Whys

4. **DESIGN** the future state (create a process map; document the standard work for the team and the leader)

5. **EXECUTE** the action plan (identify the action steps and deliverables)

WHAT	WHO	WHEN	OUTCOME

6. **SUSTAIN** the results (stabilize, reflect, and iterate)

GUIDES Cross-Functional Redesign Model

Step 1: Define Problem to Solve	Step 2: Secure Sponsorship at the Right Level of Leadership	Step 3: Assess Change Readiness and Timing Through Personal Conversations	Step 4: Align Sponsors and Stakeholders Around the Problem	Step 5: Assemble Diverse Team of Experts and Informal Leaders	Step 6: Facilitate with GUIDES	Step 7: Spread Best Practice
Collect current process metrics	Develop relationship and trust	Sponsors: How does this change align with the strategy and timing of other initiatives?	Goals	Conduct one-on-one conversations to build trust	**Gather** current state	Tell "Why Change?" compelling story
Define desired goals and metrics	Elicit sponsor needs	Formal Leaders: How do they feel about the change urgency and timing?	Metrics	Develop group norms	**Understand** problem to solve	Discuss WIIFM "What's in it for me?"
Quantify the gap (current vs. ideal or desired metric)	Develop compelling customer story	Informal Leaders: What kind of resistance to expect and why?	Scope	Align around common language and definitions	**Identify** root causes	Share pilot or new process results
Determine process boundaries and scope	Prepare "Why Change?" elevator pitch	Company Historians: How do past changes affect the future change or initiative?	Span	Cultivate "Go-getter" mindset	**Design** future state	Review GUIDES A3
Identify span (functions and departments) touched by the process or change	Identify risks if no change	Team Members: What is the team's preparedness and capacity for the change?	Definitions	Foster psychological safety	**Execute** action plan	Review new workflows and standard work
	Define sponsor role and responsibilities			Create role clarity and expectations	**Sustain** and iterate next steps	Iterate the process with local influence (adopt and adapt)

Index

Note: Page numbers in *italic* refers to Figures.